RUBBLE MUSIC

RUBBLE MUSIC

*Occupying the Ruins of
Postwar Berlin, 1945–1950*

Abby Anderton

INDIANA UNIVERSITY PRESS

This book is a publication of

Indiana University Press
Office of Scholarly Publishing
Herman B Wells Library 350
1320 East 10th Street
Bloomington, Indiana 47405 USA

iupress.indiana.edu

© 2019 by Abby Anderton

All rights reserved

No part of this book may be reproduced or utilized in any form or by any means, electronic or mechanical, including photocopying and recording, or by any information storage and retrieval system, without permission in writing from the publisher. The paper used in this publication meets the minimum requirements of the American National Standard for Information Sciences Permanence of Paper for Printed Library Materials, ANSI Z39.48-1992.

Manufactured in the United States of America

Library of Congress Cataloging-in-Publication Data

Names: Anderton, Abby, author.
Title: Rubble music : occupying the ruins of postwar Berlin, 1945-1950 / Abby Anderton.
Description: Bloomington : Indiana University Press, 2019. | Includes bibliographical references and index.
Identifiers: LCCN 2018049714 (print) | LCCN 2018051366 (ebook) | ISBN 9780253042439 (e-book) | ISBN 9780253042415 (cl : alk. paper) | ISBN 9780253042422 (pb : alk. paper)
Subjects: LCSH: Music—Germany—Berlin—20th century—History and criticism.
Classification: LCC ML275.8.B47 (ebook) | LCC ML275.8.B47 A54 2019 (print) | DDC 780.943/15509044—dc23
LC record available at https://lccn.loc.gov/2018049714

1 2 3 4 5   24 23 22 21 20 19

For Dennis.

CONTENTS

Acknowledgments   ix

Introduction   *1*

1 Berlin Soundscapes of Defeat and Occupation   *16*

2 Occupied Music: The Berlin Philharmonic and the American Military   *43*

3 Rubble Opera after 1945: East Berlin's Staatsoper and West Berlin's Städtische Oper   *67*

4 Embodied and Disembodied Voices: Listening to Sonic Ruins   *93*

5 Berlin 1945: Toward a Ruin Aesthetic in Music   *131*

Conclusion   *156*

Bibliography   163

Index   177

ACKNOWLEDGMENTS

This book project began as the flickering of an idea I had while spending the summer in Berlin. As a first-year graduate student at the University of Michigan, I visited the capital ostensibly for a course at the Goethe Institute but soon decided to develop my research project around the city's sounds, its geographies, its complicated history. *Rubble Music* is the result of the ensuing time I spent combing through the city's archives, returning as often as I could to study unpublished scores, diaries, and correspondence written by Berliners who lived through the liminal space between war and peace. Their stained pages raised new questions for me about the resonances of 1945, and I knew I had to write a book about their experiences.

There are many people to whom I am indebted for their time and generosity as I completed this project. Jane Fulcher, my doctoral adviser, supervised this work in its early stages, providing an inspiring example of how to combine rigorous research with a compelling storyline. Similarly, Steven Whiting, Charles Garrett, Silke Maria-Weineck, and Annie Randall provided wonderful advice and support throughout the many phases of writing.

I am thankful for the help and comments of my editor, Janice Frisch, who expertly guided this manuscript through its various iterations. Likewise, the comments of the anonymous readers were absolutely invaluable, and I am very appreciative of their insights and observations. My wonderful colleagues at Baruch College, City University of New York, have provided unwavering encouragement, most especially Anne Swartz, Leonard Sussman, Debra Caplan, John Maciuika, Liz Wollman, Andrew Tomasello, Phil Lambert, Andrew Sloin, Martina Nguyen, and Elizabeth Heath. I am grateful for the scholars who took time to discuss this manuscript with me—namely, Pamela Potter, Annegret Fauser, Amy Lynn Wlodarski, Danielle Fosler-Lussier, Walter Frisch, Robert G. Moeller, Monica Black, Amy C. Beal, Mike Beckerman, Joy Calico, Allan Atlas, Tina Frühauf, Anne Shreffler, Anne Stone, and Stephen Brockmann. Their insights made a world of difference in the resulting book.

To my fellow postwar-minded academics, Martha Sprigge, Emily Richmond Pollock, Kira Thurman, and Kathryn Sederberg, my thanks for sharing ideas, encouragement, and delicious cake while discussing our respective projects. Friends in Michigan, New York, and Berlin were always willing to talk through ideas—namely, Alison DeSimone, Meghan Fox, George Fragopoulos, Katie LaPorta, Nick and Anja Westray, Kim Philip, Lucy Dauner, Olivia de Paeztron, Liam Billingham, Emily Weiss, Brandon Woolf, and Tina Petereit. My thanks to Matthias Weiter and Manuela Malaszkiewicz-Weiter, our Berlin family, for generously sharing their home with us during summer research trips.

I would like to express my sincere appreciation to the funding and institutional structures that supported the research for *Rubble Music*—namely, the Fulbright Commission, the German Academic Exchange Service (DAAD), the Holocaust Educational Foundation, the Professional Staff Congress and the City University of New York, the Eugene Lang Foundation, and the AMS 75 PAYS Endowment of the American Musicological Society, funded in part by the National Endowment for the Humanities and the Andrew W. Mellon Foundation. Archives in Germany provided the bulk of the materials for this project, and I would especially like to thank Dr. Werner Grünzweig and Peter Deeg of the Akademie der Künste, Katja Vobiller of the Berlin Philharmonic Archive, Jean Christophe Gero of the Staatsbibliothek, Monika Bartzsch of the Landesarchiv, and Andreas Meurer of Ries and Erler Verlag.

I am endlessly appreciative of my parents, Dave and Mary Joyce, who provided encouragement during my early days of graduate school through *Rubble Music*'s completion. I would also like to thank my brother, my in-laws, and my sisters-in-law for their support. Finally, I would like to dedicate this book to my husband, Dennis, whom I met on a rainy summer evening in Görlitzer Park. He has been my constant supporter, willing to discuss everything from translation questions to methodological approaches. Our son, Anselm, was born shortly before I sent off the final version of this manuscript. The care and patience of my family allowed me the time I needed to complete this project, and I am looking forward to seeing what our next adventure together will be.

RUBBLE MUSIC

INTRODUCTION

As Soviet forces surrounded Berlin, preparing for their final assault on the capital in April 1945, many of the city's musicians continued their creative endeavors. Composer Paul Höffer completed a first draft of his Toccata for solo piano, noting beneath the final fermata, "born under pain, April 15, 1945."[1] On April 16, the Berlin Philharmonic Orchestra gave a concert featuring Brahms's Double Concerto and Strauss's *Death and Transfiguration*. The following day, Staatsoper coloratura soprano Erna Berger recorded Strauss's Brentano Lieder at Greater German Radio on Masurenallee.[2] As sonic, archival, and historical evidence indicates, despite the regime's collapse, the third week of April 1945 was another workweek for many of Berlin's musicians. Musical culture did not begin anew after the collapse of the Third Reich; it simply continued, as artists worked with the materials and personnel at hand—however compromised, however rubbled.

Five days after the unconditional surrender of Nazi Germany, on May 13, conductor Hans von Benda decided it was time for a concert. Benda gathered together the remaining members of the Berlin Chamber Orchestra, the ensemble he founded in 1939, along with musicians from the city's Philharmonic, Staatsoper, and Städtische Oper orchestras—about thirty players in all. With the permission of the city's newly installed Russian occupiers, the musicians decided to perform in the partially destroyed Schöneberg town hall. In lieu of posters, Benda's instrumentalists advertised the performance by writing in chalk on the ruins of their apartment buildings. As the conductor had no trouble noting for posterity, the Schöneberg auditorium was transformed "literally from a pile of debris" into "a room worthy of the occasion," only twenty-four hours before the concert.[3] Despite the hall's smashed windows, the space was freshly painted for the event as Russian soldiers covered Franz Eichhorst's Nazi war murals. The musicians performed to a packed house, playing orchestral works by Handel, Haydn, and Tchaikovsky, and arias including Giordani's emotive "Caro mio ben." In accordance with audience demand, the ensemble repeated the performance five times the following week. For Benda, "with this new life new sounds will come to us, a whole new artistic richness."[4] But for the moment, a fresh coat of paint would have to suffice.

Accounts like Benda's emphasize resilience despite the debris and ashes left behind by World War II. Yet destruction left its mark on the city's depleted ensembles, shattered institutions, and occupied radio waves, as rubble became the defining feature of postwar musical culture. Whether figurative or material, rubble was the common postwar fragmentation to be worked through, representing, in turn, the intellectual quandary of the denazification process, a rebuilding material, an audible sonic element, a performance practice, and a compositional aesthetic. The scale of this reconstructive undertaking can be seen in the now iconic visual imagery of postwar Germany, whether in film or photography, where towering urban ruins reveal the arresting and unintentionally picturesque remnants of aerial warfare. But what about the sound of such destruction and its effects on musical culture, from compromised musicians and bombed-out venues to concerts and compositions for which urban ruin was the catalyst?

Postwar accounts of the more famous (and infamous) musicians and composers provide little, if any, information that can help us answer this question. These individuals were generally not living among or in urban ruins, and, consequently, the deprivations of war scarcely ruffle the surface of their memoirs. Instead, they describe their relationships (some positive, some tense, some ambivalent) with the newly arrived Allied occupiers, carefully avoiding any mention of their former collaborations with Nazi cultural functionaries. Conductor Wilhelm Furtwängler kept track of activities in postwar Berlin from his Swiss villa, while in a bucolic village just west of Munich, Werner Egk greeted the American tanks that rolled through his garden at the end of April. Carl Orff was reunited with a former student (now an American cultural officer) who made sure the composer was rehabilitated despite his undisputed success during the regime. In Bavaria, Richard Strauss was so in demand that the Americans created a sign-up sheet for dinners in his home. And although he admitted privately in 1945, "My life's work is in ruins," his postwar compositions such as *Metamorphosis* and *Four Last Songs* returned to a neoclassical soundworld, far from the rubble of defeated Germany.[5]

Yet there is a dissonance between more privileged artists, who were largely spared violence by geography, social connections, or material circumstances, and the lived experience of the average civilian musician. In contrast to the accounts of Strauss, Egk, Orff, and Furtwängler, I found a wealth of archival material and musical scores during my research in Berlin that explicitly addressed urban trauma in 1945. These documents openly describe wartime air raids, destruction, violence, and death—in short, musical narratives of German suffering—nearly all of which remain, to this day, unpublished. The sheer amount of evidence, from diary entries and letters to cantatas about Berlin's bombings, irrefutably shows that musicians rendered the ruined cityscape in aural terms, continuing to compose and perform despite (and even because of) postwar debris. Although their material may have been unpopular with the occupiers, countless forums and institutions hosted and supported these pieces and performances.

Between the critical years of 1945 and 1950, Berlin's material devastation generated what I call rubble music, or the sound of civilian suffering after urban catastrophe, heard in public forums monitored by the Allies as well as private ones for German civilians. Musicians moved across the porous sectors of the city with relative ease, performing and composing for the occupation powers and collaborating with fellow musicians in East and West Berlin. Before the wall's construction in 1961, more than fifty thousand East Berliners were employed in West Berlin and crossed the border each day.[6]

The subject of German victimhood during and after World War II has long been taboo, and it is not one to be undertaken without caution. I am not attempting to establish a kind of continuum of suffering, nor am I arguing that there is in any way equivalency between the German, non-Jewish experience and Jewish victimhood. Furthermore, as I discuss in the ensuing chapters, there were audible tensions and resonances between German and Jewish suffering (and even German Jewish suffering), which inform, complicate, and add nuance to rubble music as a genre. Fortunately, contributions by scholars such as Robert G. Moeller, Anna Parkinson, Monica Black, and Jennifer Evans have provided a framework for discussing the complex set of issues arising from the victim-perpetrator paradigm and the gray zone of complicity after World War II. As Moeller notes, it must be possible "to write a history of the war's end in which Germans cause immeasurable suffering *and* Germans suffer immeasurably."[7] Notions of civilian victimhood informed national identity in both East and West Germany, and although these narratives developed divergent paths in the American and Soviet zones, the trauma of Allied bombing raids was a common theme.[8]

Between 1940 and 1945, the British Royal Air Force, later joined by the US Air Force, extensively bombed Germany in what became known as the

Allied air war. Allied bombers targeted industrial areas, factories, and armaments facilities, and the attacks were initially in retaliation for the Luftwaffe's raids on Coventry and London. By 1943, however, the United States and Great Britain had adopted a broader policy of morale bombing. Designed to undermine support for the Nazi war effort, the attacks decimated urban areas, killing an estimated four hundred thousand to six hundred thousand German civilians, and rendering over 70 percent of the country's homes uninhabitable. As the seat of Hitler's government, Berlin held special significance for the Allies, who mounted 363 aerial attacks, making the city the most frequently targeted of World War II. British and American intelligence, hoping to create a firestorm on the scale of Hamburg's 1943 bombing, complained that the capital's wide streets and lack of timber buildings made it difficult to light the city aflame, creating "a good deal of consternation," as one American engineer admitted.[9] The psychological toll of repeated bombings and the accompanying lethargy arguably did little to break the population's morale. Instead, the air war generated more than seventy-five million cubic meters of debris in Berlin alone, rubble that would provide a metaphorical and literal space for Berliners to stage, compose, and broadcast their traumas, however self-inflicted, by 1945.

The Zero Hour and Rubble Arts

Eyewitness accounts of music sounding in Germany's rubble have tended to focus on the idealized aspects of rebuilding, describing the destruction only insofar as it was a testament to the musicians' commitment to their craft. Rather than hearing how the rubble changed and informed musical practices, these initial responses portrayed music as life affirming and culturally redemptive. It is no surprise that the authors of these accounts had political reasons to represent their cultural work as a unique, democratic, and occupier-sanctioned form of music making.[10] Yet the speed with which concerts, performances, and recitals resumed after the war's end suggests these activities served a greater purpose than mere entertainment or distraction from harsh realities. These events suggest that music shaped a narrative of postwar national suffering even as the German nation had ceased to exist.

Immediately after Germany's unconditional surrender, artists promoted the idea of a "new beginning" in all aspects of culture. Postwar accounts took great pains to differentiate before and after 1945, using the term *zero hour* (*Stunde Null*) to describe the period of transition between the fall of the Third Reich and the establishment of semifunctioning Allied military governments. The narratives of German musicians maintained that this era represented a caesura, belaboring the difficulties of resuming musical productions and reconstituting ensembles given the extent of the air war's urban destruction. Further, these accounts claimed, music that had enjoyed frequent performances under the Third Reich was ousted in favor of Mendelssohn, as politically sound musicians eagerly reclaimed their autonomy after the fall of an oppressive regime.[11] Postwar artists in all sectors and zones had a vested interest in propagating the idea of a fresh start as there were numerous personal and professional advantages to be gained. In this version of 1945, rubble was to be cleared away quickly, not worked through piece by piece. The zero hour was not about the arduous task of sorting debris; rather, its forward momentum repressed this process altogether. Rubble became a liability as it contained the shards of 1945's exaggerations and falsehoods. The zero hour concept was a convenient narrative of urban and cultural renewal that validated Allied policies and absolved many civilian sympathizers of wrongdoing. In most contemporary accounts, Germany's musical rubble was treated as an inconvenience to be worked around, not worked through.

Consequently, a second and third generation of scholars began redefining the zero hour as a dichotomy of "continuities and discontinuities," arguing that while certain elements of culture remained the same as they had been under National Socialism, other facets such as repertoire and personnel experienced radical upheavals. This binary acknowledged, within certain boundaries, the problems and contradictions inherent in the zero hour concept.[12] Yet many assumptions about 1945 were rooted in readings of totalitarianism that argued the state unilaterally controlled all facets of German culture. More recent Third Reich historiographies, however, have questioned the extent to which the Nazis were able to regulate all areas of artistic production. Compelling new research by Pamela Potter and others calls into question assumptions that were once undisputed: that the Reich Chamber of Culture (Reichskulturkammer) rigidly controlled all facets of artistic production, and, above all, that German musicians uniformly toiled under oppressive conditions. Instead, as Potter argues, the chamber implemented a number of reforms that even helped improve everyday life for many German musicians.[13] These findings demand a reevaluation of music in the postwar period, as they unmoor many prior notions about 1945 and its supposed cultural renewal. If the zero hour was employed for political and aesthetic purposes to describe postwar German culture, then what exactly did this culture take as its primary source of inspiration? The rubble of wartime bombing left traces on mediums from film to literature to art and, as I argue in this book, on music.

Aestheticizing time's slow decay certainly had a precedent well before 1945. Visual artists since the Renaissance depicted ruins as a marker of religious and historical significance, and by the eighteenth century, Piranesi's etchings showed nature reclaiming rubbled space. The romantics created landscape paintings and fragmentary character pieces about the crumbling rubble of ancient ruins. Modern aerial warfare of the twentieth century, however, forever altered rubble's status as a quaint relic of time's passage. Now such debris could be created in a matter of seconds and on a scale humanity had never before experienced. Although Andreas Huyssen argues the rubble of Germany's aerial warfare should not be conflated with idealized ruins, many postwar photographs, paintings, films, and musical scores did just that.[14] Deliberately aestheticizing warfare's remnants rendered the urban landscape a massive canvas, removing questions of guilt and moral responsibility to recast the destruction in terms of romantic decay, creating a kind of contemplative rubble sublime.

Consequently, the country's destruction captured the imagination of artists, filmmakers, and writers who created rubble films, rubble photographs, rubble art, and rubble literature—genres that used ruin to explore themes of postwar alienation and disillusionment. The term *Trümmerfilm* (rubble film) first surfaced in 1947, and when it did, critics generally employed it pejoratively.[15] Rather than providing a mere escapist outlet, rubble films depicted urban destruction as the primary backdrop for ordinary civilians living in the bombed-out shells of their homes, often contrasting German suffering against the characters' own compromised political pasts. Filmmakers used lengthy wide-angle shots of bombed cities to fetishize and aestheticize the destruction even as the ruined landscape served as a visual signifier of the Nazi regime's moral bankruptcy. As Robert Shandley has observed, these are films that "share the fundamental *mise en scène* of a destroyed and defeated Germany."[16] Berlin alone provided the backdrop to some forty-seven rubble films between 1946 and 1948, including Wolfgang Staudte's *The Murderers Are among Us* (1946) and Gerhard Lamprecht's *Somewhere in Berlin* (1946), as well as films produced by foreign directors such as Roberto Rossellini's *Germany, Year Zero* (1948) and Billy Wilder's *A Foreign Affair* (1948).[17]

Postwar rubble literature engaged with similar themes, as Gruppe 47, a writers' collective that included Hans Werner Richter, Ilse Aichinger, Günter Eich, Heinrich Böll, and Hans Magnus Enzensberger, confronted and documented Germany's destruction. In Richter's writings for *Der Ruf*, a journal he cofounded as a prisoner of war in Rhode Island and reestablished upon his return to Germany in 1946, the author admitted, "The hallmark of our time is the ruin. . . . It lives in us, as we in it."[18] Gruppe 47's stories of bitter homecomings, the cruel aftermath of war mirrored in the country's fractured landscape, provided unvarnished texts of nonredemptive sacrifice. When contemporary critics demeaned their literary efforts, Böll argued that "to have offered our contemporaries an escape into some idyll would have been too cruel for words," or even more to the point, "We found rubble and we wrote about it."[19]

The representation of rubble in the visual arts ranged from the romantic to the surreal. Popular rubble postcards sold and circulated among the German public even showed the country's famous landmarks reduced to rubble and ash. Photojournalist Henry Ries, a German Jewish émigré serving in the US Army, captured early rubble shots of Berlin from the skies, and in Dresden, Richard Peter's book of ruin photographs, *Dresden: Eine Kamera klagt an* (1949) memorialized the decimated Baroque cityscape, selling fifty thousand copies in a little over a week.[20]

Yet rubble photographs generally recast the shattered cityscape as a romantic ruin, featuring either postwar, contemplative landscapes in the vein of Caspar David Friedrich, or a rubble flaneur wandering through the ruins. Rather than an affect of romanticized contemplation, however, Berlin artists Werner Heldt and Karl Hofer used rubble prominently in their surrealist work from 1945 until 1948. Heldt's series of postwar paintings, including *Window View with a Dead Bird* (1945) and *Berlin at Sea* (1946–48) feature destroyed houses melting into an ocean of ruins. In Hofer's *Ruins at Night* (1947), Berlin's rubble becomes garishly laughing musical facades (fig. 1). Behind the upright piano in the foreground sits a destroyed house with piano key teeth and the f-hole of a violin for an eye.[21]

How rubble was presented in film, literature, photography, and painting varied by artist, medium, and material, and yet there remained certain thematic tropes consistent across these mediums—namely, German suffering and the moral ambiguity of the politically compromised. Yet while scholars have extensively documented rubble's resonances in other areas of postwar culture, including literature, film, visual art and photography,

Figure 0.1. *Ruins at Night* (1947) by Karl Hofer. Reproduced courtesy of akg-images. ©2018 Artists Rights Society (ARS), New York/VG-Bild Kunst, Bonn.

there has been no corresponding book linking music and ruins. In spite of the ubiquitous music making that was taking place across postwar Germany, rubble histories of 1945 seldom, if ever, consider music in relation to other rubble art forms. (Broader postwar histories, with a few notable exceptions, have been reluctant to integrate music into their analyses, most likely due to the interests and fields of their respective authors.)[22] Even if the term *rubble music* (*Trümmermusik*) was absent from postwar discourses, musicians, too, explored the sonic possibilities of the rubble. In "The Aging of New Music," Theodor W. Adorno wrote, "Since the European catastrophe, culture hangs on like houses in the cities accidentally spared by bombs or indifferently patched together."[23] Music, of the new and old variety, could travel unimpeded between roofless, bombed-out houses and through courtyards.

More recent musicological scholarship has probed the material remnants of postwar Germany to unearth long-buried (or long-suppressed) counternarratives of trauma. Amy Lynn Wlodarski has explored how the postwar ruins of France informed the work of American composer George Rochberg, who traversed the battered landscape as a soldier and wrote about his experiences in his diary, creating compositional sketches he would return to some forty years later. Martha Sprigge focuses on Dresden's ruins and cantor Rudolph Mauersberger's commemorative compositions for the Kreuzkirche boys' choir. Emily Richmond Pollock's work on Munich's rubble analyzes the contested relationship between architecture, the air war, and operatic performance. Andrew Oster argues that postwar radio opera (*Funkoper*) was itself a form of rubble music, free from the visual trappings of sets and costumes which were scarce given the widespread destruction.[24] Historians of postwar music have also thoroughly documented the institutional frameworks across 1945 Germany. Elizabeth Janik's contributions on German musical culture from the late nineteenth century to 1989, David Monod's study of American musical denazification, and Toby Thacker's work on Allied musical reeducation all concern bureaucratic infrastructures and Allied policies. These excellent studies focus on the complicated relationships between occupier and occupied.[25]

Rubble and its musical possibilities extend far beyond the borders of postwar Germany. Elizabeth McAlister has linked music in the ruins of post-earthquake Haiti with efforts to reconstitute community after crisis. Krysta Ryzewski writes about the ruins of Detroit, tying together abandoned and postindustrial spaces with musical performances in the former automotive capital. Alex Cannon explores how Southern Vietnamese musicians use what he calls "the musical ruin," or a dismantling of traditional musical forms to reflect contemporary Vietnamese society. Focusing on the American government's nuclear testing in the Marshall Islands during the 1950s, Jessica Schwartz has explored the ruined voices of female survivors after the fallout, establishing important links between the body, nuclear silences, and trauma.[26] These contributions cast Berlin's unique position in stark relief to other rubbled sites of the twentieth and twenty-first century. No sudden firestorm, nuclear testing, earthquake, or economic crisis befell the German capital, but the craters of hundreds of aerial attacks left unique resonances for civilian musicians, who grappled to find new vocabularies to describe their experiences.

Accordingly, the first four chapters of *Rubble Music* concern the tangible, physical work required to reconstitute ensembles, opera companies, and radio stations from the debris. Each chapter treats rubble figuratively and literally by analyzing the metaphorical rubble of compromised, denazified citizens as well as the physical remnants of aerial bombing. The Philharmonic, the Staatsoper, and the Städtische Oper staged events within weeks of the cease-fire, despite the destruction of their concert halls. Ruined personnel and rubbled holdings remained, as civilians and soldiers worked to locate musicians, scores, and venues.

Chapter 1 focuses on the rubble sorting of the occupiers as they divided the city into four sectors and implemented their respective music policies and denazification programs. Authorities believed that Nazism had tainted the arts and that artists who had remained in Nazi Germany were gravely compromised. The Allies would need to classify the thousands of musicians remaining in defeated Germany, artists whose activities ranged from active collaboration with the regime to passive, if begrudging, acceptance of the Nazi musical establishment. Yet recognizing the "non-Nazi bricks" in the ashen rubble piles of Berlin would prove easier said than done. Chapters 2, 3, and 4 present the audible rubble work of Berliners themselves, as they reconstituted orchestras, opera companies, and radio stations from the ruins. Although the Allies supposedly monitored these institutions, they soon became sites for Berliners to perform their own suffering in public forums. As a sonic and visual trope across Germany, the towering bombed facades of churches and historic venues provided stunning aesthetic configurations for postwar concerts. Civilians used opera stagings, commissions, and broadcasts to express their victimhood, as Berlin's institutions became platforms to begin working through the trauma of war.

The last chapter of *Rubble Music*, chapter 5, turns to more private expressions of German victimhood as I look past Allied-controlled spaces to performances and compositions by and for other Berliners. While the occupiers were concerned with questionnaires and blacklists, civilians were experimenting with rubble as a performance and compositional aesthetic. Rubble, romanticized in both musical genre and textual content, was the foremost concern for the first generation of postwar composers as their *Lieder* transformed haphazard urban destruction into something much more deliberate: the ruins of German suffering.

Living in the only German city divided by all four occupiers, Berlin's musicians were uniquely poised to benefit from and toil under the ensuing Allied competition for the best players, facilities, and programming. Despite material challenges, the city became the locus of the most ambitious reeducation experiment of the twentieth century, exemplifying the tensions and contradictions of postwar Germany. To reach common ground with the German intellectual establishment, the Allies designed their respective reorientation agendas with classical music in mind. Musical production would become increasingly tied to political shifts within the city, regulated by Allied cultural officers and later checkpoint permissions, and influenced by economic and humanitarian crises such as the currency reform, polio epidemic, and Berlin Airlift (*Luftbrücke*).

The reconstruction of Berlin's cityscape was, in many ways, the earliest sound of the Cold War, with competing factions and conflicting ideas about German culture and the country's role within postwar Europe. Russian, American, British, and French occupiers were concerned with Berlin's musical culture and the symbolic capital that came with supervising some of the most prestigious ensembles in Germany. While their respective denazification and reeducation programs shared little in the way of content, the occupiers attempted to introduce Berliners to the music of their respective nations. The Americans were relatively new to using the arts to further a political ideology, having only recently treated music as a medium for propaganda through the creation of the Office of War Information.[27] The British occupiers, with limited governmental funding, worked closely with American cultural officers to promote a democratic musical culture. The French, occupying two industrial districts of Berlin with no major ensembles or venues in their sector, focused primarily on importing artists and sponsoring performances of French music. It was the Russian occupiers, however, who were most skilled at mobilizing culture for their political agenda. Soviet cultural officers created an elaborate network of organizations to support the city's artistic community, bringing German communists back from exile in Moscow to lead the cultural reconstruction of the city. By building trust between cultural officers and their German counterparts, the Soviets made early, important gains where the Western Allies struggled.[28]

Yet for all of their policy clashes and irreconcilable political differences, the great unifier in East and West Berlin was destruction, for, as Elaine Kelly notes, "the juxtaposition of culture and rubble was a common one across all four of the occupied zones in the late 1940s."[29] German civilians emerged from the cellars and bunkers of their city, and in the flotsam and jetsam of humanity it was often difficult to tell who was a former collaborator or who was simply a follower (*Mitläufer*). "Berlin was only *more* corrupt, *more* decadent, *more* degenerate than the rest of Germany," according to one American intelligence officer.[30] It was up to the Allies to mete out punishment or to show leniency to the occupied as the future of Germany, and that of postwar Europe, hung in the balance.

If the Allies had larger bureaucratic ideals in mind, however, the aims of most German civilians were more immediate, as conductor Hans von Benda and musicians like him searched the rubble for a "new life" in the form of "new sounds."[31] After his May 13 concert in the Schöneberg town hall where, only days before, the Hitler Youth burned incriminating city records of Jewish civilians, Benda marveled at "the peoples' need for culture" (*Kulturwille*), elated that artists were finally free from "the shackles of the Hitler era."[32] Yet despite the celebratory nature of his claims, musical culture was anything but liberated from the stain of collaboration. With rubble all around, how artists worked through, cleared away, or built over this debris would set the course of musical culture in both East and West Berlin for decades to come.

Notes

1. Paul Höffer, Toccata, score, 1945, Paul Höffer Papers, Carton 21, Staatsbibliothek, Berlin. "Unter Schmerzen geboren, 15.4.45."

2. Dienstbuch G 100 and 335, Berlin Philharmonic Archive; Erich Hartmann, *Die Berliner Philharmoniker in der Stunde Null: Erinnerungen an die Zeit des Untergangs der alten Philharmonie vor 50 Jahren* (Berlin: Werner Feja, 1996), 28; and Erna Berger, *Auf Flügeln des Gesanges: Erinnerungen einer Sängerin* (Zurich: Atlantis, 1998), 79.

3. Quoted in "Neues Leben—neue Klänge: Gespräch mit Hans von Benda," *Berliner Zeitung*, May 21, 1945

4. Quoted in Ibid. See also Wilfried Welz, ed., *Rathaus Schöneberg: Stationen einer politischen Karriere* (Berlin: Spitz, 1995), 60–65; Richard Brett-Smith, *Berlin '45: The Grey City* (London: Macmillan, 1967), 135; Hans von Benda, "Phoenix aus der Asche," *Tagesspiegel*, May 16, 1965; Brewster S. Chamberlin, *Kultur auf Trümmern: Berliner Berichte der amerikanischen Information Control Section Juli-Dezember 1945* (Stuttgart: Deutsche Verlags-Anstalt, 1979), 89n105; and Toby Thacker, *Music after Hitler, 1945–1955* (Farnham, UK: Ashgate, 2007), 34, 51–58.

5. Quoted in Linda Hutcheon and Michael Hutcheon, *Four Last Songs: Aging and Creativity in Verdi, Strauss, Messiaen, and Britten* (Chicago: University of Chicago Press, 2015), 53. See also Werner Egk, *Die Zeit wartet nicht: Künstlerisches, Zeitgeschichtliches, Privates aus meinem Leben* (Mainz: Schott, 2001), 369; Wilhelm Furtwängler, *Notebooks, 1924–1954*, trans. Shaun Whiteside (London: Quartet Books, 1989), 155–63; Raphael Woebs, *Die Politische Theorie in der Neuen Musik: Karl Amadeus Hartmann und Hannah Arendt* (Munich: Wilhelm Fink Verlag, 2010), 111–18; Klaus Lang, *Celibidache und Furtwängler: Der große philharmonische Konflikt in der Berliner Nachkriegszeit* (Munich: Wissner,

2010), 1–32; Michael Kater, *Composers of the Nazi Era: Eight Portraits* (New York: Oxford University Press, 2000), 138; Kurt Wilhelm, *Richard Strauss persönlich: Eine Bildbiographie* (Munich: Kindler, 1984), 398; Alex Ross, *The Rest Is Noise: Listening to the Twentieth Century* (New York: Farrar, Straus and Giroux, 2007), 373–74; and Alex Ross, "Monument Man," *New Yorker*, July 24, 2014, https://www.newyorker.com/culture/cultural-comment/richard-strauss-and-the-american-army.

6. Elaine Kelly, *Composing the Canon in the German Democratic Republic: Narratives of Nineteenth-Century Music* (Oxford: Oxford University Press, 2014), 14. For more about East and West German compositional collaborations, see Joy Calico, "*Jüdische Chronik*: The Third Space of Commemoration between East and West Germany," *Musical Quarterly* 88, no. 1 (Spring 2005): 95–122.

7. Robert G. Moeller, "Germans as Victims? Thoughts on a Post–Cold War History of WWII's Legacies," *History and Memory* 17, no. 1/2 (Spring/Summer 2005): 153. See also Anna Parkinson, *An Emotional State: The Politics of Emotion in Postwar West German Culture* (Ann Arbor: University of Michigan Press, 2015), 113–45; Monica Black, *Death in Berlin: From Weimar to Divided Germany* (Cambridge: Cambridge University Press, 2010), 16–18; and Jennifer Evans, *Life among the Ruins: Cityscape and Sexuality in Cold War in Berlin* (New York: Palgrave, 2011), 1–15.

8. Robert G. Moeller, *War Stories: The Search for a Usable Past in the Federal Republic of Germany* (Berkeley: University of California Press, 2003), 1–20.

9. Quoted in Jörg Friedrich, *The Fire: The Bombing of Germany*, trans. Allison Brown (New York: Columbia University Press, 2006), 98. See also Robert G. Moeller, "On the History of Man-Made Destruction: Loss, Death, Memory, and Germany in the Bombing War," *History Workshop Journal* 61 (Spring 2006): 107–8; Paul Steege, *Black Market, Cold War: Everyday Life in Berlin 1946–1949* (Cambridge: Cambridge University Press, 2007), 20; and Dietmar Süss, *Death from the Skies: How the British and Germans Survived Bombing in World War II*, trans. Lesley Sharpe and Jeremy Noakes (Oxford: Oxford University Press, 2010), 1–18.

10. For a few representative examples, see Ruth Andreas-Friedrich, *Battleground Berlin: Diaries, 1945–1948* (New York: Paragon House, 1984), 35; Hartmann, *Die Berliner Philharmoniker in der Stunde Null*, 29–36; Heinrich Weber, *Die Geschichte des Lehrergesangvereins Nürnberg e.V., 1878–2003* (Nuremberg: LGV, 2003), 117.

11. For accounts that perpetuate this narrative, see Ulrich Dibelius, *Moderne Musik, 1945–1965* (Munich: R. Piper, 1966); and Siegfried Borris, *Über Wesen und Werden der neuen Musik in Deutschland: Vom Expressionismus zum Vitalismus. Beiträge zu einer neuen Musikkunde* (Berlin: A. Steffan, 1948).

12. For a representative example, see Heinz Geuen and Anno Mungen, *Kontinuitäten | Diskontinuitäten: Musik und Politik in Deutschland zwischen 1920 und 1970* (Schliengen, Germany: Argus Editions, 2006), 1–17.

13. Pamela M. Potter, *Art of Suppression: Confronting the Nazi Past in Histories of the Visual and Performing Arts* (Berkeley: University of California Press, 2016), 1–47, 130–214. See also Alan Steinweis, *Art, Ideology, and Economics: The Reich Chambers of Music, Theater and the Visual Arts* (Chapel Hill: University of North Carolina Press, 1993), 32–69, 176.

14. Andreas Huyssen, "Nostalgia for Ruins," *Grey Room* 23 (Spring 2006): 7–10.

15. For one example, see "*Arche Nora* läuft vom Stapel," *Der Spiegel*, July 19, 1947. The article reported that the film *Nora's Arc*, featuring a tale of four friends rebuilding their lives while living in the hull of a wrecked ship, would feature specially designed nautical scenery

to ensure the film would "not become a 'rubble film.'" For more on the negative critiques of rubble film and rubble literature, see Stephen Brockmann, *A Critical History of German Film* (Rochester, NY: Camden House, 2011), 183; Jaimey Fisher, "Who's Watching the Rubble-Kids? Youth, Pedagogy, and Politics in Early DEFA Films," *New German Critique* 82 (Winter 2001): 92; Heinrich Böll, "In Defense of 'Rubble Literature' (1952)," in *Missing Persons and Other Essays*, trans. Leila Vennewitz (Evanston, IL: Northwestern University Press, 1994), 126; and Kathryn Sederberg, "Writing through Crisis: Time, History, Futurity in German Diaries of the Second World War," *Biography* 40, no. 2 (Spring 2017): 323–41. My thanks to Kathryn Sederberg for her thoughts about the term *rubble literature* (email correspondence with the author, September 14, 2017).

16. Robert Shandley, *Rubble Films: German Cinema in the Shadow of the Third Reich* (Philadelphia: Temple University Press, 2001), 3.

17. Eric Rentschler, "The Place of Rubble in the Trümmerfilm," in *Ruins of Modernity*, ed. Julia Hell and Andreas Schönle (Durham, NC: Duke University Press, 2010), 435; Johannes von Moltke, "Ruin Cinema," in *Ruins of Modernity*, ed. Julia Hell and Andreas Schönle (Durham, NC: Duke University Press, 2010), 406; Tony Judt, *Postwar: A History of Europe since 1945* (New York: Penguin Books, 2005), 233; and Amanda Z. Randall, "Austrian Trümmerfilm? What a Genre's Absence Reveals about National Postwar Cinema and Film Studies," *German Studies Review* 38, no. 3 (October 2015): 573–95.

18. Quoted in Alexander Rothe, "Rethinking Postwar History: Munich's *Musica Viva* during the Karl Amadeus Hartmann Years (1945–63)," in *Musical Quarterly* 90/2 (2007): 230. The original German source can be located at Hans Werner Richter, "Literatur im Interregnum," *Der Ruf* 15, March 1947. For an excellent analysis of rubble literature, see Stephen Brockmann, "German Literature, Year Zero: Writers and Politics, 1945–1953," in *Stunde Null: The End and the Beginning Fifty Years Ago*, ed. Geoffrey J. Giles (Washington, DC: German Historical Institute, 1997), 59–74.

19. Böll, "In Defense of 'Rubble Literature' (1952)," 126.

20. Douglas Martin, "Henry Ries, 86, Photographer Who Captured Berlin Airlift," *New York Times*, May 26, 2004; Martha Sprigge, "Dresden's Musical Ruins," *Journal of the Royal Musical Association* 144, no. 1 (2019): 83–121; and Ann Fuchs, "The Bombing of Dresden," in *Cultural Impact in the German Context: Studies in Transmission, Reception, and Influence*, ed. Rebecca Braun and Lynn Marven (Rochester, NY: Camden House, 2010), 36–57.

21. Stefan Rasche, *Das Stilleben in der westdeutschen Malerei der Nachkriegzeit: Gegenständliche Positionen zwischen 1945 und 1963* (Muenster: Lit Verlag, 1995), 72–81; and Ronald Taylor, *Berlin and Its Culture: A Historical Portrait* (New Haven, CT: Yale University Press, 1997), 288–89.

22. See, for example, Wolfgang Schivelbusch, *In a Cold Crater: Cultural and Intellectual Life in Berlin, 1945–1948*, trans. Kelly Barry (Berkeley: University of California Press, 1998), or Hermann Glaser, *The Rubble Years: The Cultural Roots of Postwar Germany* (New York: Paragon House, 1986), as both these cultural histories omit music. A notable exception, however, is Pamela Potter's *Art of Suppression*, which gives histories of visual and performing arts under the Nazis and in the immediate postwar period.

23. Theodor Adorno, "The Aging of New Music," in *Essays on Music*, ed. Richard Leppert, trans. Susan Gillespie (Berkeley: University of California Press, 2002), 199–200.

24. Amy Lynn Wlodarski, "Reconstruction after the Rubble: The War-Inspired Compositions of George Rochberg," AMS Rubble Seminar, November 2017; Amy Lynn Wlodarski, *George Rochberg, American Composer: Personal Trauma and Artistic Creativity*

(Rochester, NY: University of Rochester Press, 2019); Emily Richmond Pollock, "Rebuilding and Retrenchment at Munich's National Theater," AMS Rubble Seminar, November 2017; Emily Richmond Pollock, "Pride of Place: The 1963 Rebuilding of the Munich Nationaltheater," in *Dreams of Germany: Music and (Trans)national Imaginaries*, ed. Neil Gregor and Tom Irvine (New York: Berghahn Books, 2019), 145–68; Sprigge, "Dresden's Musical Ruins," 83–121; and Andrew Oster, "Rubble, Radio, and Reconstruction: The Genre of Funkoper in Postwar Occupied Germany and the Federal Republic, 1946–1957" (PhD diss., Princeton University, 2010), 139.

25. Elizabeth Janik, *Recomposing German Music: Politics and Musical Tradition in Cold War Berlin* (Leiden: Brill, 2005); David Monod, *Settling Scores: German Music, Denazification, and the Americans, 1945–1953* (Chapel Hill: University of North Carolina Press, 2005); and Thacker, *Music after Hitler*.

26. Elizabeth McAlister, "Soundscapes of Disaster and Humanitarianism: Survival Singing, Relief Telethons, and the Haiti Earthquake," in *Small Axe: A Caribbean Platform for Criticism* 39 (November 2012), 22–38; Krista Ryzewski, "Making Music in Detroit: Archaeology, Popular Music, and Post-Industrial Heritage," in *Contemporary Archeology and the City*, ed. Laura McAtackney and Krysta Ryzewski (Oxford: Oxford University Press, 2017), 69–90; Alex Cannon, "Tradition, still Remains: Sustainability through Ruin in Vietnamese Music for Diversion," *Ethnomusicology Forum* 25/2 (2016): 146–171; and Jessica A. Schwartz, "A 'Voice to Sing': Rongelapese Musical Activism and the Production of Nuclear Knowledge," *Music and Politics* 6, no. 1 (Winter 2012), https://quod.lib.umich.edu/m/mp/9460447.0006.101/--voice-to-sing-rongelapese-musical-activism?rgn=main;view=fulltext.

27. For more on the Office of War Information's musical activities, see Annegret Fauser, *Sounds of War: Music in the United States during World War II* (Oxford: Oxford University Press, 2013), 77–93.

28. Poet Johannes R. Becher was among the most illustrious artists to return, flown in by Soviet authorities to lead the Kulturbund. See Johannes R. Becher, "Manifest und Ansprachen," in *Gründungskundgebung des Kulturbundes zur demokratischen Erneuerung Deutschlands* (Berlin: Aufbau, 1945), 32–40; Joy Calico, "The Politics of Opera in the German Democratic Republic, 1945–1961" (PhD diss., Duke University, 1999), 29–36.

29. Kelly, *Composing the Canon in the German Democratic Republic*, 12.

30. Nicolas Nabokov, *Old Friends and New Music* (Boston: Little, Brown, 1951), 262.

31. Hans von Benda, *Berliner Zeitung*, May 21, 1945.

32. Ibid. See also Welz, *Rathaus Schöneberg*, 59–63.

1

BERLIN SOUNDSCAPES OF DEFEAT AND OCCUPATION

By May 1945, Berlin was an unrecognizable ruin. Hitler's wish for the city's transformation had been realized, although not in quite the manner he had envisioned. Allied bombing raids, intensifying in 1943 as the Americans bombed by day and the British by night, damaged nearly three-quarters of the city's buildings. Most of Berlin's storied music venues were completely destroyed. The Berlin Philharmonic's concert hall was a burned-out shell, complete with a horse cadaver on its steps. One American visitor was shocked to find the Kroll Opera reduced to "tangles of twisted girders, resembling empty bird cages."[1] Cows grazed at the gates of the bombed Staatsoper on Unter den Linden (fig. 1.1). The destruction and violence during the last weeks of war gave way to elation, exhaustion, and despair. Listening to the radio at the end of May, the anonymous diarist of *A Woman in Berlin* wrote, "Late in the evening they played Beethoven, and that brought tears. I turned it off. Who can bear that at this moment?"[2]

Apparently, quite a few Berliners could. Despite the regime's collapse on May 8 and subsequent occupation, concerts and broadcasts of classical music continued without pause. Aside from Hans von Benda's performances, members of the Städtische Oper broadcast a May 18 concert to Moscow, and on May 26, the Berlin Philharmonic resumed their season by playing Mozart, Tchaikovsky, and Mendelssohn to civilians and Russian soldiers in the Titania Palast, a former movie theater.[3] The culture-hungry German public attended concerts with such frequency that one British journalist admitted, "In the midst of such shambles only the Germans could produce a magnificent full orchestra and a crowded house of music lovers."[4]

This chapter explores destroyed Berlin through two separate, yet interwoven, strands: first the literal, then the figurative, rubble of 1945. The first

Figure 1.1. Cows in front of the Staatsoper. Photograph by Erich O. Krueger, F Rep. 290-02-01, Nr. 0000636. Landesarchiv, Berlin.

section concerns the capital as a rubbled site, analyzing the various occupation policies and how the sectors were governed by the occupiers' respective political agendas. The physical destruction of the city and its division into four separate sectors created the cultural fault lines that would resurface with the beginning of the Cold War. The second half of the chapter analyzes rubble as a metaphor for denazification work, with the occupiers sorting through the musicians and musical repertoire they found left in the ruins. Denazification made up much of the Allies' early effort to reform musical culture, and their decisions during the summer of 1945 would lay the groundwork for the rest of the occupation.

Rubble Clearing and Establishing Berlin's Sectors

The Russian Sector

When Alexander Dymschitz arrived in Berlin in May, the ruins were still smoking. Formerly a professor at the University of Leningrad, Dymschitz was now a Soviet cultural officer charged with supervising Berlin's cultural life after fascism. Armed with a list of names, Dymschitz spent his first days in the city searching for the leading artists of the Weimar period; he hoped to recruit their talents and gain their support for the new occupational government. The upheaval of war, however, had displaced many on his list, such as painter Otto Nagel, and much to Dymschitz's dismay, Käthe Kollwitz had recently died. He did manage, however, to locate writer Hans Fallada, now mayor of a small village outside Berlin, and cabaret singer and actor Ernst Busch, recently liberated from a Brandenburg prison. In the interviews Dymschitz conducted, he marveled at how the city's musicians, artists, and writers were spurred on by Berlin's destruction and that despite material deprivation, "the city was not dead. People reawakened to life, people who wanted to live. They wanted to work, create, to overcome destruction and hunger."[5]

Yet the transition from war to peace had not been as seamless as Dymschitz's account might suggest. Although the ceasefire on May 8 ended armed combat, disorientation and lawlessness prevailed. Soldiers raped Berlin's female population on such a widespread scale that an estimated 95,000 to 130,000 women sought medical treatment. The Soviets rounded up three million able-bodied German men for forced labor in Russia.[6] The war may have been over, but for many Berliners, liberation presented its own set of problems.

In the midst of continued violence (and perhaps because of it), the Russians immediately recognized the importance of supporting the German intelligentsia in their cultural endeavors. In the two months before the other occupiers arrived, the Soviets worked closely with the German artistic community to rebuild Berlin's music and theater culture across the city. On May 14, General Nikolai Bersarin, commander of the occupying forces, held a meeting with leading musicians and artists to discuss plans for the city's cultural reconstruction. Bersarin wanted to reopen theaters and opera houses as quickly as possible, and given the scarce number of qualified musicians, he could not afford to be selective about performers' political backgrounds. The Soviets did not bar musicians who had been former party members from participating in the city's rebuilding, believing these artists should be integrated into the city's socialist artistic fabric.[7]

Bersarin may have restarted Berlin's cultural conversation, but it was engineer Sergei Tulpanov who would dictate the terms. Educated at Leningrad and Heidelberg Universities, Tulpanov spearheaded the cultural section of the Soviet Military Administration of Germany (SMAD). British and American occupiers soon referred to him as "the Tulip," a nickname he earned for his infuriating finesse. (When Thomas Mann visited Weimar in 1949, it was Tulpanov who showed him around the city, charming Mann with anecdotes of Weimar's illustrious past.) Tulpanov supervised Dymschitz and other Soviet cultural officers who restarted music and theater activities mobilizing the German artistic community in the service of Communism.[8]

The Soviets set about creating organizations to support their artistic endeavors in Berlin. On May 30, the Soviet Military Government Propaganda and Censorship Division established the Chamber of Artists (Kammer der Kunstschaffenden) to register politically reliable actors, musicians, visual artists, and technicians, clearing them for employment. The chamber was conveniently located at Charlottenburg's Schlüterstraße 45, the former home of the Reichskulturkammer (RKK). From 1933 until 1945, the RKK, under the direction of Propaganda Minister Joseph Goebbels, supported and monitored (to varying degrees) fine arts, film, literature, music, the press, theater, and radio in Nazi Germany.[9] From its inception, the Soviet's Chamber of Artists employed Berliners to denazify other Berliners, and although lenient in issuing work permits, the rapidity with which artists were "rehabilitated" certainly had a stabilizing effect. Aside from approving new directors and *Intendanten* for Berlin's leading music ensembles and theaters, the Soviets had little interest in weeding out every party member or Nazi sympathizer affiliated with the city's cultural institutions. In the midst of the chamber's early weeks of operation, however, the artistic community was dealt yet another blow with the unexpected death of General Bersarin, who was killed in a motorcycle accident on June 16. Bersarin's leniency had allowed Berlin's cultural life to continue despite the regime change, and in his honor, all events and performances the following day were canceled.[10]

While the chamber was concerned with the logistics of restarting cultural life, the Soviets soon created another organization, Cultural League for the Democratic Renewal of Germany (Kulturbund zur demokratischen Erneuerung Deutschlands), that focused on uniting German intellectuals and Soviet cultural figures. It was a decisive move on the part of the Russians to emphasize collaboration and partnership, rather than impose their ideology from the top down. The inaugural meeting of the Kulturbund on July 3, held in the Berlin broadcast studio on Masurenallee, opened with the Berlin Philharmonic playing Beethoven's *Egmont* Overture. The Russians wanted to mold Berlin's intelligentsia into a Socialist artistic collective, and the Kulturbund would "make it apparent to the entire world that the German people do not lack the powers to extinguish the traces of Hitler's infamy, and to earnestly begin a reconstruction of spiritual life."[11] The creation of such an organization was particularly timely, as the Soviets believed culture in Germany had become "the tool of Hitler's criminal, plundering war"[12] and was desperately in need of reform. Seven male German intellectuals gave speeches, which journalist Ruth Andreas-Friedrich found to be littered with Nazi rhetoric. "Have they forgotten that there are women among us too?"[13] she wrote in her diary, discouraged even further as the speakers encouraged German men, not women, to participate in cultural activities. The last speaker was Johannes R. Becher, a German poet freshly returned from his Moscow exile and one of several artists backed by the Soviets to lead Berlin's cultural reconstruction. Becher would serve as Kulturbund president, supervised by Sergei Barsky, SMAD's music specialist and the grandnephew of pianist Anton Rubinstein. The meeting closed with the Philharmonic playing Tchaikovsky's Fourth Symphony in celebration of the new German-Russian partnership.[14]

The city's artists and musicians quickly accepted Soviet cultural officers as equals, and the Kulturbund's Jägerstraße clubhouse, named "the Seagull" (Die Möwe) after Anton Chekhov's drama, became the premier place for musicians and intellectuals to rub elbows. Members of the Kulturbund received coupons for food and drink, an immeasurable perk when the average Berliner was subsisting on roughly eight hundred calories per day. As *Time* magazine enviously reported, at the Seagull, "Russian officials and German actors and intellectuals can fraternize to their hearts' content over good food and beer."[15]

The American Sector

In August 1945, Nicolas Nabokov returned to Berlin wedged in the back seat of a dusty American military government jeep. A composer by training with dark, wavy hair and a flair for the dramatic, Nabokov's sense of adventure was piqued by his latest assignment in Berlin. As he arrived in the city, he recognized little from his days studying at the Hochschule für Musik twenty-three years earlier. The Berlin of his memory was buried beneath seventy-five million cubic meters of rubble. Nabokov was now an intelligence officer for the American military, and as one general described Nabokov's assignment, "He's hep on music and tells the Krauts how to go about it."[16]

Nabokov was among the hundreds of officers the American military hired to carry out a new and revolutionary experiment: to promote democracy in postwar Germany through strict regulation of all forms of mass media, including musical performance. Through an extensive denazification process and reeducation program, authorities hoped to purge Germany of all traces of pro-Nazi sentiment. Perceiving German classical music as tainted by Nazi ideology, officials wanted to reformat the genre to espouse the ideals of democracy rather than fascism. The Office of Military Government, United States (OMGUS) would oversee the governance of postwar West Germany and the American sector of Berlin. With culture as the new weapon in the fight against Nazism, intelligence officers were considered the first line of defense.

According to the terms established at the Yalta conference, once American and British forces arrived, the Russians receded to the city's eastern districts of Friedrichshain, Köpenick, Lichtenberg, Mitte, Pankow, Prenzlauer Berg, Treptow, and Weißensee. The Americans took up residence in the southwestern districts of Neukölln, Kreuzberg, Tempelhof, Schöneberg, Steglitz, and Zehlendorf, while the British occupied Charlottenburg, Spandau, Tiergarten, and Wilmersdorf. As the only ally who had also been a collaborator, the French were unrepresented at Yalta, and the other occupiers could not agree on who would have to cede territory to them. Although the French hoped to occupy Berlin's city center, just as the Germans had done in Paris, they were relegated to Reinickendorf and Wedding, two sparse, northern industrial districts (fig. 1.2).[17]

Apart from the territorial agreements reached at Yalta, however, there was little consensus about how to implement cultural programs in each sector. While the Allies felt that all traces of fascism needed to be extinguished, and believed classical music had defined the soundscape of Nazi Germany, there was little agreement on how to denazify and reeducate German artists. Where the Soviets heard sounds of reconciliation in early postwar concerts, the Americans considered music to be a dangerous entity that should be carefully monitored and regulated, as classical music soon became a point of contention between the Allies.

In the largest peacetime psychological warfare operation ever undertaken, US authorities were determined "to call both the key and pace of the tune"[18] when it came to denazifying music in their sector of postwar Berlin. As decreed by American Military Joint Chiefs of Staff Directive 1067 (JCS 1067), the end of the war signaled the beginning of the four

Figure 1.2. Berlin's four sectors, 1951. Herbert Eastwood/National Geographic Creative.

Ds: denazification, democratization (including reeducation and then reorientation), demilitarization, and decentralization. But beyond JCS 1067, American officials clashed on what path to take concerning Germany's rehabilitation, fluctuating between the desire for "hard peace"—that is, the return of the country to an agrarian society, as advocated by Secretary of the Treasury Henry Morgenthau—and "soft peace"—a more lenient approach advocated by the War and State Departments and one that permitted the speedy reconstruction of the German economy.[19]

Anxiety over the possible resurgence of fascism led the American military government to create the Information Control Division (ICD), responsible for monitoring all forms of mass media in postwar Germany. The ICD was the peacetime equivalent of the Psychological Warfare Division, the organization that attempted to undermine German support for the war effort. Although the Psychological Warfare Division had used less invasive measures to accomplish its goals (often in the form of pamphlets dropped from airplanes), the ICD installed hundreds of intelligence and cultural officers on the ground in German cities during July 1945.

ICD sections monitored German radio, film, theater, music, the press, and publishing industry. A final branch, intelligence, supervised denazification efforts, revealing the ICD's wholly contradictory purpose: to promote democracy through censorship and governmental control. At the height of the reeducation project, the ICD employed 35 officers and 150 German employees to monitor culture in Berlin.[20] Brigadier General Robert McClure, former leader of the Psychological Warfare Division and now head of the ICD, cautioned in regard to cultural matters, "Our policy has been to go slowly at first, bearing in mind that the Germans are still a conquered and discredited nation."[21] The ever-methodical McClure decided to implement a three-step approach to denazification and reeducation: first, a complete halt of mass communication and public performance; second, an American seizure of these mediums and the supervised reconstitution of cultural organizations; and third, a gradual return of these outlets to German control.

In a July 12 press conference, Secretary of War Robert Patterson announced that all forms of communication and public entertainment, including radio broadcasts, films, concerts, operas, and theater performances, would be carefully monitored, as "these agencies were used by the Nazis to impress their ideas on the German people. Without the most careful supervision, they might again be employed by die-hard Nazis to continue the struggle against us."[22] American officials believed German classical music was the cultural capital with the greatest value and sought to reframe its performance context by censoring concert repertoires, approving music personnel, and promoting American music. The irony of mandatory democratization of all media was not lost on everyone. As one cultural officer noted, "We have been forced to use the same methods employed by the enemy. Fire must be fought by fire."[23] Nabokov, too, recognized this contradiction, believing OMGUS was little more than "a sprawling, para-military bureaucratic octopus" that along with the Soviets, French, and British, "was supposed to govern the wreck the victorious Allies had inherited from Hitler's *Götterdämmerung*."[24] His cynicism was not unwarranted; Nabokov arrived in Berlin at a critical time for the American occupation. US authorities believed music and theater organizations could be used to spout Nazi propaganda and should be carefully supervised. Especially in Berlin, the ICD vetted theater and music officers to ensure that "top-ranking experts" would be placed in the city "to guarantee the best representation of U.S.

interests in this field toward the German public and toward the other Allied powers."²⁵

Nicolas Nabokov was an excellent choice to serve as an intelligence officer; fluent in four languages, he was a jack-of-all-trades who maintained a sense of humor about his role in postwar Germany. Born into White Russian nobility, Nabokov fled Russia during the Revolution, moving first to Greece, then to Germany and France, and finally America. Along the way, he worked as a composer for Sergei Diaghilev's Ballets Russes, lived with photographer Henri Cartier-Bresson in New York, and formed lifelong friendships with Igor Stravinsky and Sergei Prokofiev. After arriving in the United States, he taught first at Wells College in New York and then at St. John's College in Annapolis, becoming an American citizen in 1939. Once the war broke out, he worked as an analyst for the United States Strategic Bombing Survey, studying the Allied destruction of the country he would later work to rebuild. Yet even Nabokov was not above feeling overwhelmed with his new task in Berlin. "If it had not been for the fun that I got out of it, I would have given up a fortnight after I arrived," he admitted in his memoirs.²⁶

The tasks of American music officers included "the supervision of musical productions and presentations in concert halls or other places" in addition to conducting "a survey of musical facilities through the Reconnaissance Parties,"²⁷ although why reconnaissance was necessary remained unclear. Most theater and music officers stationed in Berlin had known the city during the Weimar era. Officer Frederick Mellinger was a Berlin-born émigré and former playwright who managed the Schaubühne in Munich and the Tribüne in Berlin.²⁸ Benno Frank, chief of the theater and music section, had worked at the Volksbühne during the 1920s, the same theater that would later serve as the premier venue of the Soviet sector. Though based in Berlin, Frank was responsible for coordinating the ICD's regional offices. Music officer Walter Hinrichsen was born into a prestigious Jewish family in Leipzig who were the owners of C. F. Peters Music Publishing Company. In 1939, the Nazis forced the Hinrichsen family to relinquish control of the company, and Walter fled to New York to open his own C. F. Peters branch. Music officer Eric Clarke also came to Berlin via New York, where he worked in administration at the Metropolitan Opera.²⁹

Yet the American officer most instrumental to the city's cultural reconstruction was John Bitter, head of Berlin's theater and music section from 1945 until 1948. Bitter was born in New York City, the son of Viennese émigré sculptor Karl Bitter and Ohio-born Marie Sherill. He studied flute and conducting at the Curtis Institute of Music, and after graduation he freelanced in Vienna as a flutist during the 1930s. When he returned to the United States, he took a conducting position at the University of Miami, regularly appearing as a guest conductor with the Jacksonville Orchestra, Florida Federal Orchestra, and Miami Symphony Orchestra. In 1940, Leopold Stokowski selected Bitter to help audition students for his All-American Youth Symphony Orchestra, an ensemble the maestro created to promote cross-cultural awareness by touring Latin America. The orchestra was short-lived; once the United States entered World War II, Stokowski's plans dissolved. Bitter joined the army and was quickly made an intelligence officer because of his language capabilities. At war's end, rather than return home to Florida, he decided to remain in Germany as a music officer. Bitter's first and last assignment was in Berlin.[30]

Initially, he worked closely with Henry Alter, the first theater and music officer to arrive in the city. Alter was born in Vienna in 1918 and immigrated to America shortly after the Anschluss. Although Alter's father had converted from Judaism to Catholicism decades earlier, Henry Alter still feared Nazi discrimination. He enrolled at the University of California, Los Angeles, and worked as a personal assistant to actor Paul Henreid, best known for his role as resistance fighter Victor Lazlo in *Casablanca*. Alter joined the US Army in 1943 as an intelligence officer, serving primarily in France. Once the war ended, he accepted a position as a cultural officer.

In early July 1945, Alter received orders to report to Berlin for duty. Passing through Halle on July 5, he was overwhelmed by the number of civilians who wanted to leave the city alongside the US Army in light of the city's imminent Russian takeover. The next morning, he drove his jeep on what remained of the autobahn and reached Zehlendorf, a residential neighborhood of southwestern Berlin. Alter was confident he would remember the city from his visits as a child, but much like Nabokov, he found that the Berlin of his memories no longer existed. After curfew on their first evening in the capital, Alter and another intelligence officer, Michael Josselson, decided to go on a drive. Encountering only empty, dark streets, unrecognizable in the moonlight, they found themselves wandering along the deserted Kurfürstendamm. The jeep could barely navigate the sea of ruins in what had once been an upscale shopping district. A drunken civilian flagged them down and offered them each an American cigarette.[31] Eerie and uncanny, the encounter was a sign of things to come.

The British Sector

William Henry Beveridge, a British economist sent to postwar Germany to write a government report on postwar conditions, concluded that although the Germans had perpetrated terrible crimes, "they are unequalled in music and unsurpassed in science."[32] While Beveridge's text exposes the shortcomings of his government's economic plan for the defeated country, his observations also reveal British anxiety about their cultural policies. With their nation regarded by many Germans as "the country without music" (das Land ohne Musik), the British prioritized other mass media, such as books and films, over their music denazification and reeducation programs, believing these initiatives played more to their strengths in postwar Germany.[33]

When the British occupiers arrived in early July, they took over the Chamber of Artists building at Schlüterstraße 45 to use as their denazification headquarters. Not long after moving in, officers stumbled onto nearly 250,000 RKK member files hidden in the attic. As one British intelligence officer proudly claimed, the Soviets, who disregarded the records during their tenure on Schlüterstraße, "would have happily given Molotov's—if not Stalin's—eyeteeth for those files."[34] Although many British officers had memories of visiting Berlin prior to the outbreak of war, their recollections often stood in stark contrast with the metropolis's postwar ruins. In searching for the music academy he remembered as a teenager, one soldier was surprised to find its only trace was now "that girder."[35]

To educate their soldiers on the finer points of German cultural life, the British government produced *The German Basic Handbook*—a manual detailing public services and administration from the Weimar era through the end of World War II. Select British troops were even sent to a brief training course on German cultural history at Bletchley Park, a nod to the fact that the British placed greater focus on the reeducation of German civilians rather than denazification. British planners created the Political Intelligence Division (PID) to restructure cultural life in their zone and sector of defeated Germany. The PID fell under the purview of the Foreign Office but had only eighty employees, as Britain's ruinous postwar finances meant that they had fewer resources with which to work. In comparison with the seventeen hundred workers of the ICD, officers in the PID soon felt marginalized by the Americans. British Control Commission headquarters were located at Lancaster House on Fehrbelliner Platz, and a requisitioned culture club to rival the Soviets' Seagull was located in a villa near Westend.[36]

The PID's limited funding meant their recruitment of cultural officers was restricted to a smaller pool. The intelligence branch responsible for denazification was headed by Colonel Kaye Sely, born in Munich as Kurt Seltz. His employees included George Clare, a Jewish Austrian émigré who returned to Berlin in 1946, where he worked as an interpreter on several high-profile musicians' denazification cases under British Information Services. Music and theater officer Pat Lynch was recruited while searching for work in the want ads of the *Daily Telegraph*. He applied even though he had "no idea what the job they wanted me for was" and made his way to the London interview where he "went on a bit about Wagner."[37] Days later, Lynch was working in Berlin. A supervisor at a Southampton aircraft factory, Georgiana Melrose was hired as a German radio scriptwriter and proofreader, despite not speaking the language. Melrose later wrote of her time leafing through radio programs: "I hadn't the vaguest idea of what I was supposed to be looking for, perhaps something like 'Heil Hitler' or 'Deutschland Uber [sic] Alles.'"[38] British efforts to support German musical culture in Berlin were more piecemeal and haphazard than those of their American or Soviet counterparts, and as George Clare reluctantly admitted, British cultural officers were "no match for the Dymschitzes of Berlin."[39]

The French Sector

France's dual status as an ally and a collaborator made their footing tenuous in postwar Germany. The French occupiers had the most difficult time of all the Allies establishing themselves in Berlin, as their troops were not permitted to take control of their sector until August 12. Led by General Marie-Pierre Kœnig, the French occupiers stationed most of their personnel in Baden-Baden, a more geographically advantageous location than Berlin. Kœnig made only sporadic visits to the city's French sector and was absent from many Allied meetings.[40]

Despite an uneven start, the French had one distinct advantage compared to the other occupiers—namely, the three postwar planners who wrote the cultural policy were also tasked with implementing it. In contrast to the other Allies, where cultural officers and officials rotated on a regular basis, René Thimonnier, head of the Office of Music and Drama; Raymond Schmittlein, head of the Directorate of Public Education; and Jean Arnaud, who worked for the Information Directorate, maintained their positions until the end of the French cultural program in 1956.[41]

Music reform fell under the Direction de l'Education Publique (DEP). Among the DEP's most successful initiatives was the beaux arts program that worked in tandem with German theaters, libraries, archives, literary societies, and other cultural organizations to present events, concerts, and exhibitions related to French culture for German audiences. Often, these presentations and exhibitions toured the French zone, bringing French culture to small German towns and making explicit the links between the two countries to further goodwill. Most activities took place in the Saar region, given the location of France's military government. This geographic concentration also had its drawbacks; concerts organized by the French in Baden-Baden were often attended by so many French soldiers that German civilians complained.[42]

Meanwhile, the French occupiers in Berlin were still attempting to change their districts of occupation, but to no avail. In August 1946, however, British cultural officers finally granted the French a small building on Kurfürstendamm to create a cultural center. The Maison de France opened in 1947 with an exhibition on ceramics. Other zonal-wide French initiatives included *Die Quelle*, a newspaper for French theater, music, and film, but the publication collapsed in 1948 after the East-West currency reform.[43]

The Rubble Work of Denazification

Quadripartite Denazification of Musicians

The city's four sectors were officially ratified at the Potsdam Conference, held between July 17 and August 2, 1945. Attended by Stalin, Truman, Churchill, and Churchill's successor, Clement Attlee, the conference outlined the occupiers' plans for a defeated Germany. Toward the end of their time in Potsdam, President Truman, in an attempt to charm Stalin, sat down at the piano and played Paderewski's Minuet in G, to which the Soviet leader responded, "Ah, yes, music is an excellent thing, it drives out the beast in man."[44] Truman was probably hoping for a statement of Allied unity from Stalin, but then again, he had chosen to play Paderewski, a staunch advocate for Polish sovereignty.

As the Allies discussed the landscape of postwar Germany in Potsdam, the denazification process in Berlin began. In the cultural sphere, the Soviets oversaw the Staatsoper and Staatskapelle, the Americans supervised the Berlin Philharmonic, and the British managed the Städtische Oper. Yet not all the Allies had ensembles with which to work. As Nabokov wrote, the French had to make do with only the occasional Berlin Philharmonic performance "in their part of the sprawling Berlin ruin."[45]

But the agreement on denazification policies ended with clear geographic delineations. In the American zone, the procedure was based largely on former party membership, as the Americans began the most aggressive denazification campaign of all the Allies. Authorities believed that Nazism had tainted the arts and wanted to locate "a few solid non-Nazi bricks from the mass of rubble," though it was not immediately apparent which "bricks" were sound.[46] Each ally had different policies on the denazification of artists, and furthermore, every artistic field had experienced varying degrees of autonomy under the Nazi regime. To categorically remove every party member from music ensembles might mean the cessation of orchestral activities altogether. In the film industry, which had developed close ties to the propaganda ministry during the Third Reich, the occupiers could scarcely locate anyone who was not compromised. The same challenge persisted in theater, where many film personnel also sought work. To rehabilitate visual and performing artists quickly and efficiently, they needed systems in place to establish degrees of guilt. But to implement these bureaucratic structures, massive amounts of time, energy, and personnel would be needed. And in the rubble heap of postwar Berlin, such politically reliable German personnel would prove to be few and far between.[47]

By August, the Intelligence Section of the ICD assumed responsibility for civilian denazification screenings. Artists seeking employment had to report to their district mayor (*Bezirksbürgermeister*) between August 18 and 25 to register for employment clearance, which could be granted or denied by the ICD.[48] The Americans reached these decisions based on denazification questionnaires (*Fragebogen*), forms that became a ubiquitous part of postwar life. Attorney Franz Neumann, a German Jewish émigré associated with the Frankfurt school who lived in New York, helped authorities develop many of the forms that stood between every German civilian and gainful employment. Applicants for performing arts jobs were required to fill out four personal questionnaires, four business or career questionnaires, three military government questionnaires, and four work applications; paperwork could take anywhere from three weeks to six months to process.[49] The denazification screening was also required to obtain a ration card. The card system was divided into five categories with the first receiving the most generous allotment while the last group was given the so-called "starvation card"; qualifying its recipients for only the most meager rations.

Ironically, the American-led ICD wanted to promote greater artistic independence through even greater governmental control. As a first step, cultural officers felt it was vital to do away with titles such as *Generalmusikdirektor* and *Generalintendant* as these terms "smack of officialdom and authoritative importance." Such pomp was thought to threaten the very core of the American cultural agenda, as "the Germans should be shown how unnecessary and somewhat ridiculous such titles sound in a democratic set-up."[50]

Furthermore, the divergent organizational principles of German and American cultural institutions greatly complicated the denazification process. In America, many arts organizations were privately funded, while equivalent organizations in Germany (prior to and during the Nazi period) generally depended on government subsidies to survive, and the Propaganda Ministry had to approve all upper-level arts administration nominations. Despite the American military's best efforts to streamline denazification by setting strict guidelines, confusion arose among cultural officers regarding the separate treatment of soloists and conductors. Under the Law for Liberation from National Socialism and Militarism, orchestral musicians were considered to be ordinary labor as workers in an inferior position. Soloists and conductors, however, were classified as supervisors, garnering more intense scrutiny and, in some cases, even a denazification trial.[51]

Based on his or her political credentials, not every musician qualified for a work permit in the American sector. Intelligence officers, according to Nabokov, "did a good deal of successful Nazi-hunting and put on ice a few famous conductors, pianists, singers and a number of orchestral musicians."[52] Although Nabokov was fairly optimistic about the efficacy of the American denazification program, his glib recollections hint at the difficulties of deciding who was guilty and who was innocent, or at least innocent enough. Although American planners envisioned a wholesale purge of Germany's compromised artists, the reality was far from savory. Questions for musicians and theater personnel included the well-intentioned, albeit naive query, "Have you ever resisted the Nazis in any way, or belonged to an organization which resisted the Nazis? (yes or no)."[53] Understandably eager to pass their denazification screening, musicians searched for ways to indicate that they, too, had fallen out of favor with the regime. One member of the Berlin Philharmonic claimed that the Reich Chamber of Music "barred me from my profession, and after a consultation, the ban was lifted."[54] Another

Berlin theater director mysteriously wrote that her "passive resistance" created problems for her with the Propaganda Ministry. With answers just vague enough to seem plausible, the questionnaire exposed the maddening reality that assigning blame to artists for simply for performing under Hitler would leave no artists at all with which to build the new Germany.

Only one year after the ICD began denazification, US intelligence had gathered information on ten thousand Germans in the arts and media sector, grouping these civilians into four categories: white, gray acceptable, gray unacceptable, and black. Those on the white list were allowed to hold any position, while individuals classified as gray acceptable could accept any job except an executive post. Placement on the gray unacceptable or blacklist, however, meant the applicant could perform only manual labor. Although former members of the National Socialist German Workers Party (NSDAP) and RKK were initially classified as gray unacceptable, the ICD quickly changed their stance on RKK membership once they realized the overwhelming number of German musicians who had joined.[55] "The sound of decalorized and denazified orchestras," according to Nabokov, did little for morale.[56]

In the American and British zones, after a musician was cleared by civilian-handled courts (*Spruchkammern*), specialized examination boards (*Prüfungsausschüsse*), made up of civilian practitioners in music and theater, could recommend musicians for registration. The court's decisions were still subject to approval by the Allied Kommandatura, the city's governing body with representatives from all four powers. Yet the British were not interested in taking a strictly punitive approach. The British sector cleared the highest number of returning Intendanten from the National Socialist period (twenty-two directors, as compared to ten in the Soviet sector and eight in the American sector). The French, similarly, were not in the least concerned with blacklisting, censoring, monitoring, or banning musicians and did not use the dreaded denazification questionnaire. They also permitted Germans to denazify other Germans, and each district was permitted to set its own denazification guidelines, creating massive inequalities in policy across the French zone and sector.[57]

Although German musicians in the Soviet sector still had to obtain clearance through the Chamber of Artists, the Soviets also pursued a policy of allowing Berliners to denazify other Berliners. As one American officer complained, "Even those who were beaten and persecuted to within an inch of their lives by the Nazis," were willing "to let by-gones be by-gones, if

ART is served."[58] The Russians believed, in a way the Americans did not, that party membership was only one indication of an individual's relation to National Socialism and placed far less emphasis on denazification as a means to root out fascism.

While the Allies admitted that controlling German cultural life would prove "impossible" without "a uniform quadripartite method of denazification," the occupiers could agree on little else.[59] Artists banned in one sector could simply find work in another, essentially rendering the denazification ruling null and void. By 1946, a working party of music and theater officers from the four sectors agreed to meet to discuss issues that pertained to the entire city. Yet as a subcommittee of the Allied Control Council, the occupational government of postwar Germany, the working party operated in a purely unofficial capacity and could only make recommendations, not issue directives, to the Allied Control Council. Working party meetings soon revealed that enforcing a blacklist across all four sectors of Berlin would be fraught with difficulty. The occupiers could not reach a consensus about the criteria to compile such a list, let alone agree on who should appear on it. The Russians felt that the best recommendation of an artist's character was their current behavior, while the Americans reserved the right to deny licenses to musicians even if they passed Spruchkammer clearance. The British declared that they relied fully on the denazification panels in their sector to make decisions, while the French admitted they had neither blacklists nor a uniform denazification policy.[60]

Across the board in the visual and performing arts, denazification soon became an unwieldy task due to the volume of applicants and the impossibility of thoroughly screening each person. The German public grew tired of the proceedings, which they regarded as arbitrary and unsuccessful. High-profile cases, such as those of conductor Wilhelm Furtwängler or director Veit Harlan, consumed enormous media attention and occupier resources, even though their outcomes were questionable at best. In all cases, artists eventually resumed their careers, though not without the occasional boycott or protest attached to their work or appearances.[61]

The occupiers were caught between treating musicians themselves as rubble, to be carefully cataloged and rehabilitated for their appropriate position in postwar German society, and the very pragmatic demands posed by classifying people (however politically flawed). The Allies did not have the resources or time to check every questionnaire for accuracy and had to reach verdicts as quickly as possible. Forcing civilians to fill out a questionnaire was one thing, but changing musical taste was quite another.

Quadripartite Denazification of Music

Richard Brett-Smith, a twenty-two-year-old private in the British army, arrived in Berlin during July 1945. In comparison with the inferno of the war's last days, Brett-Smith's Berlin was one of quietly belated surrender where "time seemed to hang still."[62] Yet musical reminders of the Third Reich were everywhere. While out to dinner at a crowded restaurant one evening, Brett-Smith noticed the house band was playing the *Horst Wessel Lied* as background music. Camouflaged as a waltz, only a handful of diners recognized the tune.[63]

If the denazification of musicians was difficult, then the denazification of music would prove to be the most ephemeral task of all. What fell under the purview "Nazi music," as the British deemed it, and what music could be used to build the new East and West Germany? Had composers such as Wagner and Beethoven become the unsalvageable, monolithic sound of fascism? Left with the figurative rubble of a tradition so idealized by the Nazis, how would the occupiers and Berliners reclaim German classical music from the ruins? Furthermore, music's supposed lack of political import led to widespread disagreement about its postwar treatment, despite the multitude of Nazi Party events carefully framed by German classical music.

Yet the role music performed in Nazi propaganda is not easily ascertained. As Pamela Potter has compellingly argued, notions of "Nazi music," created during the 1930s and refined after the war, advantageously served a variety of competing factions. Émigrés, hoping to be accepted in their new artistic communities and to justify their flight from National Socialism, emphasized the oppressive barbarity of the Third Reich's musical culture. After the war, artists who had remained in Nazi Germany could downplay their successes by claiming they had labored under a totalitarian state. Even Allied cultural officers, in order to justify expensive and far-reaching denazification and reeducation programs, needed a quantifiable sound enemy against which to fight. The Americans maintained that during the Third Reich, music acted as a kind of cipher, allowing listeners to connect their individual experiences to those of the collective as they participated in Nazi celebrations and holidays. Nazi music's borders shifted depending on who was trying to define it and when.[64]

Initially, it sounded as though the occupiers would attempt the impossible: to locate a discrete Nazi musical culture. British PID officer Ivor Pink called for a ban on "Nazi Music," as "we propose only to prohibit *Nazi* anthems or other *Nazi* music."[65] His suggestion was abandoned once British officers realized they were having a difficult time explaining what Nazi music was. As a subsequent document on British music control admitted, "We do not intend to treat the producers like children and to play the role of governess by producing long lists of forbidden works."[66] The British soon revised their policy to center on three distinct prohibitions: (1) No music belonging to the German military or imperial tradition, and no music associated with National Socialism; (2) No music of overtly Nazi composers; (3) No music on special occasions that might spur the population to rebel against their Allied occupiers. Fearing simple revanchism, the American ICD similarly forbade songs and marches of the Nazis and German Imperial Army with the passage of Law no. 191.

Neither the French nor the Soviets banned any music in their respective sectors. In drafting French control documents, René Thimonnier, head of the Office of Music and Drama, briefly considered prohibiting all music composed in Nazi Germany between 1933 and 1945 but decided against such a drastic course of action. Instead, he championed "positive propaganda" by planning to import French music and musicians, believing this approach would yield a better outcome.[67]

Banning select music required a simple military edict. But prohibitions were only a fraction of what cultural officers were expected to enforce. In May 1945, the American military government produced a manual with detailed instructions concerning information control in occupied Germany. Music in Nazi Germany, according to early American intelligence, emphasized "heroic compositions, among which the works of Richard Wagner came first, followed closely by those of Beethoven."[68] In June 1945, Samuel Rosenbaum, a member of the radio section of the Psychological Warfare Division, prepared the "Draft Guidance on the Control of Music," a more nuanced document outlining the American stance on classical music in postwar Germany. Draft Guidance also revealed Rosenbaum's expertise as both an attorney and Vice President of the Philadelphia Orchestra's board. For music denazification efforts to be successful, American authorities recognized that they would need to avoid coercion. Compiling a long list of compositions to ban would only replicate fascist methods, and as Rosenbaum cautioned, "We should not give the impression of trying to regiment culture in the Nazi manner."[69] American officials were understandably keen to avoid comparisons with the National Socialists, admitting, "If, for instance, Siegfried's Funeral March from "Twilight of the Gods" were [sic] prohibited as a separate piece because of its associations with National Socialism, the same argument ought to apply to the slow movements of Beethoven's Third and Seventh Symphonies."[70] It was not the musical repertoire the Americans objected to but rather any political or militaristic framework associated with the Third Reich. Consequently, rather than banning particular compositions, the "Draft Guidance" forbade certain works from being played on major Nazi holidays. Hitler's birthday could no longer be marked by performances or broadcasts of Beethoven's *Eroica* Symphony, Strauss's *A Hero's Life*, or Wagner's *Siegfried Idyll*. The Americans also decreed that celebrations of the Heldengedenktag (Heroes Commemoration Day), a national holiday held each March to commemorate German soldiers fallen in battle, could no longer be observed by broadcasts of "solemn music." Rosenbaum is vague on this point, probably because he was unaware the *Heldengedenktag* ceremonies featured recordings of marches. The "Draft Guidance" even cautioned that non-German music could serve as militarist propaganda and instructed music officers to remain vigilant to prevent "musical sabotage." Rosenbaum lists Chopin's Etude in C minor op. 10 no. 12 ("Revolutionary") and Sibelius's *Finlandia* as two pieces that could evoke anti-Russian sentiment.

Additionally, cultural officers were interested in promoting musical alternatives to German classical music. Particularly in Berlin, all four Allies interpreted *Entartete Musik* (degenerate music), or pieces supposedly banned by the Nazis on racial, political, or stylistic grounds, to their own advantage. Although the general consensus was that German music should be reformed "by positive rather than by negative means,"[71] the Allies set about importing works from their respective countries in unabashed acts of self-promotion.

Attached to the "Draft Guidance" was a list of thirty-five American composers to be promoted in Germany, including Samuel Barber, Aaron Copland, Cole Porter, and Duke Ellington. The War Department had a field office in New York responsible for shipping this music to postwar Germany, headed by composer and administrator Harrison Kerr. Although Kerr was supposed to send music requested by cultural officers, his own predilections often got in the way. Kerr generally refused to ship non-American music, preferring to send Copland, Barber, and occasionally, his own scores to postwar Germany. Officers in the Berlin office quickly became annoyed and bypassed control policies by ordering music from Switzerland or England, often paying out of pocket rather than deal with Kerr and the New York office.[72] The British began importing the work of contemporary composers such as Benjamin Britten and Michael Tippett. The Russian Kulturbund sponsored concerts that featured repertoire from Allied countries and Berliners alike, including the music of British composers Britten, Tippett, and Alan Bush; American musicians Aaron Copland, Walter Piston, and Virgil Thomson; and Berlin artists Boris Blacher, Max Butting, and Paul Höffer, in addition to one Russian work per concert.[73]

Aside from importing compositions, the Americans, in particular, encouraged music by German composers supposedly prohibited under the Nazi regime for racial or political reasons (e.g., Mendelssohn, Hindemith, Meyerbeer, and Offenbach).[74] Mendelssohn returned to German stages with a particular vengeance. In Munich, one music officer complained, "The Mendelssohn situation has become *critical, ridiculous,* and *urgent,*"[75] as nearly every concert in August 1945 opened with an overture by the composer. Across Germany, Mendelssohn's music sounded alongside symphonies by Beethoven and Tchaikovsky, a marker of newfound antifascism and a point of convergence between survivors, civilians, and the Allied occupiers.

Yet despite the Allies' certainty that the Third Reich had successfully eradicated degenerate music to create a "Nazi canon of German culture,"[76] Nazi policies were uneven and inconsistent. The RKK, with its competing factions and frequent conflicts between Propaganda Minister Joseph Goebbels, Staatsoper Chief Officer Hermann Göring, and Chief Ideologue Alfred Rosenberg did not censor all aspects of cultural production. Works by Stravinsky, Bartók, and Hindemith were performed well into the 1930s and Ravel and Kodály throughout the 1940s. The myth that no degenerate music was performed between 1933 and 1945 arose from the same impetus to classify Nazi music—two sides of the same coin that end up revealing more about the postwar occupiers' policies than Nazi Germany.[77]

The Allies presented anything but a unified stance on cultural policy in Berlin, and the only major music initiative that the four occupiers undertook together was the creation of the Inter-Allied Lending Library, a collection of musical scores housed in the Staatsbibliothek on Unter den Linden that opened in July 1946. The library consisted of carefully selected works from each of the Allied nations, meant to bring "new life into the musical Sahara which Germany became during the years of the Third Reich."[78]

By perpetuating the notion that Nazi Germany had been uniformly hostile to degenerate music, cultural officers from east and west could unite against a common adversary.

Conclusions

The Allies were dealing with the aftermath of the most highly politicized cultural sphere in modern history. In Adorno's 1945 essay, "What National Socialism Has Done to the Arts," written shortly before the collapse of the Third Reich, he contends, "It would be erroneous to assume that there ever sprung into life a specific musical Nazi culture."[79] Adorno realized the absurdity of eradicating a Nazi canon, not in the least because it had never existed in the first place. Instead, he perceived that music as political means would become a lasting cultural legacy of the Third Reich. As surely as the Allies wanted to rebuild Germany's political and economic structures from the rubble of the Third Reich, creating a framework around Nazi music and degenerate music allowed the occupiers to follow through with their respective reeducation agendas.

Even though the occupiers' music policies in Berlin were at odds from the start, the Americans were optimistic they could find common ground with Soviet cultural officers. Benno Frank, chief of theater and music, confidently proclaimed in a 1946 interview, "In spite of all political differences between the east and west it is felt that in the field of Theatre and Music complete understanding can be reached with the Russians."[80] Yet even as the Western Allies sought to compete with their rivals, cultural officers found Soviet offerings difficult to match. While the Soviets viewed art and culture as a way to cement their partnership with Berliners, the British and Americans felt these mediums had to be monitored because of their supposed misappropriation during the Third Reich, designing their music control policies from a defensive rather than offensive mind-set.[81] Despite lingering fears of inferiority when it came to waging cultural warfare, however, there was one thing the Americans had that the Soviets did not: a world-class orchestra residing in their sector. Once the most highly celebrated ensemble in Hitler's Germany, the Berlin Philharmonic was left in dire straits by the regime's collapse. The orchestra soon became the focal point of American denazification and reeducation efforts, and although intelligence officers such as Nabokov may have been "hep on music," the Philharmonic soon realized the help of the occupiers would not come without a price.

Facing the challenges of how to treat musicians as both "rubble figures" and real people living in a fraught historical moment, the Allies had the impossible task of deciding which "bricks" were sound enough to build the new Germany. Although the rubble work of the occupiers was well under way, the rubble work of Berliners was only just beginning. With the sectors divided and Allied denazification ongoing, the city's musicians began to use Berlin's institutions and ensembles to sound out their own traumas, finding the sonic space to begin working through the rubble of their former lives.

Notes

1. Webster Aitken quoted in David Monod, *Settling Scores: German Music, Denazification, and the Americans, 1945–1953* (Chapel Hill: University of North Carolina Press, 2005), 26. Aitken was a pianist visiting Berlin under the auspices of the American military government.

2. Anonymous, *A Woman in Berlin: Eight Weeks in the Conquered City*, trans. Philip Boehm (New York: Metropolitan Books, 2005), 223. In 2003, the anonymous diarist was revealed to be journalist Marta Hillers.

3. Städtische Oper, Rep. C 120, Nr. 1484, Landesarchiv, Berlin; Berlin Concert Program, May 26, 1945, Berlin Philharmonic Archive; and Amy C. Beal, *New Music, New Allies: American Experimental Music from the Zero Hour to Reunification* (Berkeley: University of California Press, 2006), 11–18.

4. Solly Zuckermann, *From Apes to Warlords: The Autobiography of Solly Zuckermann* (London: Hamilton, 1978), 192.

5. Alexander Dymschitz, *Ein unvergeßlicher Frühling* (Berlin: Dietz, 1970), 264.

6. Anthony Beevor, *The Fall of Berlin 1945* (New York: Penguin, 2003), 410.

7. Ernst Legal, Report to the Magistrat of Berlin, May 3, 1946, C Rep. 120, Nr. 1639, Landesarchiv.

8. Norman M. Naimark, *The Russians in Germany: A History of the Soviet Zone of Occupation, 1945–1949* (Cambridge, MA: Harvard University Press, 1995), 439; Nicolas Nabokov, *Old Friends and New Music* (Boston: Little, Brown, 1951), 272, 278–83; and Thomas Mann, "Germany Today: A Famous Exile's Impression of a Ruined, Vanquished Land and an Unchanging People," *New York Times Magazine*, September 25, 1949, 26, 28.

9. For more on the Reich Chamber of Culture and its activities, see Pamela M. Potter, *Art of Suppression: Confronting the Nazi Past in Histories of the Visual and Performing Arts* (Berkeley: University of California Press, 2016), 11–12, 156; and Elizabeth Janik, *Recomposing German Music: Politics and Musical Tradition in Cold War Berlin* (Leiden, the Netherlands: Brill, 2005), 99–106.

10. Hans von Benda, "Ausfall der heutigen Veranstaltung," E Rep 200–44, Nr. 23, Landesarchiv.

11. Bernhard Kellermann, et al., "Manifest und Ansprachen," in *Gründungskundgebung des Kulturbundes* (Berlin: Aufbau, 1945), 4.

12. Ibid. See also Karl-Heinz Schulmeister, *Auf dem Wege zu einer neuen Kultur: Der Kulturbund in den Jahren 1945–1949* (Berlin: Dietz, 1977), 48.

13. Ruth Andreas-Friedrich, *Battleground Berlin: Diaries, 1945–1948* (New York: Paragon House, 1984), 67.
14. Vincent Giroud, *Nicolas Nabokov: A Life in Freedom and Music* (Oxford: Oxford University Press, 2015), 197.
15. Winthrop Sargeant, "Europe's Culture," *Time*, November 4, 1946, 54; and Naimark, *The Russians in Germany*, 398–408.
16. Nabokov, *Old Friends and New Music*, 258. For more figures on Berlin's destruction, see Michael Meng, *Shattered Spaces: Encountering Jewish Ruins in Postwar Germany and Poland* (Cambridge, MA: Harvard University Press, 2011), 1.
17. Roger Gilmore, "France's Postwar Policies and Activities in Germany, 1945–1956" (PhD diss., University of Geneva, 1971), 42–43; and Dorothea Führe, *Die französische Besatzungspolitik in Berlin von 1945 bis 1949: Deprussianisation und Decentralisation* (Berlin: Weißensee, 2001), 41–45.
18. "Director of Information Control Services," August 2, 1945, RG 260, Box 133, Records of the Information Control Division: Central Decimal File of the Executive Office, 1944–49, National Archives and Records Administration II. Hereafter abbreviated NARA II.
19. Tony Judt, *Postwar: A History of Europe since 1945* (New York: Penguin, 2005), 100–126; and Cora Sol Goldstein, *Capturing the German Eye: American Visual Propaganda in Occupied Germany* (Chicago: University of Chicago Press, 2009), 6–13.
20. Cora Sol Goldstein, "Purges, Exclusions, and Limits: Art Policies in Germany 1933–1949," Cultural Policy Center, University of Chicago. For more on the ICD's programs, see Alfred Paddock, *U.S. Army Special Warfare: Its Origins* (Lawrence: University Press of Kansas, 2002); Monod, *Settling Scores*, 47, 100–24; and "Application for Employment, John Bitter," June 25, 1949, RG 260, Box 18, Records of the Education and Cultural Relations Division, NARA II.
21. "Director of Information Control Services," August 2, 1945, RG 260, Box 133, Records of the Information Control Division: Central Decimal File of the Executive Office, 1944–49, NARA II.
22. "Abstract from the Acting Secretary of War's Press Conference," July 12, 1945, RG 260, Box 63, Records of the Information Control Division: Records of Information Services Division Staff Advisor, 1945–49, NARA II.
23. Gerard Willem van Loon quoted in Wigand Lange, *Theater in Deutschland nach 1945: Zur Theaterpolitik der amerikanischen Besatzungsbehörden* (Frankfurt: Peter Lang, 1980), 105. Van Loon was a theater officer in Bavaria.
24. Nicolas Nabokov, "Boris Blacher," in Heribert Henrich and Thomas Eickhoff, *Boris Blacher: Archiv zur Musik des 20. Jahrhunderts* (Berlin: Fuldaer, 2003), 11.
25. Music and Theater Officer Appointment Files, RG 260, Box 243, Records of the Information Control Division: Records of the Division Headquarters, 1945–49, NARA II.
26. Nabokov, *Old Friends and New Music*, 271. For more on Nabokov's experiences in postwar Berlin, see Giroud, *Nicolas Nabokov*, 180–201; Frances Stonor Saunders, *The Cultural Cold War: The CIA and the World of Arts and Letters* (New York: New Press, 1999), 18; Toby Thacker, *Music after Hitler, 1945–1955* (Farnham, UK: Ashgate, 2007), 40, 101–2; and Ian Wellens, *Music on the Frontline: Nicolas Nabokov's Struggle against Communism and Middlebrow Culture* (Farnham, UK: Ashgate, 2002), 1–13.
27. Supreme Headquarters, *Manual for the Control of German Information Services*, 142.
28. "CAF Rating Mr. Mellinger," August 15, 1946, RG 260, Box 243, Music and Theater Officer appointment files can be found in the Records of the Information Control Division: Records of the Division Headquarters, 1945–49, NARA II.

29. Monod, *Settling Scores*, 102–4. For more on the Hinrichsen family and C. F. Peters, see Irene Lawford-Hinrichsen, *Music Publishing and Patronage: C. F. Peters* (Kenton, UK: Edition Press, 2000), 253–54.

30. Monod, *Settling Scores*, 13, 38, 102; and John Bitter, *What Dreams May Come* (Miami: Charlton Publishing, 1999), 27–28, 49–70.

31. Henry Alter, interview by Brewster Chamberlain and Jürgen Wetzel, May 11, 1981, B Rep. 037, Nr. 79–82, Landesarchiv, Berlin; and Henry Alter Papers 2000.248, United States Holocaust Memorial Museum Archive, Washington, DC.

32. William Henry Beveridge, "An Urgent Message from Germany" (London: The Pilot Press, 1946), 21.

33. Gabriele Clemens, *Britische Kulturpolitik in Deutschland: Literatur, Film, Musik und Theater* (Stuttgart: Franz Steiner, 1997), 79. The British founded *Der Spiegel* in 1947 as a reeducation magazine to promote a democratic agenda. For more, see Alan Bance, introduction to *The Cultural Legacy of the British Occupation in Germany*, ed. Alan Bance (Stuttgart: Verlag Hans-Dieter Heinz, Akademischer Verlag Stuttgart, 1997), 7–37.

34. George Clare, *Before the Wall: Berlin Days, 1946–1948* (New York: E. P. Dutton, 1990), 65. See also Giles MacDonogh, *After the Reich: The Brutal History of the Allied Occupation* (New York: Basic Books, 2009), 218.

35. W. Byford-Jones, *Berlin Twilight* (London: Hutchinson, 1947), 69.

36. Clemens, *Britische Kulturpolitik in Deutschland*, 68, 89, 93; MacDonogh, *After the Reich*, 250–55, 268; and George Clare, *Berlin Days* (London: Papermac, 1994), 130, 169, 203.

37. Quoted in Clare, *Before the Wall*, 82; see also pp. 1–22. Born Georg Klaar, he changed his name to George Clare after moving to the United Kingdom. For more on British cultural officers, see Thacker, *Music after Hitler*, 56–67; and Potter, *Art of Suppression*, 274.

38. Georgiana Melrose, *A Strange Occupation* (Elms Court, UK: Arthur H. Stockwell, 1988), 38. Melrose would ultimately stay in Hamburg for sixteen years to work for the NWDR. For accounts of the British reeducation efforts in Hamburg, see Thacker, *Music after Hitler*, 89–92; Humphrey Burton, *Menuhin: A Life* (London: Faber and Faber, 2000), 253; and Donald Cameron Watt, "Hamburg," in Bance, *The Cultural Legacy of the British Occupation in Germany*, 153–58.

39. Clare, *Before the Wall*, 81.

40. Gilmore, "France's Postwar Policies and Activities in Germany," 42–43; Corey J. Campion, "Negotiating Difference: French and American Cultural Occupation Policies and German Expectations, 1945–1949" (PhD diss., Georgetown University, 2010), 100; and Führe, *Die französische Besatzungspolitik in Berlin*, 41–45, 52.

41. Thacker, *Music after Hitler*, 27–29; Campion, "Negotiating Difference," 164; and Gilmore, "France's Postwar Policies and Activities in Germany," 14.

42. Gilmore, "France's Postwar Policies and Activities in Germany," 47, 136, 141; and F. Roy Willis, *The French in Germany, 1945–1949* (Stanford, CA: Stanford University Press, 1962), 176.

43. Führe, *Die französische Besatzungspolitik*, 191–94; and Claus Scharf and Hans-Jürgen Schröder, *Die Deutschlandpolitik Frankreichs und die Französische Zone 1945–1949* (Wiesbaden: Franz Steiner Verlag, 1979), 110.

44. Quoted in Gregor Dallas, *1945: The War that Never Ended* (New Haven, CT: Yale University Press, 2005), 549.

45. Nabokov, *Old Friends, New Music*, 262.

46. Quoted in Monod, "Internationalism, Regionalism, and National Culture: Music Control in Bavaria, 1945–1948," *Central European History* 33, no. 3 (2000): 347.

47. Interview with John Backer, Intelligence Officer, 82nd Airborne Division, MG Officer Import/Export Branch, Economic Division, OMGUS, B Rep. 037, Nr. 79–82, Landesarchiv. One particularly difficult denazification case was in Stuttgart, where a quarter of the Philharmonic were former party members. Memorandum, May 23, 1946, RG 260, Box 238, Records of the Education and Cultural Affairs Division: Records Relating to Music and Theater, NARA II. For more on denazification policies, see Potter, *Art of Suppression*, 100–4; and Cornelia Rauh-Kühne, "Life Rewarded the Latecomers," in *The United States and Germany in the Era of the Cold War*, ed. Detlef Junker (Cambridge: Cambridge University Press, 2004), 65–72.

48. "Control of Printing, Radio, Theater, and Music," August 16, 1945, Slide 239, Landesarchiv.

49. Monod, *Settling Scores*, 47–57.

50. Meeting of the Working Party, December 19, 1946, RG 260, Box 237, Records of the Education and Cultural Affairs Division: Records Relating to Music and Theater, NARA II.

51. Monod, *Settling Scores*, 29, 47–57, 102–17; and Benno Frank to Eric Clarke, "Denazification," June 20, 1946, and Directive no. 24, RG 260, Box 237, Records of the Education and Cultural Affairs Division: Records Relating to Music and Theater, NARA II.

52. Nabokov, *Old Friends, New Music*, 263.

53. Personal Questionnaire, Military Government of Germany Information Control, RG 260, Box 121b, Records of the Information Services Branch: Fragebogens [sic] of Film, Theater and Music Artists, NARA II.

54. Richard Wolff, Personnel Questionnaire, December 28, 1947, RG 260, Box 121b, Records of the Information Services Branch: Fragebogens [sic] of Film, Theater and Music Artists, NARA II. "Margarete Obuch," Fragebogen and Licenses for Charlottenburg, B Rep. 207, Nr. 641, Landesarchiv, Berlin.

55. Monod, *Settling Scores*, 23–32, 100–2; see also Robert McClure, "Evaluation of NSDAP and Affiliated Nazi Organizations," May 7, 1946, RG 260, Box 237, Records of the Education and Cultural Affairs Division: Records Relating to Music and Theater, NARA II.

56. Nabokov, *Old Friends and New Music*, 252.

57. Monod, *Settling Scores*, 44–95; Clemens, *Britische Kulturpolitik in Deutschland*, 251; Willis, *The French in Germany*, 150–56; and Pechoux to Working Committee, "Denazification Procedure in Theater and Music Field [sic]," December 16, 1946, RG 260, Box 237, Records of the Education and Cultural Affairs Division: Records Relating to Music and Theater, NARA II.

58. Edward Hogan, "Some Informal Notes on the *Kammer der Kunstschaffenden*," RG 260, Box 242, Records of the Education and Cultural Relations Division: Records Relating to Music and Theater, NARA II.

59. Pechoux to Working Committee, "Denazification Procedure in Theater and Music Field [sic]," December 16, 1946, RG 260, Box 237, Records of the Education and Cultural Affairs Division: Records Relating to Music and Theater, NARA II.

60. Ibid.

61. Potter, *Art of Suppression*, 102–3. At Furtwängler's appearance with the Vienna Philharmonic in November 1947, fifty former concentration camp prisoners organized a demonstration against the conductor. He was ushered through a side door of the hall to avoid public embarrassment. *Der Kurier*, November 17, 1947.

62. Richard Brett-Smith, *Berlin '45: The Grey City* (London: Macmillan, 1967), xii.

63. Ibid., 107.

64. See Potter, *Art of Suppression*, 3, 48–52, 89–130, 159–60.
65. Clemens, *Britische Kulturpolitik in Deutschland*, 142–43.
66. Quoted in ibid., 145.
67. Quoted in Thacker, *Music after Hitler*, 27.
68. Supreme Headquarters, *Manual for the Control of German Information Services*, 203.
69. "Draft Guidance on the Control of Music," June 8, 1945, RG 260, Box 134, Records of the Information Control Division: Central Decimal File of the Executive Office, 1944–49, NARA II. For more on Rosenbaum, see Monod, *Settling Scores*, 18–23.
70. "Draft Guidance on the Control of Music," NARA II.
71. Ibid.
72. Monod, *Settling Scores*, 29, 118–19.
73. Weiss, "Musik im Kulturbund der Sowjetischen Besatzungszone und der DDR 1945–1951," in *"Stunde Null": Zur Musik um 1945: Bericht über das Symposion der Gesellschaft für Musikforschung an der Musikhochschule Lübeck 24–27. September 2003*, ed. Volker Scherliess (Kassel: Bärenreiter, 2014), 249.
74. "Draft Guidance on the Control of Music," NARA II.
75. Quoted in Thacker, *Music after Hitler*, 76.
76. "Suggested Modification in *Drahtfunk* Radio Programming, August 20, 1946," and "Music Programming, August 23, 1946," RG 260, Box 134, Records of the Information Control Division: Central Decimal File of the Executive Office, 1944–49, NARA II.
77. Potter, *Art of Suppression*, 3, 89–129; Pamela M. Potter, "What Is 'Nazi Music'?" *Musical Quarterly* 88, no. 3 (2005): 428–55; and Joan Evans, "Stravinsky's Music in Hitler's Germany," *Journal of the American Musicological Society* 56 (Fall 2003): 525–94.
78. *Weekly Information Bulletin*, Office of the Assistant Chief of Staff, G-5 Division USFET, Information Branch, August 1947, 11–12, 14, http://digital.library.wisc.edu/1711.dl/History.omg1947n105.
79. Theodor Adorno, "What National Socialism Has Done to the Arts," in *Essays on Music*, ed. Richard Leppert, trans. Susan Gillespie (Berkeley: University of California Press, 2002), 383.
80. Benno Frank, *New York Star*, October 18, 1946.
81. "Activity of Prüfungsausschüsse," July 25, 1946, and "The Working Party," December 16, 1946, RG 260, Box 237, Records of the Education and Cultural Affairs Division: Records Relating to Music and Theater, NARA II.

2

OCCUPIED MUSIC

*The Berlin Philharmonic and
the American Military*

During the final days of the Third Reich, conductor Leo Borchard huddled in a Charlottenburg cellar with several friends. The group had miraculously survived Hitler's reign as opponents of the Nazi regime, yet the arrival of Russian troops brought other dangers. Once Soviet soldiers reached Borchard's street, several Werwolf agents, fanatical Nazis determined to resurrect the Third Reich, fired on the invaders. The Russians frantically searched the block for the shooters, mistaking Borchard and his group first for Werwolf operatives, and then equally as fatally, for partisans. With candles blazing and four Soviet officers staring on in stony silence, Borchard tried to placate the soldiers by singing their national anthem; his partner, journalist Ruth Andreas-Friedrich, immediately realized, "He's singing for our lives."[1] As he finished, the mood lightened as the soldiers clapped him on the back and shared their food, a small feast of bacon and sausage. Never before and never again would Borchard give such a command performance.

Fluent in Russian, Borchard soon made an impression on the Soviets, befriending General Nikolai Bersarin, commander of the occupying forces. Bersarin admired not only Borchard's talent as a musician but also his work for Onkel Emil, a small communist resistance group that hid Jews during the Third Reich and provided them with falsified documents. Borchard was just the kind of comrade that the general needed to rebuild the city's musical culture, and Bersarin quickly appointed him *Generalmusikdirektor* of the Berlin Philharmonic. With the Philharmonic's principal conductor, Wilhelm Furtwängler, living in Swiss exile, Borchard was savvy enough to realize that Bersarin's decision could mean the career opportunity of a lifetime.[2]

To the Russian occupiers, Borchard was uniquely qualified to play a leading role in the city's reconstruction. Born to German parents in Moscow in 1899, he spent most of his childhood in St. Petersburg, moving to Berlin after the Russian Revolution. Eventually, he found work as an assistant conductor at the Kroll Opera, an institution funded by the Weimar government that encouraged modernist opera stagings. With Otto Klemperer as its music director, political turmoil meant the Kroll Opera would be a short-lived experiment, and it closed in 1931. Again looking for work, Borchard briefly served as a cultural ambassador for the Reichsmusikkammer (RMK) in occupied Greece. Occasionally, he even appeared as a guest conductor with the Berlin Philharmonic, leading a March 1943 concert of contemporary music by Gottfried von Einem, Werner Egk, and Zoltán Kodály.[3]

The Philharmonic had been the most celebrated ensemble under National Socialism, and the Soviet occupiers were content to allow the musicians to continue concertizing with little oversight. In early May, with the city now under Soviet control and the Americans' arrival still two months away, Philharmonic musicians were uncertain about the ensemble's fate. On May 13, only five days after Germany's surrender, Borchard and forty Philharmonic members decided to rehearse at the Wilmersdorf home of clarinetist Ernst Fischer. In lieu of public transportation, they traveled on foot or by cycling through the ruins; double bassists pushed their instruments in wheelbarrows or in baby strollers. Among the first order of business was to assess the ensemble's performing forces and material resources. Seventy of the orchestra's 110 musicians fled Berlin in the final weeks of the war, and not all would return. Allied bombing had leveled the ensemble's hall and destroyed most of the orchestra's instruments and scores. To assist with the orchestra's rehearsals, Bersarin granted them permission to practice at Wilmersdorf's town hall, formerly the site of Wehrmacht administration offices.[4]

On May 26, the Philharmonic gave its first postwar concert at the Titania Palast movie theater in Steglitz. Tickets were handwritten and the ensemble was less than half of its regular size, yet the hall was packed with concertgoers who applauded wildly as Borchard reached the podium. The orchestra opened the program with Mendelssohn's *A Midsummer Night's Dream* Overture, a piece they had not played since 1935. (The orchestra still had Mendelssohn's scores due to the efforts of trombonist Friedrich Quante, who managed to hide select works by Jewish composers in a location he refused to divulge.) Borchard also conducted Mozart's Violin Concerto No. 5 in A Major and Tchaikovsky's Fourth Symphony.[5]

Although Ruth Andreas-Friedrich wrote in her diary that the concert erased memories of "Nazis, the lost war and the occupation forces,"[6] her claim of transcendence, while appealing within the zero hour framework, was perhaps a calculated exaggeration for the benefit of posterity. Another eyewitness was less generous about the event's resonance, describing the terror and chaos that ensued when Soviet soldiers burst through the theater's doors with their pistols brandished during the Mendelssohn Overture. When the Russian soldiers left during the final movement of the Tchaikovsky, the audience breathed a collective sigh of relief.[7]

The orchestra's rubbled personnel and repertoire were the literal and metaphorical debris of postwar musical culture. US cultural and intelligence officers supervised the Philharmonic between 1945 and 1949, and during the ambitious denazification and reeducation process, Information Control Division (ICD) officers registered compromised musicians and promoted American music and musicians. Yet as Nicolas Nabokov admitted, in the "still smoldering heap of rubble called Berlin,"[8] it was impossible to begin entirely anew in light of scarce material resources and personnel, as the occupiers began the arduous task of sorting through the rubble of musicians and conductors.

Rubbled Musicians and Conductors

In early July, when the Americans arrived in Berlin, they were unsure how to supervise the ensemble. The orchestra's close relationship to the regime had sustained the Philharmonic financially, but compromised them politically, as its members had served as cultural ambassadors and civil servants. As the most celebrated orchestra under the Third Reich (*Reichsorchester*) and the highest paid, Joseph Goebbels excused the Philharmonic from military service because he considered concert tours in occupied countries just as vital as armed combat. Even in the waning months of the regime, these musicians were exempt from serving in the *Volkssturm*, the desperate Nazi militia composed of young boys and old men.[9]

The ensemble's final concert under the Third Reich took place on April 16, 1945, in the Beethovensaal beside the ruins of their former home. (British phosphorous bombs destroyed the Philharmonic's primary concert hall in January 1944.) The program included Strauss's *Death and Transfiguration*, an apt choice for the encircled city; earlier that morning, Soviet troops had commenced their assault on the capital. To the audience wrapped in their overcoats, the concert must have had a macabre air of finality. Even as heavy shelling began on the city center, the ensemble continued to practice. On April 20, Hitler's birthday, the Philharmonic rehearsed with conductor Leopold Ludwig, although the two concerts planned for April 21 and 22 were canceled due to heavy artillery fire from the Russian advance.[10]

The ensemble prepared for the city's fall in various ways. Most, like Borchard, hid in cellars, although not without incident. In the chaotic weeks that followed, the musicians were completely at the mercy of the Soviet occupiers. Soldiers seized double bassist Erich Hartmann and placed him in a detention center along with hundreds of other German men, presumably to be deported east. He managed to escape by climbing over a wall at an opportune moment. Hartmann had no intention of returning to Russia anytime soon. Wounded on the Eastern Front in 1943, he was one of the few Philharmonic musicians to have served in the Wehrmacht. Other orchestra members faced time as conscripted laborers for the occupiers; oboist Helmut Schlövogt had to work at Sachsenhausen concentration camp for several days.[11]

But these musicians were the fortunate ones. Several artists were killed by Allied bombing, including violinists Hans Ahlgrimm and Alois Ederer, clarinetist Oskar Audilet, and timpanist Kurt Ulrich. Violinist Bernard Alt and double bassist Alfred Krueger committed suicide along with their families before the surrender.[12] Violist Curt Christkaus volunteered for the Volkssturm, only to drown in the Oder River while retreating from the advancing Russians. Harpist Rolf Naumann and oboist Willi Lenz were murdered for their bicycles as they fled west. Soviet soldiers took trumpeter Anton Schuldes into custody during the Battle of Berlin, and he was never seen again. Yet between war and peace, the orchestra kept practicing. One British officer recalled a Philharmonic rehearsal at the Theater des Westens on Kantstraße where Borchard conducted "a hundred odd men, poorly dressed by normal standards," who played "a movement of a Beethoven Symphony amid the chaos and the ruins of that shattered street."[13]

The ensemble concertized under Soviet jurisdiction until the Americans arrived in early July. The Titania Palast movie theater, the Philharmonic's primary venue, was located in the American sector. The transition was not without its share of problems; at first, the 2nd Panzer Division requisitioned the Titania Palast for American troop entertainment, while US Special Services wanted to confiscate all the Philharmonic's instruments that were stored in the basement. Borchard and music officer Henry Alter persuaded military authorities to reconsider, and they returned the instruments and granted the musicians access to the building. In acknowledgment of the Americans' arrival, the orchestra gave two concerts exclusively for troops on July 8 and 9, featuring music by "Felix Mendelssohn-Bartholdi" as posters announced.[14]

British and American cultural officers met with Borchard and the orchestra's business managers on July 31 to discuss an eight-week plan for the Philharmonic. The officers decided that concerts would take place at least every weekend in either the American sector's Titania Palast or the British sector's Theater des Westens. Aside from these venues, the orchestra would perform in the American sector's Zinnowald Saal in Zehlendorf, Cosmos-Kino in Tegel, Quick Theater in Neukölln, and the Soviet-controlled Rundfunkhaus, home of Radio Berlin.[15] Music officer John Bitter understood that the orchestra was a valuable asset in the game of cultural diplomacy between the Allies. With Bitter and Alter's help, the ensemble had amassed nearly one hundred musicians, leading Alter to conclude, "I really think that we saved the Berlin Philharmonic Orchestra."[16] Although it was questionable that the Americans were solely responsible for the ensemble's survival, they wasted no time in making adjustments to the orchestra's roster.

Cultural officers aimed to purge Philharmonic musicians whose political backgrounds they deemed suspect. Grounds for removal were simple: if a musician had joined the party before 1935 or held a leadership position under the National Socialists, they were fired. All in all, there were far fewer party members in the Berlin Philharmonic than in comparable German-speaking ensembles. More than forty of the Vienna Philharmonic's 117 musicians were former members of the Nazi Party, though these musicians faced even fewer consequences than their German counterparts. As Bitter complained in his report, "In contrast to the Berlin Philharmonic, the Vienna Philharmonic has always gotten away with murder in its prodigal use of Nazi members."[17]

Of the seventeen former party members who played for the Berlin Philharmonic (fourteen full time and three part time), the Americans dismissed nine musicians, beginning with the orchestra's business managers Joseph Stoehr and Lorenz Höber in December 1945. One aggravated music officer wrote that Höber "still can't get it through his head that the Americans can get rid of him even though he was hired by the city of Berlin,"[18] as the violist fought to remain employed by the Philharmonic. The ICD then fired seven other former party members: cellist Wolfram Kleber, horn players Georg Hedler and Adolph Handke, violinists Alfred Graupner and Hans Woywoth, double bassist Arno Burkhardt, and harpist Fritz Hartmann.[19]

Musicians who were dismissed on political grounds faced few real sanctions, however. They could relocate to other zones and sectors or, in certain cases, simply wait and resume their careers. Seven of the nine dismissed musicians found work in Berlin. The Russian-controlled Staatsoper hired Stoehr and Höber, the British-licensed Städtische Oper employed Kleber, and the American-run RIAS Symphony Orchestra recruited Hedler. Between 1946 and 1947, the Philharmonic even rehired Graupner, Burkhardt, and Handke as the ICD relaxed their denazification procedures.

During the denazification process, the orchestra struggled to maintain high performance standards as twenty instrumentalists left in search of better working conditions. Given the Philharmonic's importance for their reorientation aims, ICD officers petitioned their military superiors to increase the musicians' rations by four hundred calories per day. In his search for a scapegoat, Bitter also decided the ensemble's managers were incompetent; "As devoted as I am to this group and their welfare, I feel a certain stagnation setting in because of the way the orchestra is run,"[20] he wrote. To counteract what he believed were poor management decisions and to diversify the group's repertoire, Bitter felt the Philharmonic needed a musical director. The orchestra flatly refused, voting against the idea sixty-five to one and pleading with the Americans to "help restore democratic self-representation, just as it was before 1933."[21] Bitter was forced to drop the idea once and for all.

Orchestral musicians, classified as "ordinary labor," were but one component of the American denazification and reeducation plan. Finding suitable conductors, however, occupied the bulk of cultural officers' time and efforts. In late July 1945, Rudolph Dunbar (fig. 2.1), a thirty-seven-year-old Guyanese American conductor and former war correspondent, paid Borchard a visit to discuss music. Over coffee in Borchard's Charlottenburg apartment, they shared stories of the difficulties they experienced in establishing their careers. Borchard's German citizenship meant that to the Allied occupiers, he was indelibly linked with the Nazi regime, while Dunbar encountered skepticism about his conducting abilities because of his skin color. As a parting gift, Borchard presented him with a volume of

Figure 2.1. Conductor Rudolph Dunbar, September 1946. Carl Van Vechten photograph. ©Van Vechten Trust. Yale Collection of American Literature, Beinecke Rare Book and Manuscript Library, Yale University.

Bach cantatas, inviting him to conduct the Philharmonic sometime that fall. Andreas-Friedrich recorded the encounter in her diary, and although sympathetic to the struggles Dunbar faced, she also exoticized him: "Is it a victor, who is standing in front of us? In his elegantly styled American uniform, beautiful like a panther and passionately interested in Bach and Beethoven?"[22]

On the evening of August 23, a British officer invited Borchard and Andreas-Friedrich to his villa in Grunewald, where they spent the night eating and drinking. Around midnight, Colonel Thomas Creighton, another British officer, offered to drive Borchard and Andreas-Friedrich back to Berlin given the strictly enforced curfew for all German civilians between 11:00 p.m. and 5:00 a.m. On the way home, Creighton and Borchard chatted amicably about music, and Andreas-Friedrich listened from the back seat. As Creighton approached an American checkpoint, he noticed a swinging lantern in the darkness. Assuming it was someone trying to hitch a ride, Creighton kept driving. The lantern had, in fact, been a signal to halt, and when the vehicle did not stop, the American officer on duty fired shots, fatally wounding Borchard. According to Andreas-Friedrich, Borchard's final words were simply, "Next time, I'll play Bach for you,"[23] his utterance conveying the supreme irony of having survived the Third Reich only to be accidently shot by his liberators.

An untimely four days after his death, *Newsweek* ran an article about the conductor titled, "One Man Can Save German Music." The piece made no mention of his shooting but instead cheerfully reported, "The problem of German music involves not only what to play—but who can be trusted to play it," arguing that Borchard was "the only man, according to many critics, around whom the orchestra can hope to rebuild."[24] The entire article was a fabrication, doubly so now that the article's protagonist was dead. It was not until 1955, ten years after Borchard's shooting, that the American military government closed their official inquiry, declaring his death a *Besatzungsschaden* (occupation casualty) by concluding the British were at fault.[25]

Having accidentally killed the Philharmonic's best hope for postwar reeducation and rehabilitation, the Americans were uncertain how best to proceed. At the next concert on August 25, Robert Heger directed the ensemble, and several leading Berlin artists gave speeches in Borchard's honor, including Michael Bohnen, president of the Chamber of Artists and intendant of the British-controlled Städtische Oper, and violist Lorenz Höber, a

Philharmonic manager who would soon be fired by the Americans. Instead of closing with Richard Strauss's *Don Juan* as planned, the orchestra played the Funeral March from the *Eroica*, dedicating the movement to Borchard. Only three months earlier, the same piece had marked Hitler's suicide.[26]

With Borchard's unexpected death, Rudolph Dunbar got his chance to lead the Berlin Philharmonic sooner than he anticipated. On September 2, 1945, the orchestra, "under the direction of the famous American conductor" (fig. 2.2) performed Weber's *Oberon* Overture, Tchaikovsky's Sixth Symphony, and William Grant Still's *Afro-American Symphony*. Dunbar and Still were good friends, having played together in the Harlem Symphony Orchestra during the 1920s. The Berlin audience of two thousand applauded so vigorously that Dunbar returned to the stage five times for bows. As a goodwill gesture, he presented the Philharmonic with a Parisian contrabassoon, an instrument the ensemble lacked entirely as all of theirs had burned in Allied bombing raids. Dunbar repeated the performance the following day for five hundred Allied service members.[27]

The Allied Control Council, the governing body in Berlin comprised of representatives from the Soviet Union, United States, and United Kingdom, perceived Dunbar's appearance as "a valuable step in wiping out racial prejudice," as the *New York Times* reported, "Members of the orchestra, which has been known to ignore the conductor and play music its own way, agreed that Dunbar was a musical topnotcher."[28] Through Dunbar's concerts, the Americans hoped to create the illusion that American views on racial equality were much more progressive than those of Germans.

As the first Guyanese American and member of the military to lead the Berlin Philharmonic, Dunbar sought the professional recognition that would come with conducting the ensemble. Yet his status as a second-class citizen within the very organization he represented meant that his appearance would not be taken seriously by the military or by much of the press. *Time* magazine concluded that military authorities pushed Dunbar to conduct because "their interest was more in teaching the Germans a lesson in racial tolerance than in Dunbar's musicianship."[29] Furthermore, Germans civilians were well aware of the racial inequalities in the United States. Early Soviet propaganda emphasized the cruelty of the Jim Crow laws, and furthermore, segregation was on display in postwar Germany as black and white GIs still had separate regiments, barracks, and clubs. Military Governor Lucius Clay maintained throughout the postwar period that African American soldiers should be limited to marching in parades.[30]

TITANIA-PALAST
STEGLITZ · SCHLOSS-STRASSE 5

PROGRAMM

Sonntag, den 2. September 1945, vormittags 10.30 Uhr

BERLINER PHILHARMONIKER

unter Leitung des berühmten amerikanischen Dirigenten

Rudolph Dunbar

C. M. v. Weber . . . . *Ouvertüre "Oberon"*

William Grant Still . . . . *Afro-American Symphony*

P. Tschaikowsky . . . . *Sinfonie Nr. 6 op. 74*
(Pathétique)

I. Adagio, Allegro non troppo,　　II. Allegro con grazia
Andante, Allegro vivo,　　　　　　III. Allegro molto vivace
Andante come prima　　　　　　　IV. Finale, Adagio lamentoso

VORANZEIGE

Konzert des Berliner Philharmonischen Orchesters
Leitung: Robert Heger
am Sonntag, dem 16. September, 10.30 Uhr

Figure 2.2. Program for Rudolph Dunbar and the Berlin Philharmonic, September 1945. Courtesy of the Berlin Philharmonic Archive.

Even though many Americans of color may have experienced greater racial tolerance in postwar Germany, the country was still far from a utopia of acceptance. As Dunbar's performance revealed, his appearance elicited a range of responses from the public, not all of which were positive. Philharmonic musicians were themselves uncertain of what to make of Dunbar's appearance. An oboist in the orchestra could only register his shock by writing, "A Negro Officer Dünbar [sic] directs!"[31] in his daily planner. One French newspaper even went so far as to note that Dunbar was "a conductor of the Berlin Philharmonic that Hitler certainly hadn't expected."[32] After playing the Still symphony, one flutist confessed to a reporter, "Now at last I understand your American jazz,"[33] reinforcing the pervading stereotype that music written by African American composers would be categorized as jazz, although Still's genre-defying symphony was a hybrid of blues and classical influences. Despite Dunbar's efforts and the support of the American military, the Philharmonic never again performed Still's music.

Dunbar's appearance was temporary, however, and the question remained who would become the ensemble's permanent conductor. There were no ideal German forerunners for the position, and music officers were desperate to find a director with the necessary political qualifications and requisite experience. Yet the Americans soon banned or blacklisted nearly every major conductor who had remained in Germany during the Third Reich, including Hans Knappertsbusch (blacklisted for his Philharmonic propaganda tours), Leopold Ludwig (blacklisted as a former party member), Robert Heger (blacklisted for his frequent concertizing under the Third Reich), and Wilhelm Furtwängler (blacklisted and still awaiting denazification).[34]

There was no shortage of opinions concerning the Philharmonic's new conductor. Colonel Creighton, Borchard's driver the evening he was shot, believed the orchestra's best hope was Fritz Busch. As a German émigré, Busch's political and musical credentials were promising. After the Nazis fired him from the Dresden State Opera in 1933, he served as the first music director of the Glyndebourne Opera Festival between 1934 and 1939 before relocating to New York and conducting at the Metropolitan Opera. Creighton was so convinced of his plan that he wrote a mutual friend to inquire if Busch would be interested in the job, but the conductor would not end up returning to the ruins of Germany until 1951. With few feasible alternatives, when Philharmonic violinist Hermann Bethmann suggested his Romanian friend conduct a few performances, the Americans readily agreed. A composition student at the Hochschule für Musik, Sergiu Celibidache appeared to be the perfect fit for the ensemble: he had lived in Berlin since 1936 but had not been a member of the Nazi Party nor served in the Wehrmacht. Although Celibidache had relatively little conducting experience, he was young, energetic, and *non-German*. The occupiers were eager to dispel Nazi claims of German cultural superiority once and for all and agreed to give the conductor a chance.[35]

At the end of April 1945, Celibidache had turned down the chance to flee Berlin as it fell to the Russians. When a group of fellow Romanians offered him a place in their car heading west, he declined, reluctant to leave his compositions behind in Berlin while hoping "to experience everything with my own eyes."[36] Celibidache had a prescient sense that to stay in the city might mean better prospects for his career, foresight that would prove correct in only a few months. On August 29, the day of Borchard's funeral, Celibidache led the Philharmonic for the first time. Brimming with energy and a volatile temper, the thirty-three-year-old musician was everything Furtwängler was not. After Celibidache's first concert with the ensemble, oboist Helmut Schlövogt noted his surprise in his daily planner, writing "A Romanian directs!"[37] It would be the first of more than four hundred performances the Philharmonic and Celibidache would give together.[38]

At the end of September, the city of Berlin assumed financial responsibility for the orchestra, contributing more than 120,000 Reichsmarks (RM) to rebuild the ensemble. After passing military clearance, Celibidache signed his name to the ensemble's American-issued license along with Paul Schroer (second violin) and Ernst Fuhr (cello), the orchestra's newly elected managers. The former *Reichsorchester* was now conducted by a Romanian, supervised by the Americans, and performing for Allied troops throughout Berlin. At a September performance exclusively for American soldiers, the Philharmonic opened with Wagner's *Tannhäuser* Overture, played just before the nearly obligatory (if not clichéd) Mendelssohn selection, the *Andante* from the composer's Italian Symphony.[39]

With the issue of who would become the ensemble's primary conductor solved, American officers now used their connections with the Philharmonic to further their civilian careers. Nicolas Nabokov pushed for his own compositions to be played, and in May and June 1946, the orchestra acquiesced, performing his *Parade*. (As a point of comparison, between December 1945 and 1947, the ensemble played only three other American works.) The ensemble was hardly alone in performing the compositions of the occupation powers. As Berlin composer Max Butting noted in his memoir, "a high percentage of German interpreters preferred works by 'their' occupiers for opportunistic reasons."[40]

John Bitter, as the Philharmonic's appointed military supervisor, advised the group in many capacities, even though the lines between Bitter's military duty and personal agenda began to blur. Although he wanted "to help rebuild the good Germany; that of Beethoven, Schiller, Goethe, and Brahms,"[41] Bitter primarily used his military connections to gain valuable conducting experience for his return to civilian life. Between 1945 and 1948, he led the Berlin Philharmonic some thirty times. For his first performance with the orchestra, given for Allied troops on December 10, 1945, he began with John Philip Sousa's *The Stars and Stripes Forever* in a pointed rejoinder to the banned *Horst Wessel Lied* that had once opened the orchestra's concerts. The performance included waltzes from Strauss's *Der Rosenkavalier*, Sibelius's Second Symphony, Tchaikovsky's *Romeo and Juliet* Overture, and the German premiere of Samuel Barber's *Adagio for Strings*. In an attempt to help German audience members connect with Corporal Samuel Barber, the notes observed that aside from his musical commissions for the army, Barber's tasks included building latrines in Texas.[42] Henry Alter sat in the audience for Bitter's first performance, surprised that "he actually was not bad," although he did find Bitter rather pompous, "looming quite large in his uniform."[43] Another officer noticed that Bitter "was so nervous I was afraid he would fall off the conductor's podium."[44]

While the Berlin press was generally positive about Bitter's abilities, reviews of his concerts focused more on the orchestra's sound than on the conductor. The ICD still monitored all forms of mass media in their sector and zone, and reviewers were careful not to castigate a member of the military. Outside of the American zone, critics were more forthcoming. After a July 1947 appearance at the House of Soviet Culture, one writer complained that Bitter's interpretation of Tchaikovsky's *Serenade for Strings* sounded like Mozart due to its lack of "fervor, fire, spirit and sentiment."[45] Aside from conducting the Philharmonic, Bitter also made guest appearances with the Staatskapelle Berlin and RIAS Symphony Orchestra, the resident ensemble of the city's American-run radio station, as well as performing with the Dresden Philharmonic, Hamburg Philharmonic, Gürzenich Orchestra Cologne, and Staatskapelle Kassel. Bitter introduced these orchestras to several new works, including Bartók's Third Piano Concerto and Shostakovich's First Symphony in Hamburg, Ravel's *La Valse* in Cologne, and Hindemith's Cello Concerto in Kassel, a work the composer wrote in America.[46]

The troubling nature of Bitter's work with German orchestras, particularly the Berlin Philharmonic, was not lost on cultural officer Eric Clarke, a former arts administrator for the Metropolitan Opera. Although Clarke complained to a superior, "As the Berlin music officer who has nursed the Philharmonic along, should he [Bitter] face it in any other capacity? . . . Is he not weakening our present stand against entertaining Germans?,"[47] the military did nothing to stop the conductor. In contrast to Bitter's free rein, British cultural officers were not permitted to appear alongside German musicians, as one edict made clear, "no Military Government official may take advantage of his position to participate in German cultural activities."[48]

Philharmonic musicians were similarly skeptical of Bitter's abilities, and as Erich Hartmann admitted, "We had to work with him because he had political influence, maybe even military authority. . . . It was certain that he admired our orchestra, although the feeling was not always mutual."[49] In 1948, Electrola offered Bitter a recording contract with the Philharmonic. Eager to accept the deal, Bitter wrote to Benno Frank, offering to donate his potential earnings to charity, just as he had done with all of his German conducting engagements to date. Despite Bitter's gesture of goodwill, Frank felt the recording would be a blatant conflict of interest and refused to approve his request.[50]

Yet the subtext of American efforts to control who conducted the ensemble revolved around one question: Would the Philharmonic's principal conductor, Wilhelm Furtwängler, return to Berlin? Since February 1945, he had lived in self-imposed Swiss exile near Geneva. Although Furtwängler had never joined the Nazi Party, he had led the orchestra at select propaganda events during the 1930s and 1940s, enjoying one of the most visible and prestigious conductorships during the Third Reich. Despite Furtwängler's insistence that his music could be separated from politics, his postwar reputation was severely compromised, and in February 1946, ICD director Robert McClure announced Furtwängler's blacklisting across all zones and sectors of Germany, claiming, "It is an indisputable fact that through his activities, Furtwängler was prominently identified with Nazi Germany." McClure went on to allege, "By allowing himself to become a tool of the party, he lent an aura of respectability to the circle of men who are now on trial at Nuremberg for crimes against humanity,"[51] conflating the Nazi political and German cultural spheres. The American occupiers intended to make an example of National Socialism's most celebrated conductor through a highly publicized denazification process, though, as *Time* magazine reported, "Furtwängler himself is viewing the struggle from a secluded nook in the Swiss Alps."[52]

Evidence the Americans presented against the conductor included his one-year vice presidency of the RMK. The conductor resigned in 1934 as a result of his role in the Hindemith affair, a scandal caused by his support of the composer's *Mathis der Maler* despite National Socialist opposition to the opera. Aside from Furtwängler's activities within Nazi Germany, the Americans claimed the conductor had also participated in propaganda tours throughout occupied Europe, an allegation he denied. Occupied music, for Furtwängler, was going too far, as "I did not want to come in the wake of tanks into the countries."[53] Although it was Hans Knappertsbusch who led most of Philharmonic's propaganda tours, Furtwängler had performed in the Czech Republic and in Denmark while both countries were occupied.

Furtwängler's denazification continued for nearly two years as American authorities vacillated between wanting to punish National Socialism's most decorated conductor while retaining the possibility of his services in the American sector. Meanwhile, the Soviets openly campaigned for Furtwängler's rehabilitation, tempting him with offers to conduct at the Staatsoper to bypass American clearance. The Russians were more than willing to overlook Furtwängler's recent past for a chance to have him working in their sector. But the conductor remained steadfast; he wanted to be reinstated by the Americans in order to direct the Philharmonic. He knew it would be a symbolic victory if he could resume his former post rather than accepting the Soviets' offer. So he decided to wait.[54]

The conductor's trial took place in two installments on December 11 and 17, 1946, led by intelligence officer Alex Vogel, and as Bitter reported, "Furtwängler will be permitted the use of a lawyer, but for advice only. He must do all the talking himself."[55] Witnesses included past and present members of the Philharmonic who used the opportunity either to laud Furtwängler's courage or to wage a character assassination. Testifying in his closing remarks that he stayed in Berlin to help German music through the crisis of National Socialism, Furtwängler repeated the clichéd admonition, "No one, who was not in Germany at that time, could judge how it really looked here."[56] But the Americans' task was to judge Furtwängler, not his working conditions during the Third Reich. After four months of deliberation, on April 29, 1947, the American military government classified the conductor as a *Mitläufer* (follower) and placed him in category IV, permitting him to resume his leadership role with the Philharmonic.[57] As music officer Henry Alter later admitted of both Furtwängler's and Herbert von Karajan's denazification, to bar them from making music "would be punishing oneself."[58]

Although Furtwängler believed German music was a form resistance to the Nazis, between 1939 and 1945 it was also the sound of occupation, domination, and subjugation. Even if he found the Nazis' cultural politics distasteful, the regime still granted him a platform on which he could conduct in front of packed concert halls. Ultimately, Furtwängler's crime was not that he was Nazi but that he failed to recognize the dangerously politicized role that music had taken on during the Third Reich. In his audiences sat party officials, civilians, and even forced laborers.[59] By continuing to conduct beneath the swastika during the Third Reich, Furtwängler could not escape its presence in the postwar period either.

Ruins of Repertoire: The Act of Ruined Listening

The shattering of a collective listening experience began well before the fall of the Third Reich. A photograph of concertgoers taken during winter 1944, a year before the war's end, reveals the pride of place that music held in Berlin. The small group trudges through the winter day, some with umbrellas, their heads bent down to avoid what was presumably a chilling wind. Dark hats and threadbare coats made a stark contrast against the falling snow. In the background, only ruins, as bourgeois society made their way home from an afternoon concert (fig. 2.3).

Orchestral music, the remnants of the nineteenth-century Germanic Romantic tradition, continued to be the link between Germany's musical past, wartime cultural activities, and shattered postwar reputation. Although the Philharmonic paid lip service to Allied and Jewish composers in the postwar period, the ensemble performed mostly the same pieces as they had under National Socialism, as the orchestra made use of their standing under the American occupiers to give sonic space to German postwar suffering. Such suffering was not only expressed through repertoire but also by those who played it. When Furtwängler agreed to give a series of seven performances in the Soviet, British, and American sectors, he selected Beethoven to be the central repertoire of his programs.

Figure 2.3. Berlin concertgoers on their way home, early 1944. bpk Bildagentur. Photograph by Hanns Hubmann. Art Resource, New York.

The city's musical community was in a state of frenzy when the conductor's plane landed at Tempelhof on the morning of May 22, 1947. Potential audience members waited more than fourteen hours outside the Titania Palast to try and hear one of his concerts. Black market prices ranged from 300 to 500 RM per ticket.[60]

His first performance on May 25 eerily echoed the conductor's return twelve years earlier after his resignation from the RMK, featuring the same repertoire: Beethoven's Fifth and Sixth Symphonies as well as the *Egmont* Overture. Yet the program notes for the evening, written by Berlin musicologist Hans Heinz Stuckenschmidt, recast Furtwängler in the image of some of the nineteenth and twentieth century's greatest Jewish musicians. According to Stuckenschmidt, Furtwängler was "an eminently spiritual musician in the vein of Gustav Mahler,"[61] a champion of not only the works of Beethoven, Brahms, and Bruckner but also the music of Arnold Schoenberg. Stuckenschmidt connected prewar and postwar humanism by omitting any reference to the Third Reich, instead writing that Furtwängler's absence between 1945 and 1947 was because the conductor wanted to devote himself solely to composition, an activity he greatly enjoyed but had little time for because of the Philharmonic's schedule. At the concert's conclusion, the audience applauded for fifteen minutes, and Furtwängler returned to the stage seventeen times for bows. Eventually, he resorted to bowing in his overcoat as a signal he wanted to go home. Even though Bitter wrote in his weekly report, "It was an honest music success, no political demonstration and the Phil played beautifully,"[62] at the conductor's concert with the Staatskapelle a few days later, Bitter noted the raucous applause carried "a political tinge."[63] The Americans may have cleared Furtwängler in a court of law, but they were uncertain how to handle his presence in the divided city, especially his appearance with a Soviet-licensed ensemble.

The Berlin press reviews of Furtwängler's return were generally glowing. One Soviet news agency used battle metaphors to describe the conductor's performance ("fierce combat" or *erbitterter Kampf*), concluding that "Egmont is the victim"[64] at the overture's conclusion. Yet "victim" (*Opfer*) in 1945 certainly carried other connotations, leading to uneasy comparisons with the more recently designated "victims of National Socialism," a category of civilians who survived Nazi persecution.

Because most of the players had not performed under Furtwängler's baton, his return heralded continuity rather than a cultural zero hour. Yet the conductor's appearances were not received with wholehearted enthusiasm in all quarters. "With Furtwängler playing Brahms and Bruckner in the same way as [if] nothing happened in the past . . . all the hopes that something has changed since '45 are gone,"⁶⁵ one Berlin composer wrote a friend in England. Allied officials expressed similar misgivings; as an American official admitted, "[to] hear about Furtwängler having great triumphs in Berlin, I wonder what role music can fulfill in the political re-education of the German people."⁶⁶ The uproar surrounding Furtwängler's return concerts was also about the rubbled bourgeois concert experience. How could the nineteenth century's monumental symphonies reflect the twentieth-century postwar soundworld?

Despite his lengthy battle to be reinstated by the Americans, Furtwängler led the Philharmonic in only twelve concerts during the 1947 and 1948 season, a meager number in comparison to Celibidache's seventy-six. His life in Switzerland provided the best working conditions he had experienced in over a decade, while Berlin's rubbled cityscape could only present challenges, shortages, and controversies.⁶⁷ Yet if Furtwängler had stayed in Hitler's Reich to give the Germans hope during their darkest days, then why in the city's postwar hour of need would he retreat to Clarens, a little corner of the world seemingly untouched by recent history?

Rubble City

Conditions in Berlin were about to take a dire turn, as the June 1948 currency reform in West Germany and West Berlin so angered the Soviets that Stalin embarked on a drastic plan of action to force the Western Allies out of the city. The Russians severed all ground supply routes to West Berlin by taking advantage of a loophole in the Potsdam Agreement and beginning what would become a nearly yearlong blockade. Furtwängler was scheduled to conduct the Philharmonic in July, appearing alongside violin prodigy Patricia Travers and harpsichordist Ralph Kirkpatrick, both American musicians invited as part of the ICD's visiting artist program. The conductor canceled only ten days in advance, and the Philharmonic musicians were irate. As Celibidache admonished his senior colleague, "Your not coming was all the more incomprehensible as you were already in Munich," complaining, moreover, that Furtwängler's upcoming Beethoven cycle with the Vienna Philharmonic "also does not exactly please the orchestra."⁶⁸

The "inhuman conditions through which the Russians were trying to dominate the city,"⁶⁹ as one cultural officer wrote, made it necessary to feed West Berliners through airlifts. Burdened by travel restrictions and the currency reform alike, Bitter despaired as inflation made concert tickets unaffordable for many Germans. The blockade made the Philharmonic's schedule a point of contention between Allied cultural officers, as the Americans began pressuring the orchestra to stop performing under Soviet auspices. Thomas R. Hutton, the acting Information Services Branch chief (in lieu of John Bitter, who was away at a conducting engagement in Göttingen), wanted the ensemble's managers to cancel all upcoming concerts in Russian-occupied territory, despite scheduled appearances at the broadcasting studio on Masurenallee for "The Voice of Moscow," and other performances planned across the Soviet zone in Halle, Schkopau, Leipzig, and Wolfen. Even though Hutton was loath "to hear democracy, democratic government, and Military government in Germany villified [sic],"[70] he did not have the military authority to ban the orchestra from appearing under Russian auspices. While an October 7 article titled, "Terror against the Philharmonic," appearing in the Soviet organ *Neues Deutschland*, claimed it was the Americans who forbade the ensemble from performing in Soviet territory, the ensemble put the issue to a vote the following day. The orchestra realized that if they wanted to remain in the American sector, certain sacrifices would have to be made, and voted seventy-three to one (with seven musicians abstaining) to stop giving concerts at the Soviet broadcasting studio. Although decided by a democratic process, there was little doubt the Americans were pleased.

Destroyed venues, compromised musicians, and the ruins of a once monumental repertoire became the sound of German suffering in the Berlin Philharmonic's postwar performances. The orchestra became a sort of ensemble in residence in its own city as American authorities regulated the Philharmonic's repertoire, musicians, conductors, and performance schedule. From *Horst Wessel Lied* to *The Stars and Stripes Forever*, the ensemble survived because it was adaptable, heeding first the demands of the National Socialists and later those of the occupiers to continue concertizing.

Notes

1. Ruth Andreas-Friedrich, *Berlin Underground: Diaries, 1945–1948* (New York: Paragon House, 1984), 310.

2. Thomas Eickhoff, *Politische Dimensionen einer Komponisten-Biographie im 20.Jahrhundert: Gottfried von Einem* (Stuttgart: Steiner, 1998), 76; and Matthias Strässner, *Der Dirigent Leo Borchard: Eine unvollendete Karriere* (Berlin: Transit, 1999), 213.

3. Berlin Philharmonic Program, March 1943, Berlin Philharmonic Archive.

4. "Das Berliner Philharmonische Orchester nach dem zweiten Weltkrieg," 2–4; and Dienstbuch, G 100, Berlin Philharmonic Archive.

5. Berlin Philharmonic Programs, May 26, 1945, and March 11, 1935, Berlin Philharmonic Archive. For information about the recovery of music by Jewish composers, see Erich Hartmann, *Die Berliner Philharmoniker in der Stunde Null: Erinnerungen an die Zeit des Untergangs der alten Philharmonie vor 50 Jahren* (Berlin: Werner Feja, 1996), 37.

6. Andreas-Friedrich, *Battleground Berlin*, 35.

7. Anonymous account in Peter Muck, ed., *Einhundert Jahre Berliner Philharmonisches Orchester* (Tutzing: H. Schneider, 1982), 2:190.

8. Nicolas Nabokov, "Boris Blacher," in Heribert Henrich and Thomas Eickhoff, eds., *Boris Blacher: Archiv zur Musik des 20. Jahrhunderts*, vol. 7 (Berlin: Fuldaer, 2003), 9.

9. Wolf Lepenies, "Eine (fast) alltägliche deutsche Geschichte," in Misha Aster, *Das Reichsorchester: Die Berliner Philharmoniker und der Nationalsozialismus* (Munich: Siedler, 2007), 19; and Hartmann, *Die Berliner Philharmoniker in der Stunde Null*, 6–7.

10. There are some discrepancies concerning the date of the last Philharmonic concert before Germany's surrender. April 16 is confirmed by Hartmann and by the daily planners of several other musicians, yet a 1956 pamphlet printed by the ensemble titled, "Das Berliner Philharmonische Orchester nach dem zweiten Weltkrieg," lists April 8 as the final concert. Pamela Potter names April 11 as the final performance, held as "a concert for Mr. Speer." For more information, see Aster, *Das Reichsorchester*, 326; Pamela Potter, "The Nazi 'Seizure' of the Berlin Philharmonic," in Cuomo, *National Socialist Cultural Policy*, 58; Hartmann, *Die Berliner Philharmoniker in der Stunde Null*, 28; and Dienstbuch G 100 and 335, Berlin Philharmonic Archive.

11. Schlövogt, Dienstbuch 335, January 1945 to December 1945, Berlin Philharmonic Archive.

12. Suicide had grown increasingly common. In 1945 alone, some 7,057 Berliners killed themselves rather experience an uncertain postwar world.

13. W. Byford-Jones, *Berlin Twilight* (London: Hutchinson, 1947), 69.

14. Henry Alter, interview by Brewster Chamberlain and Jürgen Wetzel, May 11, 1981, B Rep. 037, Nr. 79–82, Landesarchiv, Berlin; and Philharmonic Concert Program, July 8, 1945, Berlin Philharmonic Archive.

15. Strässner, *Der Dirigent Leo Borchard*, 230. Although the broadcasting studio on Masurenallee was in the British sector, the Soviets refused to relinquish the most powerful radio transmitter in all of Germany.

16. Henry Alter, interview by Brewster Chamberlain and Jürgen Wetzel, May 11, 1981, B Rep. 037, Nr. 79–82, Landesarchiv. The German original reads "Ich glaube wirklich, dass wir das Berliner Philharmonische Orchester gerettet haben."

17. Bitter, "Weekly Theater and Music Report," April 30, 1947, RG 260, Box 241, Records of the Education and Cultural Affairs Division (E&CR): Records Relating to Music and Theater, NARA II. For more information on the denazification of the Berlin Philharmonic, see Walter Hinrichsen, "Members of the Philharmonic Orchestra Berlin Being Discharged in Accordance with Denazification Policy in the U.S. Zone," June 25, 1946, RG 260, Box 237, Records of the Education and Cultural Affairs Division: Records Relating to Music and Theater, NARA II; Forck, *Variationen mit Orchester*, 20, 43, 54; and Fritz Trümpi, *Politisierte Orchester: Die Wiener Philharmoniker und das Berliner Philharmoniche Orchester im Nationalsozialismus* (Vienna: Böhlau, 2011), 113.

18. Hogan, "Weekly Report," May 23, 1946, RG 260, Box 239, Records of the Education and Cultural Resources Branch, Records Relating to Music and Theater, NARA II.

19. Frederic Mellinger, "Commandatura Meeting, Denazification—Berlin Philharmonic," May 29, 1946, RG 260, Box 237, Records of the Education and Cultural Affairs Division: Records Relating to Music and Theater, NARA II.

20. John Bitter to M. Wohlthat, October 2, 1948, RG 260, Box 97, Office of Military Government, Germany (OMGUS), Records of the Berlin Sector, NARA II. See also John Bitter, "August 15–31, 1947 Report," National Archives Records: Shipment 4, Box 8-1, Folder 2, May 1946 to November 1948, B Rep. 036 Nr. 4/8-1/2, Landesarchiv; and Michael Josselson, "Ration for Berlin Philharmonic Orchestra," January 7, 1948, RG 260, Box 97, Office of Military Government, Germany (OMGUS), Records of the Berlin Sector, NARA II.

21. Berlin Philharmonic Management to Information Control Services, January 3, 1948, RG 260, Box 97, Office of Military Government, Germany (OMGUS), Records of the Berlin Sector, NARA II.

22. Andreas-Friedrich, *Battleground Berlin*, 27.

23. Ibid., 312.

24. "One Man Can Save German Music: Leo Borchard," *Newsweek*, August 27, 1945, 62–64.

25. Klaus Lang, *Celibidache und Furtwängler: Der große philharmonische Konflikt in der Berliner Nachkriegszeit* (Munich: Wissner, 2010), 19.

26. Strässner, *Der Dirigent Leo Borchard*, 235; Philharmonic Concert Program, August 25, 1945, Berlin Philharmonic Archive.

27. "Music: Rhythm in Berlin," *Time*, September 10, 1945; Amy C. Beal, *New Music, New Allies: American Experimental Music from the Zero Hour to Reunification* (Berkeley: University of California Press, 2006), 15; and the Foundation for Research in the Afro-American Creative Arts, "W. Rudolph Dunbar: Pioneering Orchestra Conductor," in *The Black Perspective in Music* 9/2 (Autumn 1981): 193–225. With banjo players hard to find in Europe, Dunbar had already obtained Still's permission to omit the part in the symphony's third movement. Charles William Latshaw, "William Grant Still's Afro-American Symphony: A Critical Edition" (PhD diss., Indiana University, 2014), 8.

28. "Negro Wins Plaudits Conducting in Berlin," *New York Times*, September 3, 1945.

29. "Music: Rhythm in Berlin," *Time*, September 10, 1945.

30. Heide Fehrenbach, *Race after Hitler: Black Occupation Children in Postwar Germany and America* (Princeton, NJ: Princeton University Press, 2005), 17–45; David Monod, *Settling Scores: German Music, Denazification, and the Americans, 1945–1953* (Chapel Hill: University of North Carolina Press, 2005), 240; and Eugene Davidson, *The Death and Life of Germany: An Account of the American Occupation* (New York: Knopf, 1959), 277. For more recent work on the intersections of race and classical music in Germany, see also Kira Thurman, "Singing the Civilizing Mission in the Land of Bach, Beethoven, and Brahms: The Fisk Jubilee Singers in Nineteenth-Century Germany," *Journal of World History* 27, no. 3 (September 2016): 443–71; and Kira Thurman, "Black Europe: A Useful Category for Historical Analysis," *Black Perspectives: African American Intellectual History Society Blog* (December 2016).

31. Helmut Schlövogt, Dienstbuch G 335, September 2, 1945, Berlin Philharmonic Archive.

32. "W. Rudolph Dunbar: Pioneering Orchestra Conductor," 205.

33. "American Conducts Berlin Philharmonic," *Journal-Courier*, September 3, 1945.

34. Toby Thacker, *Music after Hitler, 1945–1955* (Farnham, UK: Ashgate, 2007), 56.

35. "National Socialists Oust Busch as Orchestra Conductor of Dresden Opera House," *New York Times*, March 7, 1933; Fritz Busch, *Pages from a Musician's Life* (Westport,

CT: Greenwood, 1971), 198–211; Hartmann, *Die Berliner Philharmoniker in der Stunde Null*, 43; and correspondence from T. R. M. Creighton to Leonie [last name unknown], undated, Max-Reger Institut, Brüder-Busch-Archiv, Karlsruhe. My thanks to Peter Berggren for sharing this letter with me.

36. Quoted in Lang, *Celibidache und Furtwängler*, 26.
37. Schlövogt, Dienstbuch 335, August 28, 1945, Berlin Philharmonic Archive.
38. Lang, *Celibidache und Furtwängler*, 389.
39. Beschluss des Magistrats in der Sitzung am 24. September 1945, C Rep. 120, Nr. 1692, Landesarchiv; "License no. 501 Issued to One Sergiu Celibidache for the Berlin Philharmonic Orchestra," November 1945, RG 260, Box 238, Records of the Education and Cultural Affairs Division: Records Relating to Music and Theater, NARA II; Lang, *Celibidache und Furtwängler*, 77; Muck, *Einhundert Jahre Berliner Philharmonisches Orchester*, 205; and Berlin Philharmonic Program, September 15, 1945, Berlin Philharmonic Archive.
40. Max Butting, *Musikgeschichte, die ich miterlebte* (Berlin: Henschel, 1955), 233. See also Monod, *Settling Scores*; and Sergiu Celibidache, *The Berlin Recordings, 1945–47*, Audite, 2013. Bitter was also an amateur composer who looked for opportunities to perform his work, organizing the premiere of his First String Quartet at Haus am Waldsee, an outdoor concert venue in Zehlendorf.
41. John Bitter, interview by Brewster Chamberlain and Jürgen Wetzel, November 6, 1981, B Rep. 037, Nr. 79–82, Landesarchiv.
42. Berlin Philharmonic Program, December 10, 1945, Berlin Philharmonic Archive. See also Beal, *New Music, New Allies*, 15–16. For more concerning Bitter's conducting, see Monod, *Settling Scores*, 119–21.
43. Henry Alter, interview by Brewster Chamberlain and Jürgen Wetzel, May 11, 1981, B Rep. 037, Nr. 79–82, Landesarchiv.
44. W. Phillips Davison, *A Personal History of WWII: How a Pacifist Draftee Accidentally Became a Military Government Official in Postwar Germany* (Lincoln, NE: iUniverse, 2006), n.p.
45. Heinz v. Cramer, "John Bitter im Haus der Kultur," *Berlin am Mittag*, July 12, 1947.
46. Dr. John Bitter Collection, Box 1, Folder 2, University of Miami Libraries, Coral Gables, Florida. See also Monod, *Settling Scores*, 119–21.
47. Eric Clarke, "Memorandum: Captain John Bitter, Conductor," January 15, 1947, RG 260, Box 243, Records of the Information Control Division (ICD): Records of the Division Headquarters, 1945–49, NARA II.
48. Quoted in Gabriele Clemens, *Britische Kulturpolitik in Deutschland 1945–1949: Literatur, Film, Musik und Theater* (Stuttgart: Franz Steiner, 1997), 201.
49. Hartmann, *Die Berliner Philharmoniker in der Stunde Null*, 42.
50. Eric Clarke, "John Bitter," January 14, 1948, RG 260, Box 134, Records of the Information Control Division (ICD): Central Decimal File of the Executive Office, 1944–49, NARA II.
51. Robert McClure, "For Release 21 February 1946," RG 260, Box 43, Records of the Information Control Division (ICD): Records of Division Headquarters, 1945–49, NARA II.
52. Winthrop Sargeant, "Europe's Culture," *Time*, November 4, 1946, 56.
53. Wilhelm Furtwängler, Denazification File, December 17, 1946, RG 260, Box 237, Records of the Education and Cultural Resources Branch, NARA II.
54. Elizabeth Janik, *Recomposing German Music: Politics and Musical Tradition in Cold War Berlin* (Leiden, the Netherlands: Brill, 2005), 134–39.
55. John Bitter, "Theater and Munich Report," October 24, 1946, RG 260, Box 239, Records of the Education and Cultural Resources Branch, NARA II.

56. Furtwängler, Denazification File, December 17, 1946, RG 260, Box 237, Records of the Education and Cultural Resources Branch, NARA II.
57. Susanne Stähr, "Die Ära Furtwängler," in Forck, *Variationen mit Orchester*, 195–96.
58. Interview with Henry Alter conducted by Brewster Chamberlain and Jürgen Wetzel, May 11, 1981. B Rep. 037, Nr. 79–82, Landesarchiv.
59. Ian Baruma, *Zero Hour: A History of 1945* (New York: Penguin, 2013), 4. Baruma's father, then a Dutch law student brought to Germany as a forced laborer, recalled Furtwängler's concerts as one of his few happy memories from the war years.
60. "500 Mark für Furtwängler-Karte," *Der Spiegel*, May 31, 1947.
61. Hans Heinz Stuckenschmidt, Berlin Philharmonic Program Notes, May 25, 1947, Berlin Philharmonic Archive.
62. John Bitter, "28 May 1947 Report," National Archives Records: Shipment 4, Box 8-1, Folder 2, May 1946 to November 1948, B Rep. 036 Nr. 4/8-1/2, Landesarchiv. See also "Furtwängler wieder in Berlin," *Frankfurter Neue Presse*, May 5, 1947.
63. John Bitter, "17 July 1947 Report," National Archives Records: Shipment 4, Box 8-1, Folder 2, May 1946 to November 1948, B Rep. 036 Nr. 4/8-1/2, Landesarchiv.
64. Allgemeine Deutsche Nachrichtendienst, May 27, 1947, Berlin Philharmonic Archive.
65. Boris Blacher to William Glock, undated letter, Boris Blacher Papers, Folder 362, AdK.
66. Davidson Taylor quoted in Monod, *Settling Scores*, 214.
67. Lang, *Celibidache und Furtwängler*, 102. Elisabeth Furtwängler, the conductor's wife, claimed there were several reasons her husband did not resume his former Philharmonic schedule: the vitriol of the international press, numerous other conducting invitations, and his desire to devote more time to his first love, composition.
68. Lang, *Celibidache und Furtwängler*, 176–78.
69. Eric Clarke, "Review of Activities for August 1–15," Records of the Education and Cultural Relations Division (E&CR): Records Relating to Music and Theater, RG 260, Box 242, NARA II; Ernst Fischer and Ernst Fuhr, Berlin Philharmonic Schedule, September 26 to December 25, 1948, RG 260, Box 97, Office of Military Government, Germany (OMGUS), Records of the Berlin Sector, NARA II; and John Bitter, "July 1948 Report," National Archives Records, Shipment 4, Box 8-1, Folder 2, May 1946 to November 1948, B Rep. 036, Nr. 4/8-1/2, Landesarchiv. For nearly a year, the Western Allies, and particularly American forces, piloted 277,500 flights to Tempelhof Airport, delivering 2.3 million tons of food. The Soviet Blockade lasted until May 12, 1949. See also Tony Judt, *Postwar: A History of Europe since 1945* (New York: Penguin, 2005), 146; and Monod, *Settling Scores*, 183–95.
70. Tom R. Hutton, "Philharmonics [sic] Concerts under Soviet Auspices," October 7, 1948, RG 260, Box 97, Office of Military Government, Germany (OMGUS), Records of the Berlin Sector, NARA II.

3

RUBBLE OPERA AFTER 1945

*East Berlin's Staatsoper and
West Berlin's Städtische Oper*

Staging Opera's Rubble Hour

Wandering through the ruins of Hamburg shortly after its 1943 firebombing, writer Hans Erich Nossack asked of the cratered landscape, "Was all this just scenery for a fantastic opera?"[1] The air war's destruction annihilated urban Germany, as old town timber buildings and narrow passageways were transformed into kindling by phosphorus bombs. Opera houses, often centrally located, were damaged along with military targets and homes, as the flames made no distinction. Walking past Berlin's Gendarmenmarkt to the Staatsoper in early May 1945, aspiring actress Sabine K. noted the opera's decrepit condition in her diary: "Vehicles and artillery stood in ruins.... This [the opera] was as much my home as our flat and it should be made so once again.... We have truly suffered, and now this."[2] Sabine K. saw the operatic ruins as a visual metaphor for German victimhood, as hardly any opera houses remained standing. By the Third Reich's defeat, the Wiesbaden opera house was the only one in Germany left unscathed.[3]

Opera provided ripe grounds for the staging of German postwar suffering, as the stunning visual display of these bombed structures became a garish spectacle. Venues that remained partially intact were often repurposed by the Allies to billet or entertain soldiers. Winifred Wagner, the composer's daughter-in-law, was horrified to hear American GIs playing jazz on her piano and to see Italian opera and other "desecrations" staged at Bayreuth. The Nuremberg opera house became home to the Stork Club, a popular nightclub for soldiers. At Munich's Prinzregententheater, Allied troops threw out the seats so they could sleep in the balcony.[4]

Neither the Western Allies nor German civilians could reach a consensus about how to rebuild operatic culture. In April 1945, Richard Strauss wrote a manifesto about the genre's way forward, proposing a radical plan of reconstruction. According to the eighty-year-old composer, each German city should (re)build two opera houses: a smaller venue for Spieloper and serious operas, and a larger hall reserved for Wagnerian opera and, of course, Strauss's own works. Other musicians, however, were more reluctant to perform canonic nineteenth- and twentieth-century Germanic repertoire. When asked by Melos magazine how he envisioned opera's reconstruction, the intendant of Stuttgart Opera argued that companies should begin with Gluck and Mozart, or even French and Italian Spieloper, absolutely avoiding monolithic works by composers such as Wagner.[5] Amid shattered halls and rubbled repertoires, what was the sound of German opera in 1945?

After the cease-fire, Berlin was left with the ruined shells of its four opera houses: the Staatsoper, Städtische Oper, Volksoper, and Komische Oper. Initial efforts to rebuild the city's operatic culture centered exclusively on the British-supervised Städtische Oper (renamed the Deutsche Oper in 1961), and the Russian-licensed Staatsoper. The Komische, now located in the Soviet sector, reopened only in 1947, and the Volksoper closed entirely. Of primary concern for the Städtische Oper and Staatsoper was to find serviceable venues, or detour theaters (*Ausweichtheater*). With their home on Unter den Linden destroyed, Staatsoper singers and staff helped install the opera company at the Admiralspalast on Friedrichstraße, a theater chosen for its roof. Städtische Oper management began making plans to move to the Theater des Westens on Kantstraße, formerly the home of the Volksoper, as their regular Bismarkstrasse house was in ruins. The Kantstraße venue was hardly in perfect shape, with soldiers' bodies in the lobby and its roof partially collapsed into the orchestra pit, but it was smaller and would be easier to repair.[6]

On May 15, General Nikolai Bersarin appointed conductor Heinz Tietjen to lead the reconstruction of the city's opera houses, placing Soviet military administration resources at his disposal. An excellent musician and unrelenting opportunist, Tietjen had served as director of the Städtische Oper in the 1920s, artistic director of the Bayreuth Festival between 1931 and 1945, and director of the Staatsoper under Hermann Göring as minister-president from 1936 onward. On June 8, Bersarin abruptly released Tietjen from his duties, most likely having learned of the conductor's activities under

National Socialism. Bersarin did not ban him from further employment in the cultural sector, however, suggesting the Soviets could tolerate Tietjen's past as long as he was not the figurehead for the city's operatic reconstruction. The Russians then appointed actor and director Ernst Legal to lead the Staatsoper, conductor Robert Heger as head of the Staatskapelle, and singer and actor Michael Bohnen to serve as director of the Städtische Oper. Legal, Heger, Bohnen, and Tietjen, all artists who had been active under National Socialism, would find they awaited completely disparate, if entirely arbitrary, denazification processes at the hands of the Allied occupiers.[7]

In planning the 1945/46 season, material and personnel shortages had to be quickly accounted for, as many singers had fled Berlin or were otherwise missing. The initial offerings of each house revealed a great deal about their artistic and political trajectories, as well as the divergent Cold War paths on which they would soon embark. The cultural occupation of East and West Berlin played out through opera and its production, staging, and financing—a point of convergence and controversy for the Allied occupiers and German civilians alike. Unlike orchestral music, opera could claim a new, antifascist orientation by simply changing its venues, sets, and costumes as the tense contradictions of the country's years of National Socialism revealed themselves on postwar opera stages. While the Allies wanted to introduce German opera-goers to works from their respective nations, Berliners themselves were interested in exploring themes of civilian suffering through their staging choices. By hearing the city's rubble in literal and figurative senses through operatic restitution, personnel decisions, and repertoire selection, civilians used opera to stage occupier-sanctioned forms of German victimhood.

Rubble and Restitution

While the Philharmonic and other ensembles began the arduous process of locating musicians, instruments, and venues, Berlin's opera companies had the added responsibility of reassembling costumes, props, and set pieces. During the war, holdings from various German music institutions (as well as goods stolen from occupied countries) were hidden in rural salt mines and palaces. After the 1944 closing of most theaters and opera houses to mobilize personnel for the war effort, both major Berlin opera houses evacuated large parts of their collections to off-site locations.[8]

The Staatsoper sent more than one hundred fifty thousand costumes and seven tons of musical scores, including their "non-Aryan works" (*nicht arischen Werke*) and three boxes from the Wagner library, to Heimboldshausen salt mine in central Germany. Smaller groups of scores and costumes were also shipped to shafts in Bad Landeck (including twenty thousand props), and Salzdettfurt (ten thousand pairs of shoes and another forty-six thousand costumes). The Städtische Oper sent instruments and musical scores to Seesen in lower Saxony, a second shipment of musical scores to Neuenhagen bei Berlin, and another set of instruments valued at 127,000 Reichsmarks (RM) to Schloß Raduhn near Königsberg. Although the goods may have been protected from aerial attacks, they were susceptible to post-war pillaging, as German civilians, soldiers, and displaced persons depleted most of these caches once they discovered them. The Städtische Oper employee sent to retrieve the instruments at Raduhn, for example, found every case had already been ripped open and each instrument removed.[9]

Materials remaining in palaces and salt mines in August 1945 became the property of their respective occupation power. The Heimboldshausen salt mine (fig. 3.1) used to store the Staatsoper holdings was now located in the American zone. Cultural officers authorized thirteen German civilians to organize the collection, "for loan to BERLIN opera companies,"[10] to use in the 1945/46 Staatsoper and Städtische Oper seasons. Yet, as the word "loan" suggests, the Americans begrudgingly relinquished only a fraction of the items, as cultural officers did not want to surrender the materials to the Soviets, despite the fact that the costumes belonged to the Russian-licensed Staatsoper. US cultural officers also kept much of the Staatsoper's music, removing three truckloads of scores to become the American-controlled music lending library in Frankfurt. As late as February 1947, Sergei Tulpanov was still demanding the return of the items, and the Americans seemed delighted to finally have the upper hand, responding to Tulpanov's inquiries that "there exists no authority under which your request for the return of the collection can be fulfilled."[11]

The redrawing of Germany's postwar borders further complicated questions of restitution. Bad Landeck reverted to Polish territory (Lądek-Zdrój) after the Germans were expelled as part of the Potsdam Agreement, and the Staatsoper could no longer lay claim to the materials stored there either. Between their forfeited goods at Heimboldshausen and Bad Landeck, the company estimated their material losses to be approximately 53 million RM. As Staatsoper director Ernst Legal reported in 1946 concerning the

Figure 3.1. Eric Clarke and Benno Frank inspect opera costumes in a salt mine near Heimboldshausen. Library of Congress Mission to Germany. Photograph by Richard S. Hill.

prior year's events, "The situation of opera was the most difficult imaginable. They [the Staatsoper] had lost their house and all their warehouses that held all kinds of decorations, costumes, materials, and furniture. We had, in the material sense, absolutely nothing."[12] Yet despite the lack of scores, instruments, and costumes, the Soviets wanted Berlin's opera houses to produce operas as quickly as possible, however compromised, however rubbled each company's personnel might be.

Rubble and Personnel: Denazification

Erna Berger felt no pressing urge to leave Berlin in April 1945. As the Staatsoper's star coloratura soprano, Berger was still performing in the city on April 15, giving a concert with several other Staatsoper singers featuring Mozart and Verdi arias. On April 17, she recorded Strauss's *Brentano Lieder* at the broadcasting studio on Masurenallee, although Berger herself admitted in her memoir, "When I think of that today, it appears to me to be completely insane."[13] Hiding in her Dahlem cellar with friends and neighbors throughout the invasion, Berger survived, resuming her work with the Staatsoper, for, "in the middle of total devastation, cultural life was fascinatingly quick to begin again."[14] Aside from Berger, other principal singers who had remained reclaimed their former positions, including bass Josef Greindl, baritone Willi Domgraf-Faßbender, mezzo-soprano Margarete Klose, soprano Tiana Lemnitz, tenor Peter Anders, and bass-baritone Jaro Prohaska. Although the Staatsoper's financial ledgers from April and May 1945 were destroyed, an estimated 85,000 RM remained in their coffers, some 63,330 RM of which was paid to staff who assisted in moving the company to the Admiralspalast, their new Friedrichstraße venue. The transition was not without incident, as the theater's owner, Staatsoper management, and city officials argued for the next year about how much the city owed the Admiralspalast for repairs.[15]

Bersarin gave Staatsoper director Ernst Legal orders to begin staging operas by August 1, and to speed up the process, the general granted former party members permission to resume work. Some fifty former party members at the Staatsoper (including singers and technicians) helped with reconstruction. As Legal reported to city authorities, "It was only logical if the commandant's office gave the order to resume working that party members would also be used."[16] In line with Bersarin's recommendation, Staatsoper management would also turn a blind eye to the former political activities of its members. Karl August Neumann, a baritone engaged at the Staatsoper since 1933, could not believe there were no sanctions imposed on former party members, and in a letter to Erich Otto, president of the German Actors' Union, Neumann complained, "As opposed to the cleaning methods that the Nazis used in the fields of Art and Propaganda . . . one encounters today an incomprehensible tolerance in all places."[17] Neumann even went so far as to attach a list of Staatsoper party members, complete with a description of their activities under the Third Reich.

By the beginning of July, Legal began casting for the rapidly approaching fall 1945 season. There were "violent arguments at the first meeting of the soloists in the foyer of the Opera," as the director was reluctant to decide whether former party members should be allowed to sing, refusing "to set himself up as a judge."[18] Legal feared the Russian occupiers could change their lenient denazification policy, as Bersarin's untimely death in June left many unanswered questions. For the fall 1945 season, Legal finally decided that for each role sung by a former party member, even as an understudy, he would hire a non–party member in case Soviet officials objected to any casting choices. As he later reported to the magistrate, for *Eugene Onegin*, the acclaimed bass Josef Greindl served as an understudy to Ludwig Hofmann's Count Gremin, a choice motivated by Greindl's former party membership and popularity under National Socialism.[19]

When the Staatsoper season opened with a celebratory concert on August 23, one quarter of its soloists were former party members. In a performance featuring music by Beethoven, Gluck, Rossini, Saint-Saëns, Tchaikovsky, Verdi, and Weber, Johannes Schüler directed the Staatskapelle, and Karl Schmidt led the opera chorus. Soloists included Josef Greindl, Willi Domgraf-Faßbender, Erna Berger, and Peter Anders.[20]

Across town, similar denazification questions plagued the Städtische Oper. The company had already begun staging concerts on July 2, featuring excerpts from ballets, several Verdi arias, and other pieces to please the Russian occupiers, including Rimsky-Korsakov's *Scheherazade*. Despite the rapidity with which the Städtische Oper resumed performances (some six weeks earlier than the Staatsoper), not everyone was in agreement that the Soviet's permissive attitude regarding former party members was the best way to stamp out fascism. (The British would also adopt a lenient policy once they were installed in their sector later that summer.) Concerned that so many politically compromised employees continued working for the Städtische Oper, one Berliner complained to German city officials, "Above all a clean house must be built, and like the swastika was once esteemed, so today must it be despised."[21] German authorities responded that because Bersarin had permitted the Städtische Oper to reopen "without inspecting the political affiliations" of its members, paradoxically, all of the "strongly-exposed" Nazis had self-selected not to report for work.[22] Despite German authorities' confidence that due diligence had been served, following the initial impulse to rebuild and restart operatic performance, denazification scandals would plague both opera houses.

Arguments and infighting between personnel hampered the rebuilding of the Städtische Oper, unchecked by the occupation powers as the British, newly arrived in July, took little interest in opera's denazification. On September 10, director Michael Bohnen decided to fire the opera's business manager, Ludwig Hülsen. "Laments and complaints have piled up concerning the haphazard and sheer negligence of your so-called management,"[23] Bohnen wrote in a letter to Hülsen, appointing Hugo Diederich as his replacement. It would be the first of many personnel disagreements in the early postwar years, as Bohnen alienated many of his colleagues with his unpredictable behavior. In April 1946, rumors began to circulate that he had been a Nazi informant. In response to numerous letters from Bohnen's colleagues complaining about his brusque handling of the Städtische Oper's affairs, the magistrate's Department of Volksbildung made an inquiry with the German examination board, asking them to open an investigation on the director.[24]

By October 1946, the accusations against Bohnen had been made public. The Russian sector's *Neues Deutschland* ran a feature article titled, "What's Going on at the Städtische Oper?," which revealed Bohnen had appeared in the Nazi propaganda film, *Achtung, Feind hört mit!* (1940). An accompanying photograph from the film showed Bohnen in a dark suit with a swastika lapel pin.[25] On Bohnen's denazification questionnaire from May 1946, he had neglected to mention a film career, simply listing his work at the Städtische Oper between 1935 and 1944 and his compulsory work at a Siemen's factory as a result of his refusal to join the party. Whether or not Bohnen was an informant remained unconfirmed, but his propaganda film work did not help his cause to remain employed at the Städtische Oper. The Department of Volksbildung demanded Bohnen's resignation, and in response, the British military brought Bohnen's case before the Berlin Denazification Commission. After two witnesses claimed Bohnen had been a Nazi informant (and with no witnesses giving testimony to the contrary), the British felt unable to award Bohnen denazification clearance. Forced to leave the Städtische Oper, as of June 1947, he could not find work in either sector.[26]

Rubble and Personnel: Operatic Rubble Women

Even if denazification failed to accurately sort through compromised personnel, at least one postwar effort to clear rubble remained effective: the rubble woman (*Trümmerfrau*). The rubble woman dominated postwar accounts of German reconstruction, as it was she who cleared away the debris of urban bombing. In an economy where men were absent for a variety of reasons, from wartime casualties, to infirmity and prisoner-of-war internment, this ubiquitous figure was charged with sorting through the wreckage to feed her family. With 170 women for every 100 men, or 7.3 million more female civilians than male, even by 1950, nearly one third of all German households were supported by female labor. Rubble was more than the mere physical remnant of war; it was also the remainder of psychological trauma. For the postwar female civilian, as Robert Moeller writes, "Removing these social and psychological ruins and 'rebuilding men' (*Wiederaufbau der*

Männer) was essential, and as accounts of this devastation made apparent, this too was women's work."[27]

Yet rubble women were also sorting through the shards of their own traumatic pasts. The violent experiences of mass rape that prevailed in Berlin and the greater Soviet zone until 1947 meant that German suffering beyond the air war took on a distinctly gendered dimension. An estimated one in three women in Berlin were raped. In Hans Magnus Enzensberger's introduction to *A Woman in Berlin*, a diarist's account (recently revealed to be journalist Marta Hillers) of Berlin's early days of Soviet occupation, Enzensberger observed, "When their husbands and lovers returned, paralyzed by defeat, it was women who cleared the rubble."[28] But often the same women had their own traumas to work through, as the diarist herself writes after experiencing repeated rapes. She, too, resumes her career as a journalist, despite the difficulties and dangers of traversing the ruined landscape to reach her new office.

There remains a disconnect between narratives that discuss the reconstruction of high culture and the lived experience of much of Berlin's female population. Yet early postwar concerts were also spaces of violence, in the case of one Philharmonic performance where the Soviets interrupted the music with weapons drawn. In the first row of the balcony, female audience members fled from the hall, fearing rape. Henry Alter pondered the contradiction between Soviet cultural policies and the violence with which they governed the city, noting that the Russians were "quite humane as administrators of the occupied city . . . especially in the cultural domain," albeit, "if one does not take into account the violent first weeks."[29] Looting, mass rape, and occupier-supported cultural ventures took place concurrently, though they were not easily reconcilable with one another.

Consequently, gendered violence and the figure of the rubble woman made their mark on the way postwar operas were viewed, staged, and consumed by a primarily female audience. Opera provided a space for women to take on leading roles as artistic advisers, directors, and performers, positions that would have been unthinkable in other cultural organizations. Ernst Legal realized he could not reopen with Staatsoper without assistance from its foremost dramatic soprano, Frida Leider, and retained her services as a consultant. Before the war, Leider had frequently performed at the Metropolitan, Chicago, and Covent Garden opera houses, specializing in Wagnerian roles such as Brünnhilde and Isolde. After 1939, she continued singing in Spain, Italy, and Germany while her husband, German Jewish violinist Rudolf Deman, remained in Swiss exile. Leider spent the final years of the war at her country cottage in Pausin, but after receiving Legal's summons in July 1945, she hitched a ride back to the city with the Russian military. The urban center of her memories was replaced by desolate ruins, as "Berlin exceeded my worst apprehensions."[30] Although Legal first offered her a chance to return to the Staatsoper stage, she declined. At fifty-seven and in the twilight of her career, Leider had no desire to mount a comeback. She did, however, accept his offer to serve as an adviser, a position she maintained between 1945 and 1952, in addition to her work as a professor at the Hochschule für Musik from 1948 onward. To help cultivate and train artists, Leider started her own studio as an incubator for young talent, dedicating herself to filling the critical pedagogical gaps caused by war, deprivation, and military service. It was in this capacity that Leider auditioned Dietrich Fischer-Dieskau in 1946, newly returned from an American prisoner-of-war camp, and she urged Legal to give him a contract with the Staatsoper immediately. Legal demurred, offering Fischer-Dieskau a spot in Leider's studio. Much to Leider's chagrin, Fischer-Dieskau turned the offer down and was soon appearing frequently at the Städtische Oper instead.[31]

Both Berlin houses selected opening postwar operas that dealt with themes of female empowerment and thwarted romance; storylines that more clearly paralleled the experience of the rubble woman in 1945. In *Fidelio*, the Städtische Oper's first staged production, Leonore rescues her husband from imprisonment and almost certain death, a heroine with whom rubble women, rebuilding the country brick by brick, could identify. Leonore dresses up as a man to conceal her identity, a trick tried by more than a few postwar women (among them actress Hildegard Knef) in hopes of avoiding rape by Soviet troops. Inversely, in the Staatsoper's production of Gluck's *Orpheus and Eurydice*, a husband is unable to save his wife from death, mirroring the emasculation of German manhood in the wake of World War II. Rehearsals for *Orpheus and Eurydice* began on July 9, and the opera opened on September 8. In an all-female production directed by Wolf Völker, *Orpheus* featured Tiana Lemnitz as Eurydice, Ilse Mentzel as Eros, and Anneliese Müller as Orpheus.[32] The chorus of nymphs and shepherdesses, likewise, consisted exclusively of women. Lacking props and set pieces with which to work, *Orpheus and Eurydice* relied primarily on contrast lighting.[33] Publicity photos show Müller's Orpheus with a bandaged right foot, revealing that bodily affliction had to be overcome in the service of rubble opera (fig. 3.2).

Figure 3.2. *Orpheus and Eurydice*, Staatsoper, September 1945. SLUB Dresden/Deutsche Fotothek. Photograph by Abraham Pisarek.

Figure 3.3. The dungeon scene from *Fidelio*, depicted as part of a Städtische Oper advertisement for coming attractions. F Rep. 280, 305-1384, Slide 33. Courtesy of the Landesarchiv.

In September 1945, the Städtische Oper opened their season with *Fidelio*. The opera's themes of liberation and redemptive love served as a musical allegory for the postwar rubble woman's suffering, providing an attractive escape from the stark realities of bombed homes, occupation powers, and insufficient rations. The company first gave a private performance for soldiers and occupation officials on September 2 and only two days later for a German audience. Featuring Karina Kutz (Leonore) and Günter Treptow (Florestan) and conducted by Robert Heger, *Fidelio* was performed six times that fall. The poster advertising the event proudly proclaimed it was the first of its kind in the city, touting that its opening had beaten the Staatsoper's by just under a week.[34] Another advertisement for *Fidelio* prominently featured a sketch of the prison's foreboding dungeon (fig. 3.3). The imagery evoked parallels with the confines of an air raid shelter, scenery with which the audience would have been familiar. Already in 1944, writer Ursula von Kardorff had written of Berlin's Zoological Garden bunker, "The walls of the shelter, made of massive blocks of stone, look like a stage-set for the prison scene in *Fidelio*"[35] (fig. 3.4).

Figure 3.4. Zoo bunker, 1946. Photograph by Erich O. Krueger. Courtesy of the Bundesarchiv.

Aside from parallels in the staging's aesthetics, *Fidelio*'s characters even embodied the contradictions of the postwar period; Rocco, the prison warden who watches over Florestan, is torn between his duty to the tyrant Pizarro and his own moral sense of justice. When Rocco admits in act 2, "I do what my duty demands. Though I hate all brutality" ("Ich thu', was meine Pflicht gebeut. Doch hass' ich alle Grausamkeit"), he walks the ambiguous line between collaboration and unwilling acceptance. Rocco's willingness to follow many of Pizarro's demands (with the notable exception that he refuses to kill Florestan himself) mirrored the nearly ubiquitous defense of many war criminals in 1945. Performances of *Fidelio* soon took place across ruined Germany. Eleven days after the opera's opening in Berlin, singers in Dresden performed a concert version to benefit the city's rebuilding, and in November, the Munich Staatsoper staged *Fidelio* at the Prinzregententheater.[36]

Ultimately, the highest grossing opera of Berlin's rubble years was *Madame Butterfly*; the Staatsoper performed the piece twenty-four times in 1947 alone. In West Germany, too, Puccini's opera was among the most frequently programmed twentieth-century works, second only to Strauss's *Der Rosenkavalier*.[37] Cio-Cio-San's disgrace and ultimate suicide after her marriage to the insincere American lieutenant undoubtedly resonated with the occupied German population. Though not all scholars have heard her suicide as defeat; Linda Hutcheon and Michael Hutcheon have argued that Cio-Cio-San's decision to take her own life can be heard as a gesture of female empowerment rather than one of submission.[38] Suicide was another social issue of astounding contemporary relevance for Berlin audiences; in 1945 over 7,000 Berliners took their lives, an astounding number when compared with the 2,000 of 1938.[39]

Rubble and Repertoire: Reconstructing the Städtische Oper and Staatsoper

After *Fidelio*, the Städtische's season continued with *Cavalleria Rusticana* (Mascagni), *Pagliacci* (Leoncavallo), *The Bartered Bride* (Smetana), *Otello* (Verdi), *Martha, or The Market at Richmond* (von Flotow), *Simon Boccanegra* (Verdi), and *The Barber of Seville* (Rossini). By 1947, as Bohnen's denazification defense was unraveling, the Städtische Oper was mounting its first contemporary opera production since the war. Information Services Control had secured the rights for *Peter Grimes*, and it was subsequently produced in other British-occupied cities, including Hamburg, Düsseldorf, and Mannheim. The opera's misunderstood and spurned protagonist paralleled, in many ways, Bohnen's own expulsion from the fold, and more broadly, *Peter Grimes* was the ideal operatic parable for postwar Germany with its themes of alienation, repression, and mistrust. Conducted by Robert Heger and directed by Werner Kelch, the opera opened at the Städtische Oper on May 23, 1947, starting a weeklong celebration of English culture in Berlin. To ensure its pedagogical import was not lost on the audience, the opera was sung in German, and the cast received thirty-three curtain calls after the Berlin premiere.[40] A critic for *Die Welt* considered Britten's topic, "the mass and the individual," to hold such relevance for the Berlin audience that he observed "not only demonstrative applause, but also tears of devastation"[41] on opening night.

Yet *Peter Grimes* received mostly mixed reviews in the press. Another critic for *Melos* could hardly contain his anti-British sentiment by rendering Britten in Wagnerian terms, arguing that the composer would have been better off writing a "Volksoper" rather than a "Musikdrama," as the piece in its current form was of little interest to German audiences.[42] *Berliner Kurier* remained skeptical about the Städtische Oper's motivations for staging *Peter Grimes*, noting the production could be considered a success only "if the house's acceptance means more than a curtsy before the licensor."[43]

Two more premieres would follow shortly after *Peter Grimes*, though not during Bohnen's tenure. Heinz Tietjen was named the new Städtische Oper director for the fall 1948 season, his career having survived his work under National Socialism, his dismissal by the Soviets, and a hefty denazification fine.[44] Among the works Tietjen programmed for his first season were Verdi's *Don Carlos*, in which the young Dietrich Fischer-Dieskau made his Berlin debut as Rodrigue, and *Die Flut*, a contemporary work by Berlin composer Boris Blacher. Werner Egk's *Circe*, premiering in December 1948, was the high point of the season. Egk was the former leader of the composer's section of the Reichsmusikkammer (RMK) under the Third Reich, and another musician who continued his career in West Germany unimpeded by his activities during National Socialism. (In contrast, the Soviets premiered only two other German operas between 1945 and 1950, in Zwickau and Radebeul, hardly urban centers where such performances would have attracted much attention or scrutiny.)[45]

Meanwhile, the Soviet-licensed Staatsoper's 1945 season consisted of operas carefully tailored to appeal to both Russian and German audiences: *Rigoletto* (Verdi), *Eugene Onegin* (Tchaikovsky), and *Hansel and Gretel* (Humperdinck). As Legal admitted in a report to the magistrate, the repertoire selection "could of course not be completely free choice," but was mostly dependent on "the possibilities of obtaining the materials."[46] Leider was more forthcoming in her assessment: "The management had to take into consideration the preference of the Russians for their own operas." [47] *Eugene Onegin* opened on November 7. Starring Josef Burgwinkel, Erich Witte, and Ludwig Hofmann, and directed by Wolf Völker, the opera's set, designed by Karl Doll, was reminiscent of a Caspar David Friedrich painting, uniting the Russian classic with German Romanticism. Legal was ecstatic to report that *Eugene Onegin* earned Staatsoper management the support of Lieutenant Colonel A. Sudakow, leader of the Department of Volksbildung, the division responsible for supervising German cultural life. Legal was pleased; the number of Russians in the audience began to climb.[48]

Staatsoper productions were soon successful in attracting all of the occupation powers, not just the Soviets, collapsing the new borders of the city. In December, Erna Berger played Hansel in the December production of *Hansel and Gretel*, directed by Frida Leider. Enthusiastically received, British soldiers threw real chocolate onstage. Marjorie Clay, wife of American military governor Lucius Clay, loved the production so much that she invited the singers to give a benefit performance in the American sector. The set featured a real gingerbread house, which Berger ate parts of after the performance.[49]

The Staatsoper's three 1946 productions—*Tiefland* (d'Albert), *Madame Butterfly* (Puccini), and *Tales of Hoffmann* (Offenbach)—found increasing financial success. Already in September 1945, the Staatsoper took in 100,000 RM, which grew to 250,000 RM in November, and by January 1946 had topped 500,000 RM per month. The 210 Staatsoper performances between September 1945 and May 1946 produced a gross sum of 3.5 million RM. At the invitation of the Soviets, Nicolas Nabokov reluctantly attended *Madame Butterfly* during winter 1946. Arriving late to the performance, he squeezed past officers from all occupation powers, finally reaching his seat in the eighth row. He could scarcely sit down before an American general began pestering him with questions about the opera's plot, relieved Nabokov could "tell us what this G.D. thing is all about."[50] Nabokov's description only enraged the general, who took offense that an American officer, Lieutenant Pinkerton (or "Linkerton" as the program notes called him), behaves so dishonorably.[51]

Just as opera was a status symbol of bourgeois culture in prewar Germany, so too would the opera house become a place for the Allies to flaunt their cultural reeducation programs and musical achievements. The Soviets cultivated Russian German operatic culture as a formative part of Socialist Unity Party (SED) politics, inviting German officials and other Allies to the Staatsoper as a form of cultural diplomacy. As Frida Leider recalled, "Audiences came from all four sectors of Berlin, and one saw Berliners, English, French, Americans and Russians sitting peaceably side by side in the stalls. . . . Every language was spoken in the intervals."[52] The Russian occupiers catered to the needs of the German operatic community, providing better rations, improved working conditions, and higher salaries than the western occupiers.[53] In the late 1940s, there remained great optimism concerning the creation of a socialist, antifascist state, as Joy Calico has noted, and the Soviets quickly mobilized Berlin's operatic culture to create a partnership between the Soviet Union and East Germany.[54]

Rubble and Repertoire: Germans, Jews, and the Ruins of Operatic Works

Aside from works like *Peter Grimes* and *Eugene Onegin*, programmed in a deferential nod to their respective occupiers, the repertoire of both Berlin houses remained largely the same as it had been during the National Socialist years. Beethoven was the most frequently performed composer in 1945 Berlin, and *Fidelio* became a staple of the Städtische's offerings. Wagner, too, was often performed in Berlin's opera houses.[55] Yet what did it mean to stage works by these composers in ruined spaces, monolithic operas of the nineteenth century amid the shattered debris of aerial warfare? As Leon Botstein notes of 1945, "The appearance of innocence in the normalcy and presumed neutrality of musical life during and after the war is strikingly seductive. That alone recommends it as an object for scrutiny."[56]

Critical reception of *Fidelio* in postwar Germany was overwhelmingly positive, with reviewers hearing a polyphony of connections to contemporary events. In Berlin, one critic argued that Beethoven's music was well suited "to describe a totalitarian system."[57] Suggesting Fidelio's imprisonment was a result of his antifascist ideals and making him into a kind of resistance fighter was certainly an appealing reading of the opera in the immediate postwar period, an era searching for a redemptive narrative of German cultural production. Similarly, musicologist Georg Knepler, who returned to East Berlin in 1949, argued that *Fidelio* encouraged the idea "that one must be prepared in the struggle against injustice to take up arms."[58] Antifascist interpretations of Beethoven's opera represented a speedy reversal from its many stagings during the Third Reich, collapsing historical eras to suggest that the opera could be heard as a critique of totalitarianism. As Thomas Mann, despaired to a friend in 1945, "For what utter apathy (*Stumpfsinn*) was required to be able to listen to *Fidelio* in Himmler's Germany without covering one's face and rushing out of the hall!"[59] Yet how could *Fidelio* be both a marker of fascism's perversion of German culture and a work embodying resistance to the Third Reich? A playbill in Munich went even further, deeming the opera to be "an anti-concentration camp"[60] work and problematically conflating German and Jewish suffering. By relating the nineteenth-century cultural sphere to Nazi barbarity, the review revealed the absence of adequate language to discuss the camps and problems of representation in postwar evaluations of them. Effacing Jewish suffering by recasting the genocide as largely perpetrated against Germans (and not by them), the reviewer's response was endemic of postwar erasure. As Joy Calico and Amy Lynn Wlodarski have pointed out, there were no models in 1945 around which these discussions and critiques of musical works and the Holocaust could be based. The genocide had not yet been given the name of the Holocaust, and it is unsurprising that postwar German debates about who did the most suffering (and where they did it) largely omitted Jewish narratives.[61]

But if Beethoven's music represented one set of postwar reception challenges, Wagner's presented quite another, especially when considering the Nazis' patronage of the Bayreuth Festival or the oft-repeated axiom of Wagner as Hitler's favorite composer. The composer's music had sounded at countless propaganda events, from the 1935 Nuremberg rally, at which Hitler promulgated the race laws formally excluding Jewish citizens from German public life, to Hitler's birthday celebrations and various Nazi Party events at Bayreuth.[62] As Carolyn Birdsall argues, during the Nazi period, "the unity and synthesis associated with the *Gesamtkunstwerk* offered ideological currency as a metaphor for the national community."[63] But did the destruction of one signal the downfall of the other?

Even the collapse of the Third Reich was rendered by many eyewitnesses in Wagnerian terms. As the Russians encircled Berlin in April 1945, Albert Speer attended a concert that featured, among other repertoire, Brünnhilde's final aria from *Götterdämmerung*. The architect and armaments minster described the performance as "rather bathetic and also melancholy,"[64] recalling that afterward, he walked across the rubbled Potsdamer Platz for the last time. Similarly, Allied occupiers and historians from Nicolas Nabokov to Ian Kershaw could not resist the metaphor of the *Götterdämmerung* to describe the downfall of the regime, linking the ruinous urban landscape with the end of Valhalla. The monumental, as Andreas Huyssen notes, was perceived in the postwar era as "politically suspect," considered to be "representative of nineteenth-century nationalisms and of twentieth-century totalitarianisms."[65] Adorno, however, heard the regime's Wagnerian tendencies slightly differently. He argued that the Germans fully expected revenge after National Socialism, and therein lay the Third Reich's enduring connection to the composer. It was the anticipation of retribution, and not a shattering downfall, Adorno wrote, that "may suffice as an example for speculations on the innermost secrets of Nazi mentality and Nazi reality as suggested by the Wagnerian work."[66]

Whether due to themes of retribution, monumentality, or collapse, Wagner's music was never absent from German stages or concert halls. The composer was heard frequently on postwar concert programs for everyone from German civilians, American troops, and even displaced Jewish survivors.[67] In 1947 and 1948 alone, the Staatsoper staged *Tristan and Isolde*, *The Flying Dutchman*, and *The Mastersingers of Nuremberg*, while the Städtische Oper produced *The Valkyrie*. RIAS (Radio in the American Sector) sponsored weeklong celebrations of Wagnerian opera, including concerts at the Titania Palast. Further afield from Berlin, as Emily Richmond Pollock notes in her work on Munich's Bavarian State Opera, the public clamored for the composer, demanding his music be played with increasing frequency.[68] Although Wagner might have been unsoundly in the zero hour narrative of new beginnings, he was as much the sound of Germany's rubble years as Mendelssohn.

The Staatsoper's most eagerly anticipated opera of the postwar period was *Tristan and Isolde*, conducted in 1947 by the recently denazified Wilhelm Furtwängler. Frida Leider directed the production, which starred Ludwig Suthaus as Tristan, Erna Schlüter as Isolde, Margarete Klose as Brangäne, Jaro Prohaska as Kurwenal, and Gottlob Frick as King Mark. Legal and Leider decided to pare down the Staatsoper's *Tristan*, as Leider believed "the younger generation of music lovers, after their bitter experiences, would hardly have had much sympathy for an exaggerated romantic approach."[69] Furtwängler's three performances (and two concerts with the Staatskapelle) proved to be the highest grossing five events in the house's history to date. Management raised ticket prices to double and even triple their standard cost, as Legal recognized that Berliners were willing to pay top price to hear Furtwängler. Perhaps even more astonishing was that the conductor was able to command 10,000 RM per appearance, a staggering sum in postwar Berlin, and one that not even the Philharmonic could pay for their director.[70]

Aside from his performances for German civilians, Furtwängler also conducted the Staatskapelle in an open rehearsal on October 2 for Jewish refugees living in Schlachtensee, the largest displaced persons camp in Berlin. The rehearsal featured the Beethoven Violin Concerto (with visiting artist Yehudi Menuhin), Gluck's *Alceste* Overture, and perhaps surprisingly, the act 1 prelude from *Tristan and Isolde*, the same music they would perform for their German audience that evening.[71] There is a strange asymmetry in thinking about one of the more famous conductors of the Third Reich, in the ruins of Berlin, leading his ensemble in a rousing performance of Wagner's *Tristan and Isolde* for Jewish survivors.

And yet, throughout the latter part of the twentieth century, the myth persisted that Wagner's music had somehow been taboo or even banned in the immediate postwar period. This reckoning, as Pamela Potter and Celia Applegate have noted, was part of "a worldwide backlash against anything that seemed a reflection or a product of German nationalism."[72] Paradoxically, the Wagner myth served several pragmatic functions—namely, if his music could become the postwar locus of anxieties concerning Nazi music, then he could serve as the *Persilschein* (whitewash) for the rest of German classical music. By supposedly excising the offending element, German musical culture could be quickly and simply rehabilitated.

In the 1950s, Wagner was recast as a hero of the German Democratic Republic, while in the west, productions emphasized his internationalist qualities, as Wieland Wagner's stagings at the "New Bayreuth" eschewed realism and featured sparse set designs with experimental lighting. (It is worth noting, however, that he had already dabbled with more streamlined stagings of *The Ring* during the 1930s.) As Adorno wrote in the 1960s, to stage Wagnerian opera for contemporary audiences, one must "force what is false, flawed, antinomical out into the open, rather than glossing over it," concluding that "only experimental solutions are justified today; only what injures the Wagner orthodoxy is true"[73]—the rubbled music of a rubbled people.

In the immediate postwar period, opera became a sonic platform to explore notions of German suffering through repertoire choices such as Beethoven and Wagner, staples of the nineteenth-century operatic tradition now resounding in the ruined shells of once grand venues. Through its use of literal and figurative rubble, opera presented a unique forum for visual and sonic representations of German victimhood through staging choices, repertoire selections, and personnel. Questions of restitution were complicated by postwar political and geographic divisions, as well as the difficulties of moving materials across a cratered landscape. Compromised singers and other managerial personnel resumed their work immediately, reinstalling their respective companies in new venues, rarely (if at all) slowed by denazification proceedings. Women's roles in rebuilding operatic culture empowered them to leading positions within the Staatsoper and Städtische Oper, yet they, too, took on the arduous job of sorting through the rubble. Operatic repertoire remained much the same after the war as during (with the notable exception of productions that featured music of Allied composers), creating the illusion of continuity. Perhaps Wagner's inexhaustible hold on audiences in postwar Germany is not so surprising. After all, it is the redemption leitmotive that features most prominently at the conclusion of *Götterdämmerung*; resonating above the flames, ashes, and rubble.

Notes

1. Hans Erich Nossack, *The End: Hamburg, 1943*, trans. Joel Agee (Chicago: University of Chicago Press, 2004), 38.

2. Sabine K. quoted in Susanne zur Nieden, ed., *Alltag im Ausnahmezustand: Frauentagebücher im zerstörten Deutschland 1943 bis 1945* (Berlin: Orlanda Frauenverlag, 1993), 194. Sabine would later join the ensemble of the Maxim-Gorki Theater.

3. Andrew Oster, "Rubble, Radio, and Reconstruction: The Genre of Funkoper in Postwar Occupied Germany and the Federal Republic, 1946–1957" (PhD diss., Princeton University, 2010), 114–17.

4. David Monod, *Settling Scores: German Music, Denazification, and the Americans, 1945–1953* (Chapel Hill: University of North Carolina Press, 2005), 24; Alex Ross, *The Rest Is Noise: Listening to the Twentieth Century* (New York: Farrar, Straus and Giroux, 2007), 347; and "De-Requisition of the Opera House of Nürnberg thru the U.S. Army," Box 20, Records of the Office of Military Government, Bavaria: Records of the Education and Cultural Relations Division, NARA II.

5. Richard Strauss, "The Artistic Testament of Richard Strauss," *Musical Quarterly* 36, no. 1 (January 1950): 1–8; Alfred Mann Papers, Box 6, Sibley Music Library, Eastman School of Music, Rochester, NY; and Bertil Wetzelsberger, "Wie sollen wir aufbauen?" *Melos*, November 1946, 15. My thanks to Dr. David Peter Coppen, who was kind enough to send me copies of the materials on Strauss.

6. The Staatsoper's Unter den Linden house was damaged by an aerial attack in April 1942 and destroyed in February 1945, while the Städtische Oper on Bismarkstraße was

bombed in November 1943. Hans Heinz Stuckenschmidt, "Theaterstadt Berlin. Die Oper nach 1945," folder 2015, Stuckenschmidt Papers, AdK; "Wiederaufbau der alten Städtischen Oper: Michael Bohnen über seine Pläne," *Der Berliner,* February 2, 1946; Allied Forces, Supreme Headquarters, *Manual for the Control of German Information Service,* May 12, 1945, 196; and Memorandum, May 11, 1945, B. Rep 207, Nr. 645, Landesarchiv.

7. Heinz Tietjen Papers, "Bescheinigung Nr. 125," May 15, 1945, and "Von der zweitweiligen Ausübung der Befugnisse . . . ," June 8, 1945, Folder 27, AdK; Michael Kater, *Composers of the Nazi Era: Eight Portraits* (New York: Oxford University Press, 2000), 8–9; Hans Heinz Stuckenschmidt, "Theaterstadt Berlin. Die Oper nach 1945," folder 2015, AdK; and "Stadtkommandanten von Berlin für Opern und Konzertwesen," Rep. C 120, Nr. 1484, June 11, 1945, Landesarchiv.

8. For more on the restitution of art objects, see Lynn Nicholas, *The Rape of Europa* (New York: Vintage Books, 1995), 327–406.

9. Legal to Magistrate, March 27, 1947 and March 2, 1949, C Rep. 120, Nr. 1639, Landesarchiv; Rihoko Ueno, "Monuments Men inside the Mines," Archives of American Art Blog, https://www.aaa.si.edu/node/3516; Memorandum, June 11, 1945, B. Rep 207, Nr. 645, Landesarchiv; J. H. Hills, "Inventory of Orchestra Scores in Salt Mine near Heimboldshausen," August 30, 1945, RG 260, Box 134, Records of the Information Control Division: Central Decimal File of the Executive Office, 1944–49, NARA II; and "Städtisches Symphonie Orchester," C Rep. 120, Nr. 294, Landesarchiv.

10. "In Accordance with Arrangements Made, Information Control Division," August 11, 1945, RG 260, Box 134, Records of the Information Control Division: Central Decimal File of the Executive Office, 1944–49, NARA II.

11. William M. Kinard to Colonel S. Tulpanov, February 3, 1947, RG 260, Box 134, Records of the Information Control Division: Central Decimal File of the Executive Office, 1944–49, NARA II; and "Operations at Mippe Salt Mine, Heimboldshausen, Germany," November 9, 1945, RG 260, Box 134, Records of the Information Control Division: Central Decimal File of the Executive Office, 1944–49, NARA II.

12. Legal, Report to the Magistrate, March 27, 1947, and May 3, 1946, C Rep. 120, Nr. 1639, Landesarchiv.

13. Erna Berger, *Auf Flügeln des Gesanges: Erinnerungen einer Sängerin* (Zurich: Atlantis Musikbuch, 1998), 79.

14. Ibid., 80.

15. "Über die Prüfung der Kasse und Wirtschaftsführung der ehemaligen Staatstheater," November 22, 1946, C Rep. 120, Nr. 1639, Landesarchiv.

16. Ernst Legal, Report to the Magistrate of Berlin, May 3, 1946, C Rep. 120, Nr. 1639, Landesarchiv.

17. Karl August Neumann to Erich Otto, "Betrifft Deutsche Staatsoper (ehem. Staatsoper), jetzt Admiralspalast," undated, C Rep. 120, Nr. 1676, Landesarchiv. See also Karl August Neumann, Bach Cantatas Website, http://www.bach-cantatas.com/Bio/Neumann-Karl-August.htm.

18. Frida Leider, *Playing My Part, 1888–1975* (New York: Da Capo, 1959), 199.

19. Ernst Legal, "A Report Concerning the Number of Party Members in the Staatsoper," October 8, 1945, C Rep. 120, Nr. 1676, Landesarchiv.

20. "Report of the Intendant of the Former Staatstheater," August 9, 1945, C Rep. 120, Nr. 1486, Landesarchiv; and Neumann to Otto, "Betrifft Deutsche Staatsoper (ehem. Staatsoper), jetzt Admiralspalast," undated, C Rep. 120, Nr. 1676, Landesarchiv.

21. Quotation from Georg Rebentisch to Charlottenburg District Office, June 19, 1945, B Rep. 207, Nr. 645, Landesarchiv. Information on the repertoire can be found in "Programm für Woche vom 2. bis 8. Juli 1945," B. Rep 207, Nr. 645, Landesarchiv.

22. Amt für Volksbildung, Charlottenberg to Georg Rebentisch, June 23, 1945, B Rep. 207, Nr. 645, Landesarchiv.

23. Michael Bohnen to Ludwig Hülsen, C Rep. 120, Nr. 1485, Landesarchiv.

24. Hans Heinz Stuckenschmidt, "Theaterstadt Berlin. Oper nach 1945," folder 2015, Stuckenschmidt Papers, AdK; and Abteilung für Volksbildung beim Magistrat der Stadt Berlin to Deutschen Prüfungsausschuss für die Kulturschaffenden, April 18, 1946, C Rep. 120, Nr. 1485, Landesarchiv. See also Elizabeth Janik, *Recomposing German Music: Politics and Musical Tradition in Cold War Berlin* (Leiden, the Netherlands: Brill, 2005), 140–41.

25. The piece failed to mention that Bohnen had also appeared in *Gold* (1934), a Nazi science fiction film where he played a greedy English businessman, and in *The Rothschilds* (1940), an anti-Semitic propaganda film about the illustrious family's finances during the Napoleonic Wars.

26. Janik, *Recomposing German Music*, 140–42; "Was geht in der Städtischen Oper vor?" *Neues Deutschland*, October 20, 1946; and Michael Bohnen, Fragebogen, May 15, 1946, B Rep. 207, Nr. 641, Landesarchiv. About Bohnen's work in film, see Rolf Giesen, *Nazi Propaganda Films: A History of Filmography* (Jefferson, NC: McFarland, 2003), 106, 235; "Kino Lorber Releases *Gold* on Blu-ray and DVD," https://www.kinolorber.com/news/article/id/29.

27. Robert G. Moeller, *Protecting Motherhood: Women and the Family in the Politics of Postwar West Germany* (Berkeley: University of California Press, 1993), 11. See also Geoffrey Giles, ed., *Stunde Null: The End and the Beginning Fifty Years Ago* (Washington, DC: German Historical Institute, 1997), 6; and Heide Fehrenbach, *Cinema in Democratizing Germany: Reconstructing National Identity after Hitler* (Chapel Hill: University of North Carolina Press, 1999), 95.

28. Introduction to *A Woman in Berlin: Eight Weeks in the Conquered City*, trans. Philip Boehm (New York: Metropolitan Books, 2005). For more on the gendered experience of the cease-fire, see Norman M. Naimark, *The Russians in Germany: A History of the Soviet Zone of Occupation, 1945–1949* (Cambridge, MA: Harvard University Press, 1995), 69–140; Atina Grossmann, *Jews, Germans, and Allies: Close Encounters in Occupied Germany* (Princeton, NJ: Princeton University Press, 2007), 48–87; and Ruth Andreas-Friedrich, *Battleground Berlin, 1945–1948* (New York: Paragon House, 1984), 16–17.

29. Henry Alter, interview by Brewster Chamberlain and Jürgen Wetzel, May 11, 1981, B Rep. 037, Nr. 79– 82, Landesarchiv, Berlin. For an account of the first postwar Philharmonic performance, see Peter Muck, ed., *Einhundert Jahre Berliner Philharmonisches Orchester* (Tutzing: H. Schneider, 1982), 2:190.

30. Leider, *Playing My Part*, 197.

31. Ibid., 205–9.

32. "Report of the Intendant of the Former Staatstheater," August 9, 1945, C Rep. 120, Nr. 1486, Landesarchiv; "Aufnahme des Betriebes nach dem 1.5.1945," C Rep. 120, Nr. 1639, Landesarchiv; and Hans Heinz Stuckenschmidt, "Theaterstadt Berlin. Oper nach 1945," folder 2015, Stuckenschmidt Papers, AdK.

33. As *Time* magazine noted, early postwar Staatsoper productions were "done with a sort of theatrical efficiency that is typically German and intensely dramatic." Winthrop Sargeant, "Europe's Culture," *Time*, November 4, 1946, 54.

34. Michael Bohnen, "Bericht über den Aufbau der Städtischen Oper in der Zeit vom 1. Mai 1945 bis 30. April 1946," May 6, 1946, Rep. C 120, Nr. 1484, Landesarchiv; and F Rep. 290 Photograph, and Deutsches Opernhaus Berlin, B. Rep 207, Nr. 645, Landesarchiv.

35. Ursula von Kardorff, *Diary of a Nightmare: Berlin 1942–45* (New York: John Day, 1966), 85.

36. That the opera spoke to this cultural moment can perhaps best be heard in Swiss composer Rolf Lieberman's twelve-tone "peace opera" (*Friedensoper*), titled, *Leonore 40/45*, a work he wrote as a kind of homage to Beethoven's *Fidelio*. With a libretto by Heinrich Stroebel, the opera premiered in Basel in 1952, and featured the story of Alfred, a German soldier in occupied France, and Huguette, the young Parisian woman with whom he falls in love. Hans Heinz Stuckenschmidt, "Leonore 40/45," *Die Neue Zeitung*, March 28, 1952.

37. Oster, "Rubble, Radio, and Reconstruction," 123–24; Erläuterungen zum Jahresabschluss 1947," C Rep. 120, Nr. 1639, Landesarchiv. *Madame Butterfly* grossed 408,229 RM by December 1947. See also Hans Heinz Stuckenschmidt, "Theaterstadt Berlin. Oper nach 1945," Folder 2015, Stuckenschmidt Papers, AdK.

38. Linda Hutcheon and Michael Hutcheon, *Opera: The Art of Dying* (Cambridge, MA: Harvard University Press, 2004), 135.

39. Monica Black, *Death in Berlin: From Weimar to Divided Germany* (Cambridge: Cambridge University Press, 2010), 147; and Paul Steege, *Black Market, Cold War: Everyday Life in Berlin, 1946–1949* (Cambridge: Cambridge University Press, 2007), 60.

40. Toby Thacker, *Music after Hitler, 1945–1955* (Farnham, UK: Ashgate, 2007), 91–92; Gabriele Clemens, *Britische Kulturpolitik in Deutschland 1945–1949: Literatur, Film, Musik und Theater* (Stuttgart: Franz Steiner, 1997), 194; Kurt Westphal, "Internationale neue Musik in Berlin," *Melos*, August/September 1947: and 292–94; Hans Heinz Stuckenschmidt, "Theaterstadt Berlin. Oper nach 1945," Folder 2015, Stuckenschmidt Papers, AdK.

41. Josef Marein, "Brittens *Peter Grimes*," *Die Welt*, March 27, 1947, http://www.zeit.de/1947/13/brittens-peter-grimes.

42. H. W. Kulenkampff, "Auf dem Weg zur englischen Oper," *Melos*, April 1947: 176–78.

43. "Blick in die Zeit," *Melos*, April 1947: 175.

44. After Bohnen's dismissal in 1947, the Städtische Oper was led by a series of interim directors, including Peter von Hamm, Robert Heger, and Werner Kelch, all of whom had conflicting visions for the future of the company. Entnazifizierungskommission für Kunstschaffende to Heinz Tietjen, Folder 28, Heinz Tietjen Papers, AdK. The fine amounted to 2,185 DM. See also Kater, *Composers of the Nazi Era*, 8–9; and Janik, *Recomposing German Music*, 140–42.

45. Joy H. Calico, "The Politics of Opera in the German Democratic Republic, 1945–1961" (PhD diss., Duke University), 33. In Zwickau, Robert Hanell's *Der Bettler von Damaskus* was staged in May 1947, and in Radebeul, Fritz Reuter's *Ein Funken Liebe* premiered in January 1948. See also Ernst Kroll, "Berliner Opern-Chronik in drei Teilen," in *Musikstadt Berlin zwischen Krieg und Frieden: Musikalische Bilanz einer Viermächtestadt* (Wiesbaden: E. Bote & G. Bock, 1956), 76; Hans Heinz Stuckenschmidt, "Theaterstadt Berlin. Oper nach 1945," Folder 2015, Stuckenschmidt Papers, AdK; and Kater, *Composers of the Nazi Era*, 3–30.

46. Ernst Legal, Report to the Magistrate of Berlin, May 3, 1946, C Rep. 120, Nr. 1639, Landesarchiv. "Die Wahl des Spielplanes konnte unter den geschilderten Umständen natürlich keine ganz freie sein, sondern sie wurde wesentlich mit durch die Möglichkeit der Materialbeschaffung beeinflusst, fand jedoch alles in allem neben dem wachsenden Publikumserfolg auch die Billigung der Presse."

47. Leider, *Playing My Part*, 201.
48. Hans Heinz Stuckenschmidt, "Theaterstadt Berlin. Oper nach 1945," Folder 2015, Stuckenschmidt Papers, AdK; Ernst Legal, Report to the Magistrate of Berlin, May 3, 1946, C Rep. 120, Nr. 1639, Landesarchiv; Edward N. Johnson, *Fünf Monate in Berlin: Briefe von Edward N. Johnson aus dem Jahre 1946*, ed. Werner Breunig and Jürgen Wetzel (Munich: de Gruyter, 2014), 181; and Brewster Chamberlin, *Kultur auf Trümmern: Berliner Berichte der amerikanischen Information Control Section Juli-Dezember 1945* (Stuttgart: Deutsche Verlags-Anstalt, 1979), 55.
49. Berger, *Auf Flügeln des Gesanges*, 81–82.
50. Nicolas Nabokov, *Old Friends, New Music* (Boston: Little, Brown, 1951), 258.
51. Ernst Legal, Report to the Magistrate of Berlin, May 3, 1946, C Rep. 120, Nr. 1639, Landesarchiv; Staatsoper Program, *Madame Butterfly*, 1946, F Rep. 280, 305–1384, Slide 42, Landesarchiv; "Erläuterungen zum Jahresabschluss 1947," C Rep. 120, Nr. 1639, Landesarchiv; and Hans Heinz Stuckenschmidt, "Theaterstadt Berlin. Oper nach 1945," Folder 2015, Stuckenschmidt Papers, AdK.
52. Leider, *Playing My Part*, 206.
53. In 1948, the Staatskapelle concertmaster earned 1,500 RM per month, compared to the concertmaster's 1,000 RM at Städtische Oper.
54. Ibid. For more on East Germany identity and opera, see Calico, "The Politics of Opera in the German Democratic Republic, 1945–1961," 1–47; and Joy H. Calico, *Brecht at the Opera* (Berkeley: University of California Press, 2008), 109–39. See also Janik, *Recomposing German Music*, 140; and "Bezüge der Orchestersolisten," July 21, 1948, C Rep. 120, Nr. 1692, Landesarchiv.
55. Janik, *Recomposing German Music*, 314.
56. Leon Botstein, "After Fifty Years: Thoughts on Music and the End of World War II," *The Musical Quarterly* 79, no. 2 (Summer 1995): 227.
57. *Der Kurier*, June 7, 1949. "Beethoven ist nicht von ungefähr darauf gekommen, ein totalitäres System zu beschreiben."
58. Quoted in Elaine Kelly, *Composing the Canon in the German Democratic Republic: Narratives of Nineteenth-Century Music* (Oxford: Oxford University Press, 2014), 48.
59. Thomas Mann to Walter von Molo, *Briefe, 1937–1947*, ed. Erika Mann (Frankfurt: Fischer, 1961), 2: 444. See also William Kinderman, *Beethoven* (Oxford: Oxford University Press, 2009), 130.
60. Quoted in Friedrich Prinz, *Trümmerzeit in München: Kultur und Gesellschaft einer deutschen Großstadt im Aufbruch 1945–1949* (Munich: Prinz, 1984), 146. From playbill, November 18, 1945, Archiv der Bayerischen Staatsoper, Munich.
61. For more, see Joy H. Calico, "*Jüdische Chronik*: The Third Space of Commemoration between East and West Germany," *Musical Quarterly* 88, no. 1 (Spring 2005): 95–122; Joy H. Calico, *Arnold Schoenberg's* A Survivor from Warsaw *in Postwar Europe* (Berkeley: University of California Press, 2014), 1–40; and Amy Lynn Wlodarski, *Musical Witness and Holocaust Representation* (Cambridge: Cambridge University Press, 2015), 1–35.
62. For more on the relationship between the regime and Bayreuth, see Pamela Potter, *The Most German of the Arts: Musicology and Society from the Weimar Republic to the End of Hitler's Reich* (New Haven, CT: Yale University Press, 1998), 1–27; Pamela Potter and Celia Applegate, "Germans as the 'People of Music': Geneaology of an Identity," in *Music and German National Identity*, ed. Pamela Potter and Celia Applegate (Chicago: University of

Chicago Press, 2002), 24; and Michael Kater, *The Twisted Muse: Musicians and Their Music in the Third Reich* (Oxford: Oxford University Press, 1997), 1–42, 200.

63. Carolyn Birdsall, *Nazi Soundscapes: Sound, Technology and Urban Space in Germany, 1933–1945* (Amsterdam: Amsterdam University Press, 2012), 142.

64. For accounts of final concerts under the Third Reich that featured Wagner's music, see Albert Speer, *Inside the Third Reich*, trans. Richard Winston and Clara Winston (Toronto: Macmillan, 1970), 463; and Nicolaus von Below, *At Hitler's Side: The Memoirs of Hitler's Luftwaffe Adjutant, 1937–1945* (London: Greenhill Books, 2001), 234.

65. Andreas Huyssen, *Present Pasts: Urban Palimpsests and the Politics of Memory* (Stanford, CA: Stanford University Press, 2003), 189. See also Nicolas Nabokov, "Boris Blacher," in Henrich and Eickhoff, *Boris Blacher: Archiv zur Musik des 20. Jahrhunderts* (Berlin: Fuldaer, 2003), 7:11; and Ian Kershaw, *The End: The Defiance and Destruction of Hitler's Germany, 1944–1945* (New York: Penguin, 2011), 3–15.

66. Theodor Adorno, "What National Socialism Has Done to the Arts," in *Essays on Music*, ed. Richard Leppert, trans. Susan Gillespie (Berkeley: University of California Press, 2002), 375.

67. Historian Toby Thacker writes that the French banned Wagner's music in postwar Germany, along with the music of Richard Strauss and Anton Bruckner. Toby Thacker, "'Gesungen oder musiziert wird aber fast in jedem Haus': Representing and Constructing Citizenship through Music in Twentieth-Century Germany," in *Citizenship and National Identity in Twentieth-Century Germany*, ed. Geoff Eley and Jan Palmowski (Stanford, CA: Stanford University Press, 2008), 169.

68. Emily Richmond Pollock, "Pride of Place: The 1963 Rebuilding of the Munich Nationaltheater," in *Dreams of Germany: Music and (Trans)national Imaginaries*, ed. Neil Gregor and Tom Irvine (New York: Berghahn Books, 2019), 145–68.

69. Leider, *Playing My Part*, 207.

70. "Erläuterungen zum Jahresabschluss 1947," C Rep. 120, Nr. 1639, Landesarchiv; Abteilung für Volksbildung to the Berliner Philharmonische Orchester, December 11, 1947, C Rep. 120, Nr. 1692, Landesarchiv.

71. For more on Menuhin's visit and his performances with Furtwängler, see Tina Frühauf, "Five Days in Berlin: The 'Menuhin Affair' of 1947 and the Politics of Jewish Post-Holocaust National Identity," in *The Musical Quarterly* 96, no. 1 (Spring 2013): 14–49.

72. We might contrast this 1947 dress rehearsal with the 2001 Berlin Staatskapelle's performance of the prelude to *Tristan and Isolde* under Daniel Barenboim. Arguably, the context was markedly different and separated by decades, with a German orchestra playing in the traditional Jewish homeland, and the conductor himself was an Israeli citizen. Barenboim played the prelude as a surprise second encore but performed it only after he had taken a poll of the audience to gauge support for the idea. He paused before the piece to allow those who wished to leave time to do so. Potter and Applegate, "Germans as 'The People of Music'," in Potter and Applegate, *Music and German National Identity*, 30–31; and Anthony Tommasini, "Music: A Cultural Disconnect on Wagner," *New York Times*, August 5, 2001.

73. Theodor Adorno, "Wagner's Relevance for Today," translated by Susan Gillespie. In *Grand Street* no. 44 (1993): 32–59. The quotation is from pp. 57. See also Kelly, *Composing the Canon in the German Democratic Republic*, 67–71; Patrick Carnegy, *Wagner and the Art of the Theatre* (New Haven, CT: Yale University Press, 2006), 263–309; and Monod, *Settling Scores*, 260.

4

EMBODIED AND DISEMBODIED VOICES

Listening to Sonic Ruins

As Henry Gluski flew over Berlin before landing at Tempelhof Airport in August 1945, he could scarcely believe the cityscape he witnessed. The ruins stretched as far as he could see—monuments to carpet-bombing and the violent street fighting of the war's final weeks. Nineteen-year-old Gluski had just accepted a broadcasting position with Berlin's American Forces Network (AFN), the radio station of the American military government designed for American GIs stationed in Berlin. Because he was the youngest and most inexperienced, Gluski was given the radio programs no one else wanted to moderate. His assignments included the early, early morning show and the weekly Quadripartite Symphony Hour. He chose mostly nineteenth- and twentieth-century repertoire—namely, the works of Jewish composers, including Mahler and Mendelssohn, believing their music held reeducational value for any German listener who might be tuning in.[1]

In a city that more closely resembled a moonscape than a metropolis, radio provided a link to the outside world. As historian Monica Black writes of the rubbled landscape of 1945, "Ruins and the graves of the dead had come to comprise the city's topography and become part of a new, postwar way of seeing."[2] Yet the war had also created a new postwar way of hearing, as the destruction left its imprint on the aurality of the city. Without walls, doors, windows, or roofs, the ruins allowed sound to travel from dwelling to dwelling without any impediment. Radio blurred the boundaries of musical/sonic publicness and privacy, to evoke Georgina Born's terms, as sound could now freely travel. Radio waves lacing through one ruin to another created what R. Murray Schafer has called schizophonia, or the confusion between sound happening in real time and its electroacoustic counterpart. As British officer George Clare recalled, "My most striking first impression was not visual but aural: the muted echoes of a battered city."[3] Other visitors found the ruins even took on a melody of their own: "Amid the sour wreckage of a spotted city this music of a sweet and nostalgic nature was often to be heard,"[4] Allied soldier Richard Brett-Smith noted in his memoir.

While much scholarship has focused on the visually arresting aspects of ruins, less attention has been paid to their sound. One did not just see the ruins; one also heard them. These "musically imagined communities,"[5] created and informed by postwar German radio, offer a window into the shared traumatic experiences of the air war. This chapter explores the tensions between ruin listening in the private and public spheres. The disembodied voice of the radio created a community of listeners while still dividing the listening public who had to choose between the American- and Soviet-supported stations. Yet radio heard in the privacy of one's home stood in sharp contrast to the proliferation of public concerts in the ruins throughout postwar Germany. As Berlin musicians returned to the bombed craters of their former venues to stage performances, these ruin concerts permitted ensembles to engage with notions of German suffering by reclaiming churches, palaces, and concert halls destroyed by Allied bombing. These performances were among the first overt expressions of German victimhood, as they aestheticized the rubble left by the air war. Through radio waves and ruin performances, Berlin's embodied and disembodied soundscapes brought political conflict and musical production in direct confrontation with each other.

Rubble Radio

As tensions between East and West Berlin waxed and waned, radio had the ability to easily cross the city's borders, unifying its listeners not by geography but by aurality. With fewer spaces in which to give concerts and considering the difficulties to arrive at these venues, radio provided the Allies and German civilians with a practical alternative. The sonic ruins of the city soon became their own recital halls, creating what Benedict Anderson has termed unisonality, by generating the possibility for "people wholly unknown to each other to utter the same verses to the same melody."[6] To form these aural communities across urban divides, the Soviets emphasized the affinities between German and Russian classical composers, taking a socialist realist approach, while the Americans promoted modernism and new music over the airwaves. The war and its sonic aftermath radically changed the way in which Germany's composers heard their music, and radio was at the center of this revelation. Even though their methods may have differed, both stations commissioned a number of important postwar works from the city's composers. These compositions used various musical forms such as cantatas and radio plays to broadcast traumatic experiences of bombing, injury, and death. Although the Allies may have believed they tightly controlled all aspects of radio production, the airwaves provided mass media possibilities to broadcast experiences of civilian suffering in occupied Berlin.

During the Nazi era, German radio had been a political instrument intimately tied to the regime. In Weimar Germany only an estimated five hundred thousand Germans subscribed to radio; by 1930, there were more than three million listeners. As the harbinger of news, entertainment, distraction, and propaganda, radio ownership skyrocketed in 1933 after Goebbels commissioned the cheap and readily available *Volksempfänger* (people's receiver). With the declaration of war in 1939, radio's mass media possibilities were needed to keep the morale of civilians and soldiers high, as Germany became the second largest radio-listening public in Europe, just behind England. Music on the radio reassured the population of final and ultimate victory, creating and strengthening a sense of a national community through the broadcast medium. When Hitler wrote in the late 1930s, "We should not have conquered Germany without . . . the loudspeaker,"[7] the statement did not seem an exaggeration.

Popular radio programs such as the *Request Concert for the Wehrmacht*, a bimonthly broadcast featuring musical dedications connected the people's community (*Volksgemeinschaft*) at home with soldiers at the front. (The program even inspired the 1940 Nazi propaganda film *Request Concert*, which used the radio broadcast as a vital component in the love story between pilot Herbert Koch and Inge Wagner.) Celebrations like Heroes' Commemoration Day (*Heldengedenktag*) were broadcast throughout the country, opening with music from the Staatsoper.[8]

In January 1945, as the Wehrmacht suffered crippling losses in the east and the Allies accelerated their bombing campaigns against German cities, Goebbels turned on his radio, catching the final movement of the *Eroica* Symphony featuring conductor Wilhelm Furtwängler and the Vienna

Philharmonic. "How beautiful and refreshing it is to immerse oneself in this world,"[9] Goebbels wrote in his diary before returning to the stark realities of the Soviet offensive. Radio played a vital role in the sonic landscape of fascism, and yet, as Annegret Fauser notes, "The lived sonic experience of that world war often remains unrecognized."[10] A large part of this lived soundscape was the air raid. After the radio sounded an initial warning, sirens would wail. Larger cities had thousands of them, as the alarm's radius was only sixteen hundred feet. Through its tones, the siren signaled the four stages of the raid: (1) stay alert, (2) seek shelter within the next ten minutes, (3) bombing may be over, and (4) the raid is finished. Once in the cellar, many Germans brought their radios with them for updates and entertainment purposes. Radio sets permitted the government to enter the private sphere at any time to interrupt with announcements and warnings. In order to ensure that radio broadcasts could continue uninterrupted during evening bombing raids, Reich Radio (*Reichsrundfunk*), the most powerful transmitter in the country, broadcast from a Berlin bunker on Masurenallee.[11]

But radio's possibilities cut both ways for the Reich as propaganda posters warned that "Enemies listen!" ("Feinde hört mit!")—suggesting that civilians not discuss political or military matters in public or over the phone where enemy ears might hear. These attempts to criminalize information sharing and illegal acts of listening extended to prohibitions on foreign radio stations, though there were few real sanctions for tuning into channels from abroad. By dictating how to listen, and how not to listen, Kurt K., a teenager during the Third Reich, later recalled, "These state-subsidized radio sets (*Volksempfänger*) had the purpose of keeping the people acoustically under control."[12]

Hitler's fifty-sixth and final birthday was marked with broadcasts of Beethoven's Seventh Symphony while his suicide ten days later was mourned with the Funeral March from the *Eroica* Symphony. It is for this reason that Brian Currid notes the stereotypical soundtrack of Nazi Germany involves "the roar of a crowd, the echo of a goose step, the sound of march music, and the resonant voice of Adolf Hitler." Such a sonic imaginary forms a stark contrast with musical metaphors of the regime's collapse—of "the music of the roaring of enemy planes" and "a crescendo in the fighting."[13] Radio was the voice of the people's community, and it would soon become the most powerful and far-reaching mass medium in destroyed Germany.

Soviet and American Broadcasting in Berlin

With Nazi Germany's unconditional surrender, the Allies quickly broke up Greater German Radio, controlled by the Reich Broadcasting Corporation, and instead reestablished regional stations according to the model used before 1933. The Americans ran five radio stations across Germany: RIAS Berlin, Radio Bremen, Radio Frankfurt, Radio Munich, and Radio Stuttgart. The Soviets, British, and French Allies supported one station each: Radio Berlin, Northwest German Broadcasting (NWDR), and Southwest Broadcasting (SWF), respectively. The Soviet Radio Berlin and American RIAS created reeducational programing "to make available to the German people something of the cultural heritage of which they have been kept ignorant during the Nazi period."[14] Berlin broadcasts included everything from programs promoting new music to news bulletins. The stations also commissioned works from the city's composers, who produced scores about the trauma and suffering of war. The broadcast medium allowed compositions about civilian victimhood to resound freely through the ruined spaces of Berlin.

Yet combing through the files related to radio in postwar Berlin raises certain challenges—namely, that these early postwar broadcasts survive only on paper, not through recordings. In their work on British broadcasting in the interwar period, Paddy Scannell and David Cardiff admit, "There is an inescapable paradox at the heart of this project of which we have been acutely aware all along—our object of study no longer exists."[15] A lack of recordings need not constitute a methodological gap, however, as scholars such as Josephine Dolan have pointed out. Physical materials can reveal the inherent tension in the medium of radio, as "an interface between writing and talk; between the written and the spoken word; between the competencies of reading and listening."[16] In the case of rubble music, there exists a wealth of archival radio documents in the form of memorandums, scripts, and musical scores.

By analyzing where the sonic and the written archives intersect, this section hears rubble music through broadcasts supervised by the Allies but largely written, staffed, and heard by German civilians. "Sound is an artifact of the messy and political human sphere,"[17] Jonathan Sterne wrote in *The Audible Past*, and rarely was sound so fraught as in the destroyed capital. Gathering around the radio, a prized possession, remained the most ubiquitous form of information sharing possible in the postwar period.

Figure 4.1. Berlin Radio Repair Workshop, Radio Ohnesorg, 1947. SLUB Dresden/Deutsche Fotothek. Photograph by Richard Peter.

A functioning radio meant a link to other city-dwellers as well as the outside world, a connection that made having access to a functioning radio a necessity (fig. 4.1).

Once the Soviets arrived in Berlin, they seized Germany's most powerful radio transmitter on Masurenallee in Charlottenburg. By mid-May, Radio Berlin (*Rundfunk Berlin*) broadcast news, special programs, and music for nineteen hours a day, as one of the few sites of cultural production to remain in prewar condition. The station also aired live concerts, the first of which took place on May 18 and was also broadcast to Moscow. Another live performance on May 27 showcased musicians from the city's opera houses led by Leopold Ludwig. The program contained pieces by German and Russian composers, including excerpts from Mozart's *The Marriage of Figaro* and *Don Giovanni*, Beethoven's *Fidelio*, and Tchaikovsky's Fifth Symphony. The broadcast was a symbolic gesture that was as much about showing unity between two former enemy countries as it was about who was left in Berlin to perform.[18]

In the first few weeks of broadcasting, the Soviets primarily played the music of Russian composers like Tchaikovsky, Rimsky-Korsakov, and

Glazunov, and Austro-Germanic composers such as Brahms, Haydn, Mozart, and Schubert. The station marked Richard Strauss's eighty-first birthday on June 11 with a special broadcast featuring nearly two hours of his music. Radio Berlin also featured news, morning gymnastics, and *Volksmusik*, in addition to programs tailored to the perceived taste of German audiences such as "Music for the Housewife," "The Heartbeat of Berlin," and "The ABCs of the Lighthearted Muse," a program that featured interviews with artists persecuted by the regime. The Soviet occupiers sought to use the airwaves to promote a common musical ideology, as their station would maintain the longest hours of all the Allies, often broadcasting past midnight.[19]

When the American military arrived in Berlin in early July, they, too, wanted to establish a radio presence as quickly as possible. On July 17, several GIs reached the city with orders to create Berlin's AFN in under seventeen days. (AFN stations accompanied troop movement, and there were also branches in Munich and Bremen.) On August 4, AFN Berlin began broadcasting with a wire antenna strung between two trees, a 250-watt transmitter, and two trucks that contained additional equipment. Signing on with Gershwin's *Rhapsody in Blue*, the station could broadcast to only a two-mile radius. Despite its modest range, the station provided valuable news and music in the first several weeks of the occupation. By mid-August, AFN relocated to 28 Podbielskiallee, the requisitioned twenty-seven-room mansion of former Nazi foreign minister Joachim von Ribbentrop. (Ribbentrop was tried at Nuremberg and executed for war crimes in 1946.)[20]

Because AFN was designed for American GIs stationed in Berlin, the Americans realized that in order to rival the Soviet's Berlin Radio, they would need to create another station tailored exclusively to German listeners. Wired Radio in the American sector, or DIAS (*Drahtfunk im amerikanischen Sektor*), began broadcasting on February 7, 1946. In a nod to the Soviet presence in the city, the Americans recognized Berlin's "strong radio competition and the necessity for the *Drahtfunk* [radio] to stand out as a cultural instrument,"[21] and by September, DIAS became RIAS, or Radio in the American Sector (*Rundfunk im amerikanischen Sektor*), after the station acquired a transmitter and greater broadcasting abilities. RIAS reserved approximately 55 to 60 percent of its airtime for music, much more space than the political or news departments received, and strictly broadcast only music between 12:00 a.m. and 6:00 a.m.[22]

The Americans also created the RIAS Chamber Choir, the RIAS Symphony Orchestra, and the RIAS Dance Orchestra to perform on air and to give live concerts. There was money for these "extras" by American standards due to the difference in the way German and American radio stations were funded. In Germany, stations were nationalized, collecting a subsidy from the government that freed them any dependence on commercial sponsors. Due to their state-guaranteed backing, they had the financial freedom to fund orchestras and choirs of extremely high caliber. As a noncommercial venture, the stations were nonprofit and paid their musicians and personnel well, making West German radio a highly desirable place to work. New music was supported because there was no risk of losing sponsors. This proved in striking contrast to the American system, where the roughly one thousand privately run stations were dependent on advertising.[23]

Bringing American music to postwar Germany was first suggested on May 23, 1945, by Information Control Division (ICD) radio section director Davidson Taylor. In civilian life, Taylor was CBS's head of classical music broadcasting. An inordinately pragmatic man, Taylor recognized it would be difficult to distribute physical scores of American music in Germany. Radio provided an attractive alternative, for as an American military newsletter admitted, "In the absence of former entertainment sources—from cafes to concert halls—the German public expects radio to provide them with entertainment of a caliber comparable to pre-1933 production."[24] American planners were also aware that radio's powers of distribution exceeded every other form of mass media and were keen to differentiate between mere entertainment and high culture, as "artists in the fields of music, theater, and radio can carry out a function of great importance in the fields of reeducation."[25] Radio would not become the mere mouthpiece of the Allies, however, because each power still needed the help and talent of German civilians to create programs tailored to the wider civilian population.

Among the reeducation aims of the occupiers was to reintroduce music supposedly banned during the Third Reich, and radio became the most accessible method for the distribution of this music. Maintaining the pervasiveness of the "Nazi canon" or "Nazi index" of musical works under the Third Reich, the Americans used the legacy of degenerate music (*Entartete Musik*) to legitimate the importation of American classical music for the radio. Accordingly, RIAS created the program *Studio for New Music* (*Studio für neue Musik*). Because the ICD was interested in promoting "German composers prohibited under the Nazi regime for racial or political reasons" and "composers from outside Germany,"[26] *Studio for New Music* aimed to reintroduce Berliners to music supposedly banned by the Nazis, including works by Igor Stravinsky, Paul Hindemith, and Anton Webern. Unbeknownst to the ICD, a number of the featured composers had, in fact, tried to align their work with the goals of the National Socialist state during the 1930s; as late as 1938, Stravinsky was trying to secure an invitation from his publisher, Schott & Sons, to conduct his music in Germany. Hindemith's relationship to the Nazis was also less than one of staunch resistance ("I have been asked to co-operate, and have not declined,"[27] he wrote to Ernst Toch in 1933), although in 1945, this was not widely known. Webern, too, had appealed to Nazi authorities in Austria, trying to convince them of twelve-tone's merits.[28]

As the director of *Studio for New Music*, Hans Heinz Stuckenschmidt was to become an integral part of the American cultural agenda. Educated in Berlin, Ulm, and Magdeburg and self-taught in theory and musicology, Stuckenschmidt had worked as a freelance writer and composer in Paris, Hamburg, Prague, and Bremen before coming to Berlin in the 1930s. Stuckenschmidt's support for new music made his scholarship unwelcome in the Third Reich, and after his November 1934 *Berliner Zeitung* review of Berg's *Lulu-Symphonie* (performed to a full house at the Staatsoper), he received an edict from the *Reichsverband der deutschen Presse* that his criticism possessed "a direction indubitably influenced from the Jewish side,"[29] barring him from publishing in Germany. In the early 1940s, Stuckenschmidt was conscripted into the Wehrmacht as a translator and, after 1945, was held in an American-run prisoner-of-war camp in France where he again served as a translator, this time for the American military. While at the Atichy POW camp, Stuckenschmidt passed the time by drafting musicology lectures for fellow prisoners on topics from "Modern Opera" ("Die moderne Oper") to "Wagner's Prospects" ("Wagners Aussichten"). Returning to Berlin in 1946, Stuckenschmidt was offered a job by the ICD as the director of the *Studio for New Music*, to air Friday evenings on RIAS. He quickly realized his new alliance with the Americans could prove mutually beneficial; they provided him with a platform and financial support for his work, while the military government gained a vocal German ally for new music.[30]

Stuckenschmidt's pro-and-contra episode format appealed to skeptical listeners and proponents of new music alike as he scripted every detail, recognizing the importance of these broadcasts as a way to (re)introduce Berliners to modern music. In "A Talk about Dissonances," broadcast in November 1946, a musician (Stuckenschmidt) and a "friend of music"

(Hermann Schindler) discussed the role of dissonance throughout Western classical music. Paul Höffer played music examples on the piano. The broadcast opened with an excerpt from Ernst Krenek's Toccata and Chaconne op. 13, a piece based on the Bach chorale, *Ja ich glaub an Jesum Christum*. (Krenek fled Nazi Germany in 1938 and settled in the United States, although this is not mentioned in the dialogue.) The following conversation ensued:

FRIEND OF MUSIC (ENTERS QUICKLY): What is that noise you are making in here? It's terrible!

MUSICIAN: (keeps playing)

FRIEND OF MUSIC: But would you please stop; that is absolutely unbearable!

MUSICIAN: (has continued to play, but now stops) What are you raving about? What you have just heard was a chorale from Krenek that was written more than twenty years ago.

FRIEND OF MUSIC: Do you seriously call this garble music?[31]

The musician points out that what might today be a consonance (i.e., a major triad) would have been considered a dissonance five hundred years ago ("You think only modern music brings about this impertinence?").[32] Stuckenschmidt's character even compares Hindemith's case, who, as he points out, left Germany on account of "his dissonances" ("seiner Dissonanzen") to J. S. Bach's, as the composer left his job in Arnstadt after his "novel sounds" ("neuartige Klänge") greatly disturbed the congregation. Stuckenschmidt's comparison rings hollow; fleeing Nazi Germany in the early 1930s and leaving Arnstadt for better working conditions in the early 1700s were widely disparate experiences. "A Talk about Dissonances" ultimately resists engaging with the trauma of exile. Similar scripts for "degenerate music" ensued, including music by Alban Berg, Béla Bartók, Arnold Schoenberg, Igor Stravinsky, Darius Milhaud, and Kurt Weill. It was, of course, no accident that all the featured composers who had fled Nazi Germany made their way for longer and shorter periods to the United States.

Aside from Stuckenschmidt's broadcasts, RIAS frequently incorporated other programing that linked the American continent with the European musicians who had fled fascism. The station celebrated the centenary of Mendelssohn's death with a weeklong series of his music from October 28 until November 4, 1947. But as much as the broadcasts were about Mendelssohn, they were also about promoting the safe haven that America had given many European-born conductors. With recordings featuring the Boston Symphony Orchestra led by Serge Koussevitzky and Dimitri Mitropoulos and the New York Philharmonic by Artur Rodziński, the broadcasts emphasized the fruitfulness of the American-European partnership.[33]

Despite RIAS's efforts to reeducate Berliners, the station had difficulties building an audience in its early years. The primary problem was RIAS's signal quality, which was not as strong as Radio Berlin. As a result, most Berliners in 1946 and 1947 were listening to the Soviet station regardless of the sector they lived in or their political views. An October 1946 RIAS survey revealed that 67 percent of the city listened to Berlin Radio compared to only 16 percent for RIAS. Despite these setbacks, the Americans were still convinced of RIAS's strategic worth as a reeducation tool, acquiring a more powerful transmitter in January 1948 to improve their audibility and build a larger audience.[34]

East and West Berlin Commissions

American-controlled RIAS and Soviet Radio Berlin remained committed to commissioning works from Berlin's composers. While this patronage fulfilled a didactic purpose—teaching audiences about the terrors of warfare and the moral bankruptcy of National Socialism—these pieces also served as sonic memorials to the suffering and trauma of German victims, a state- and occupier-sanctioned form of public mourning. In the period before the Berlin Wall or the Berlin Blockade, the occupiers freely commissioned works from composers on both sides of the city, regardless of the sector in which they lived.

Among the most prolific and politically savvy composers, and one who managed to win favor with both the Russians and the Americans, was Boris Blacher. Born in Russian-speaking Manchuria in 1903, Blacher studied music in Siberia and Harbin, China, before moving to Berlin to study architecture in 1922. Dissatisfied with his choice, Blacher soon enrolled at the Hochschule für Musik to study composition with Friedrich Ernst Koch. He enjoyed a moderately successful career as an arranger and composer and a brief appointment at Dresden Conservatory in 1938, although the Nazis dismissed him a year later. Blacher was one quarter Jewish and considered to be stateless, exempting him from service in the Wehrmacht and, of course, party membership. By 1945, Blacher and his wife, pianist Gerty Herzog-Blacher, were uniquely poised to become key players in Berlin's musical scene. The composer took at position first at Paul Höffer's International Music Institute and then at the Hochschule in 1946. John Bitter and Nicolas Nabokov were frequent guests in the Blachers' Wilmersdorf home and secured extra food rations for the musicians. Nabokov, in particular, took an interest in the composer's work and soon found that "Blacher was a living encyclopedia of music's torturous and complex history,"[35] as they spent long evenings discussing culture and politics.

Blacher's postwar works frequently engaged with the individual's struggle against societal injustice, and his radio opera, *The Flood* (*Die Flut*) (1946), a commission from Radio Berlin, was a thinly veiled allegory of the deprivations and corruption of the postwar period. The plot concerned four stock characters (young woman, young man, fisherman, old banker) who become trapped on a shipwreck awaiting low tide. Eventually, the young man murders the banker for his gold, departing with the young woman, who both dream of wealth and a life of leisure. The fisherman remains with the body as well as his delusions of a relationship with the young woman. The boat itself is a thinly veiled metaphor for National Socialism, and as musicologist Andrew Oster notes, the work is "a creative testament to postwar Berlin." Scored for only five woodwinds and a string quartet, the radio opera premiered on December 20, 1946, over Radio Berlin (the first newly composed radio opera since the war) and was also staged in Darmstadt, Dresden, Hannover, and Heidelberg the following year.[36]

One year after Berlin's fall to the Soviets, Radio Berlin also commissioned the composer to write music for a radio play, *The Last Days of Berlin* (*Die letzten Tage von Berlin*), by Wilhelm Hoffmann, director of the State Library at Württemberg. Blacher's score accompanies Hoffmann's retelling of the Soviet invasion, though references to unsavory elements such as rape or looting are, of course, omitted. *The Last Days of Berlin* premiered on April 30, 1946, marking the one-year anniversary of the occupation. Radio Berlin's weekly magazine, *The Radio*, featured a synopsis of the radio play, calling *The Last Days of Berlin* "a radio kaleidoscope from the year 1945."[37] The article is accompanied by a series of drawings detailing the destruction, showing Berliners huddling in basements, buildings toppling onto tram tracks, and explosions near subway stations as civilians hurry for cover as Hoffmann called the Battle of Berlin "a witches' sabbath,"[38] describing the chaos and uncertainty of April 1945.

The score is typical of Blacher's style, featuring driving rhythms and a clarity of line strongly influenced by Stravinsky, Milhaud, and Satie rather than by Austro-Germanic composers. Scored for piccolo, flute, oboe, two clarinets, bassoon, trumpet, trombone, bass, drum, and piano, the music is divided into six sections. Military drumbeats and diminished triads prevail within Blacher's music, which accompanies the city's fall. The second section is scored only for solo snare drum, presumably signaling the Nazi's last stand and the realization their efforts were futile. Sections 5 and 6 are written *alla Marcia*, and with the sudden introduction of a march in the piano, marking the arrival of the Russians in Berlin.[39]

Across town in the eastern district of Prenzlauer Berg, Max Butting also resumed his work as a composer. Although a former party member, like many of his contemporaries, joining the Nazi Party did little to impede Butting's postwar career, and in 1947, he became director of Radio Berlin's Music Section. He drew from his previous experience working for Reich Radio during the 1930s, where he felt that the absence of an artistic director (a common practice in radio before 1933) meant that the station's programming would sink to "the level of the listeners."[40] Butting preferred airing live performances rather than recordings, and he worked tirelessly to rectify what he perceived to be shortcomings in radio production, composing for ensembles and both Berlin radio stations.

When RIAS commissioned Max Butting to write a piece in 1948, the composer produced *After the War: Four Cantatas for Mixed Choir and Chamber Orchestra*. Among the few surviving documents concerning Butting's work with the station is a brief autobiography. The composer writes that his music had been unwelcome since 1933 and that "public and private obstructions caused a creative pause"[41] during the Nazi regime. In reality, he had turned his attention to running the family's iron business. Yet no one at RIAS followed up on Butting's claims of persecution; rubbled reputations and cityscapes went hand in hand.

Each cantata featured a text by the composer, representing the difficulties of life in postwar Berlin through the four seasons. In "IV. Winter," Butting sums up life in Nazi Germany by writing, "Ten years ago we built a fortress, in the ashes and rubble of which we grovel today."[42] The cantata concludes with the plea, "Give us peace," repeated five times, and the hope that the following spring will awaken Berliners from their "rubble misery."[43] These works are testaments to German suffering in the early postwar years, specific in regard to the deprivations but vague as to their causes. Instead, the seasons themselves present certain challenges for the narrator and are often the culprits of the city's destruction. Butting's text begs the question of whether he intended for his audience to identify each season with one of the occupiers—unpredictable and swift to render punishment? Most likely sung by the RIAS soloists and orchestra, no recording of this broadcast exists.

Ultimately, it was the Soviet Blockade of West Berlin, beginning on June 24, 1948, that did the most to boost RIAS listenership, giving the American station 80 percent of Berlin's ears as RIAS increased their broadcasting to eighteen hours a day, double their previous amount. AFN broadcast twenty-four hours a day in order to keep American and British pilots awake as they flew in and out of Tempelhof Airport to deliver supplies.

Henry Gluski left AFN after two years at the station, relinquishing his work as moderator of the Symphony Hour. He had opened each show with the national anthems of all four Allied powers until 1946. An American general who heard the broadcast complained that Gluski should not include the Soviet anthem, and he was subsequently ordered to remove the music from the program. Circumventing the rules, he decided to open the Symphony Hour with excerpts from Prokofiev's *The Love for Three Oranges* instead. He waited for a reprimand from his commanding officer, but it never came; none of his superiors knew the piece, or for that matter, who Prokofiev was. Engaging in his own kind of "musical sabotage," Gluski continued broadcasting the Prokofiev throughout the resonant ruins of the city.[44] The aurality of the cityscape forever changed, these radio broadcasts transformed craters and facades into sites of sonic protest, juxtaposing Allied propaganda with the sounds of German suffering.

Rubble Concerts

While the radio invited Berliners to contemplate the city's destruction from the ruins of their former homes, other musical experiences in the rubbled cityscape were more public. In one of his first official outings in the capital, John Bitter heard the Berlin Chamber Orchestra perform the music of Haydn, Gluck, and Beethoven. Under the direction of Hans von Benda, who, in Bitter's rendering, resembled, "a long, gaunt, emaciated, Christ-like figure,"[45] the Dahlem concert proceeded smoothly until it began to storm. The roof, looming some forty feet above, was filled with holes that poured rain onto the listeners seated below. For the remainder of the concert, audience members rearranged their benches in a futile effort to avoid the water.

The orchestra kept playing, and Bitter was both impressed and puzzled by the tenacious attempts to continue. Observing a similar contradiction between the urban debris and feverish cultural activity, one *Time* magazine correspondent wrote, "This vitality seems to bear an inverse relation to the amount of ruin that surrounds it."[46]

The war's destruction profoundly reshaped everyday musicalizing. In Berlin, Munich, Dresden, and Nuremberg, concerts continued in spite of, and sometimes even because of, the city's physical devastation. German ensembles used urban rubble to give performances that were visually arresting, uncanny, and macabre as musicians returned to spaces destroyed by Allied bombing. The ruin concert expressed civilian suffering as musicians returned to the rubble of their former venues. These performances broke out across the country, staged by and for civilians and featuring the music of classical and romantic Austro-German composers. Berlin proved to be the paradigmatic location for ruin performances, and the cityscape took on a particular ruined aesthetic due to its largely nineteenth- and twentieth-century architecture. With steel girders providing the structural support for most buildings, rather than timber beams as in other city centers, the capital's ruins towered skyward.[47]

As the city where, as Svetlana Boym wrote, "East and West play hide-and-seek with one another," Berlin's destroyed spaces soon became sites of public mourning and commemoration. Yet at the center of debates about German suffering and postwar culture remains the contentious issue of silence. Did the Germans openly embrace their role as victims of the air war? Or was the nation unwilling or unable to acknowledge the air war's staggering death toll? In the wake of 1945, according to the well-trodden psychological diagnosis of Margarete and Alexander Mitscherlich, Germany experienced an "inability to mourn" for their depraved leader, thereby preventing the German people from working through their grief concerning the death, destruction, and defeat of their country. Hannah Arendt was similarly disappointed by what she considered "a lack of response" on the part of German intellectuals who were taciturn in regard to the country's ruin. Even forty years later, literary scholar W. G. Sebald's charge that postwar writers failed to document the Allied destruction of German cities, engaging in a kind of collective amnesia where only three novelists grazed the "landscape of ruins,"[48] resounded through all forms of postwar culture. No genre or discipline seemed immune to accusations of silence.

Contrary to these claims, however, more recent scholarship has definitively shown that notions of German suffering played a prominent role in the country's reconstruction. What Eric Langenbacher has termed German-centered memory, or the presumed experience of the average German civilian, reemerged almost immediately after the collapse of the Third Reich. As Robert Moeller argues, notions of German victimhood informed national identity in both Germanys. In the east, the perpetrators were Anglo-American imperialist bombers who had attacked German cities between 1942 and 1945, while in the west, the mass rapes committed by Red Army soldiers and the fate of prisoners of war still in Soviet captivity informed public debates about German victimhood. Similarly, Anna Parkinson condemns the "melancholic scholarship" resulting from the Mitscherlichs' argument, noting that there were many early attempts to work through Nazi crimes intellectually and emotionally. Notions of German suffering after 1945 depended on where one looked or, perhaps more accurately, where one listened.[49]

Ruin music making was included in these initial responses to trauma. The city took on a particular soundscape, as music in the ruins distracted laborers from the monotony of their backbreaking tasks in more informal iterations of rubble music making. The ruins could be a place to rehearse (fig. 4.2) as workers tossed bricks to each other while the training choir (*Der Aufbauchor*) from Berlin's Deutsches Theater sang, accompanied by an accordion and a double bass. The pun of "Aufbau," literally meaning "to build up" (from *aufbauen*), could not have been lost on the singers and workers as the music accompanied the city's physical reconstruction. Rubble music provides temporary relief from the work at hand: the painstaking effort to rebuild Berlin, brick by brick. A community of workers becomes a community of listeners as their workspace is transformed into a concert hall. Similarly, a trio of musicians in East Berlin celebrated Frauentag (Women's Day) by playing for workers (fig. 4.3), because, as the accompanying newspaper article concluded, "with music, everything is easier,"[50] a phrase that draws uncomfortable parallels to concentration camp uses of music. As scholars such as Shirli Gilbert, Guido Fackler, Joseph Toltz, and Wolfgang Benz elucidate, music making in the camps was often used as a terror tool. The problematic blurring of German civilians and forced Jewish laborers conflated their suffering in disconcerting ways.[51]

Figure 4.2. Music for the Reconstruction, 1953. Photograph by Hans-Günter Quaschinsky. Courtesy of the Bundesarchiv.

Music in Ruins

Aside from impromptu music making, performers also staged events that made full use of the ruin's aesthetic possibilities. Many cities used their urban decay as a ready-made backdrop for performances featuring German musicians playing German music. Staged displays of cultural resilience, despite the destruction and suffering caused by the air war, proliferated across the country. As historian Michael Meng notes, "In film, literature, and photography, rubble became an integral component of German cultural memories of victimization,"[52] and music, too, was part of this narrative thread.

On July 29, 1945, in the bombed ruins of St. Sebald Church in Nuremberg, a small group of musicians performed part 1 of Haydn's *The Creation* (*Die Schöpfung*) for the first oratorio performance in postwar Germany. By the time members of the Teacher's Choral Association (*Lehrergesangverein*) and the Nordbayerisches Landesorchester organized the rubble concert, the Americans had already occupied Nuremberg for more than three months. Because military

Figure 4.3. A trio plays for *Frauentag*, 1953. Photograph by Schmidtke. Courtesy of the Bundesarchiv.

authorities dissolved all organizations that had existed under the Nazis, conductor Karl Demmer recognized that he would need to obscure his musicians' recent pasts (as well as his own) in order to perform. As the director of both ensembles, Demmer renamed them the innocuous-sounding Choir and Orchestra of the Concert Society (*Chor und Orchester der Konzertgesellschaft e.V.*). (Considering the Teacher's Choral Association had 400 singers in 1938 and only 37 members by 1945, the organization scarcely resembled its prewar iteration.) Ostensibly, the St. Sebald parish office (*Pfarramt*) organized the performance, rather than the singer's association (*Verein*), another attempt by Demmer to make the ensembles appear newly constituted after the cease-fire.[53] For the July performance, the Nuremberg audience sat on tavern benches brought to the ruined choir of the church. Among the listeners were seventy members of the Wehrmacht still in uniform, and as one soldier later recalled, "After everything we lived through, we had to perceive it as a gift to be able to hear *The Creation*. . . . I was long defenseless against my tears, overcome by the music and by our misery."[54]

Shortly after the first concert, the Americans fired Demmer for his activities under National Socialism and hired conductor Rolf Agop to conduct the remaining performances. One witness likened the placement of the musicians and audience members to the Sermon on the Mount as Jesus delivered his message to the disciples, while another music critic marveled, "The audience was sitting on top of debris and rubble. In their hearts burned the longing for the indestructible."[55] By the time the five-concert series finished in September, around fourteen hundred people had visited the church to hear either part 1 or part 2 of *The Creation*.

In Munich, musical culture was similarly rubbled. In an article for the Paris edition of the *Herald Tribune*, American composer Virgil Thomson reported the city resembled "a construction in pink sugar that has been rained on,"[56] though, like Berlin, concerts resumed immediately after the surrender. In August 1945 (fig. 4.4), a chamber ensemble performed in the ruins of Munich's Grottenhof, a surviving courtyard of the city's Residenz. Once a centerpiece of the city's cultural heritage, the Residenz had previously housed Bavarian nobility and served as the seat of the German government before World War I. Audience members and musicians alike are dressed formally despite the structure's decrepit condition.

That same month, Dresden staged a rubble performance of its own. The city had been destroyed by a firestorm in February 1945, ignited by American and British bombers, a catastrophe that claimed an estimated forty thousand lives. Now under Soviet jurisdiction, on August 4, 1945, in the ruins of the

Figure 4.4. Grottenhof concert, 1945. Photograph by Tino Walz. Courtesy of Bildarchiv, Bayerische Staatsbibliothek, Munich.

Kreuzkirche, director and composer Rudolf Mauersberger led the Kreuzchor in the first vesper service since the regime's collapse. Eleven of the Kreuzchor's boy choristers had perished in the firestorm, and Mauersberger chose the repertoire accordingly. Among the works the choir sang were the Renaissance motet, "Behold How the Righteous Dies" (*Ecce, quomodo moritur Justus*) by Jacobus Gallus Carniolus, "When Once I Must Depart" (*Wenn ich einmal soll scheiden*) from J. S. Bach's St. Matthew Passion, and the Lutheran chorale "Eternal Sun of God" (*Die güldene Sonne*). To honor the firebombing victims, Mauersberger also composed two mourning motets, "You were like Us" (*Ihr wart wie wir*) and "How Desolate Lies the City" (*Wie liegt die Stadt so wüst*). Using passages from the Lamentations of Jeremiah as its text, the sparse harmonies of "How Desolate Lies the City" are reminiscent of Hugo Distler as well as the early polyphony of Heinrich Schütz, both composers whom Mauersberger greatly admired. The apocalyptic, poetic imagery speaks to the end of a city as well as to the end of the regime, survived by a narrator who recalls the terrible scene. As Martha Sprigge notes, the motet "was conceived harmonically, its voices crushed under the oppressive weight of destruction."[57] Mauersberger not only staged a ruin concert; he was also writing rubble music.

Figure 4.5 Benefit concert, Kaiser Wilhelm Memorial Church, Berlin, 1952. Courtesy of *Süddeutsche Zeitung*.

Although ruin concerts occurred throughout occupied Germany, they took place with greatest frequency in Berlin, beginning with Benda's May 13 concert in the partially destroyed Schöneberg Rathaus.[58] Concerts in Berlin ruins continued throughout the late 1940s and early 1950s, taking place in Dahlem, Mitte, Steglitz, and Charlottenburg. In 1947, the Bach Choir of Berlin's Kaiser Wilhelm Memorial Church began staging a series of Bach cantatas in the ruins. The first performance was on Easter Sunday, featuring *Christ lag in Todesbanden*, BWV 4, in the rubble of the St. Matthäuskirche in Steglitz, and thereafter, the choir performed cantatas every two weeks in the Kaiser Wilhelm Memorial Church. As one of the city's most iconic bombed spaces, the church also hosted rubble performances to raise money for its reconstruction. In the photograph from a benefit concert (fig. 4.5), umbrellas block the sight lines of most audience members.[59]

Music, Ruins, and Film

The city's ensembles returned to the rubble not only to make music for a contemporary audience; some of these performances were also staged for the camera, permanently capturing the destroyed temporality of the city. In 1950, the Berlin Philharmonic Orchestra gathered in the ruins of their former concert hall to play Beethoven's *Egmont* Overture. The performance, filmed as part of a documentary about the ensemble, *Ambassadors of Music* (*Botschafter der Musik*), featured the orchestra sitting on the sunken rubble of their former stage, aestheticizing, and in many ways romanticizing, the bombed hall on Bernburger Straße. Even conductor Sergiu Celibidache's podium was stylized to appear as though it was emerging from a crater. The film turns the notion of rubble music on its head; now we are the only audience sitting alone with the musicians (fig. 4.6).

In a style owing much to film noir, director Hermann Stöß presents a highly edited version of the ensemble's performance history. *Ambassadors of Music* was ostensibly about the orchestra's role as messengers of goodwill, and the film emphasizes the positive to completely omit the negative—that is, the ensemble's recent years of National Socialist patronage. Originally planned as a short film, Stöß decided he had enough material to expand his documentary to a full-length showcase, featuring preexisting footage of Furtwängler and Bruno Walter as well as new scenes with Celibidache. The city's Department of Finance, Business, and Education agreed to support *Ambassadors of Music*, giving Stöß 75,000 DM to complete the project, as "the film will use rich archival materials to give a comprehensive account

Figure 4.6. Celibidache and the Berlin Philharmonic in the ruins of the *Alte Philharmonie*, 1950. From *Ambassadors of Music*, dir. Hermann Stöß.

of the past and present meaning of the Philharmonic orchestra for Berlin's cultural life."⁶⁰ Yet both Furtwängler and Hans Heinz Stuckenschmidt would disagree with the department's assessment. After viewing the film privately, Furtwängler was so angry over the director's fictionalized portrait that he demanded to see the script, while Stuckenschmidt concluded the entire effort was a waste given the film's inaccuracies.⁶¹

The most egregious misrepresentations in the film include Stöß's use of propaganda footage from Philharmonic concerts in occupied and war-torn Europe. As Hans Knappertsbusch conducts the orchestra in plush locales such as Granada's Alhambra and the Paris Opera House, Stöß depicts the ensemble as spreading the life-affirming message of music throughout the world. The attentive (captive?) audience listens closely. While the orchestra's 1943 propaganda tour actually featured Beethoven symphonies, *Ambassadors of Music* replaces the audio track with other Philharmonic recordings. Stöß's film depicts the ensemble performing Tchaikovsky's *Pathétique* Symphony in Granada and Debussy's *Prelude to the Afternoon of a Faun* in Paris to reflect a more cosmopolitan worldview. The propaganda footage is now a palimpsest for music's universal, rather than strictly German, qualities.

Central to the film are a series of ruin scenes in the ensemble's destroyed concert hall. The sequence begins with concertmaster Siegfried Borries playing Beethoven's *Romanze*, op. 40, presumably accompanied by the Philharmonic, whose music we can hear but not see. The camera alternates between tight shots of Borries's face to panoramas of the hall's interior. The viewer has the eerie sensation of being alone with the violinist amid a sea of ruins and ashes. After the *Romanze*, Stöß pans out to reveal the orchestra is also sitting in the rubble, arranged as if on their former stage. The ensemble performs the *Egmont* Overture, a work with a delicate political subtext about occupation and resistance. Beethoven wrote the overture in 1810 to accompany Goethe's tragedy about the sixteenth-century Netherlandic count. The Spanish Habsburgs eventually beheaded Egmont for resisting their occupation, making him a martyr for Holland's sovereignty. As Michael P. Steinberg notes, the Nazis revered the *Egmont* Overture, hearing in Beethoven's composition "the musical correlative of the kind of heroism they wished to extol."[62] In 1945, American cultural officers even banned performances of Goethe's *Egmont*, fearing its "opposition to foreign occupation forces"[63] might encourage a German uprising.

The *Egmont* scene alternates between interior shots of the bombed shell to close-ups of Celibidache's face engaged in the epic struggle required to play Beethoven's music in the ruins. Stuckenschmidt described the conductor's performance as "possessed."[64] Although the ensemble is arranged as if the stage is still standing, the back wall is missing, and we can see past the musicians to the ruined city beyond. The orchestra's performance is trapped in aspic, and only we, as contemporary viewers, notice anything awry. There is something highly unsettling about these musicians returning to the site of the Philharmonic, dressed in tuxedos, to reenact a scene that never occurred in the first place. Celibidache never conducted the ensemble before or during the war, nor had he ever performed in the Bernburger Straße venue. By revisiting their hall six years after its bombing, the orchestra raised questions concerning their own victimhood and complicity. Aerial attacks had killed four Philharmonic members, and four more musicians lost their lives during the Soviet invasion. Only by returning to the ruined monumentality that was once their concert hall could the group shed their image as a propaganda orchestra, reclaiming Beethoven from the rubble by carefully staging their own suffering.

Still other postwar films with wider distribution made use of music and ruins to explore notions of German victimhood and suffering. As Robert Shandley writes, these films use the ruins "as a background and metaphor of the destruction of [the] German's own sense of themselves,"[65] as the subject matter drew contributions from both German and foreign directors. A central scene of Roberto Rossellini's *Germany, Year Zero* (1948) features a phonograph recording of Hitler's voice ringing through the desolate rubble. The film's twelve-year-old protagonist, Edmund, sells the device to Allied soldiers who have literally and figuratively inherited the aftermath of fascism. At the film's conclusion, after Edmund poisons his invalid father, he wonders alone through the ruins when music of a church organ interrupts his amblings. Rossellini blurs the distinction between diegetic and nondiegetic for a moment, until he cuts to shots of an organist playing in the rubble of a church (fig. 4.7). The chorale chords, vaguely reminiscent of Bach, emanate from the bombed shell, stopping passersby in their tracks (fig. 4.8). After pausing for a moment to listen, Edmund continues on, climbing into a ruined apartment building and jumping to his death. The church organ scene suddenly takes on new meaning as a benediction for his short life.

In Billy Wilder's *A Foreign Affair* (1948), music and ruins suggest an altogether different form of victimhood—namely, that the occupiers themselves are the victims of German deceit, as Wilder's film pokes fun at both the denazification and fraternization processes. The Americans look rather buffoonish for most of the film, unable to catch a former high-ranking Gestapo agent who is hiding in their sector. Hoping that he will resurface at a show of his former lover, cabaret singer Erika von Schlütow (played by Marlene Dietrich), the occupiers permit her to continue performing. But as Erika sings "The Ruins of Berlin," written by Friederich Hollaender, himself a German Jewish exile who makes a cameo in the film as Erika's accompanist, it is clear that the musical ruins in *A Foreign Affair* are not only traumatic remnants. The song's lyrics, written in four languages as a nod to each of the occupiers, show that the ruins are alive and teeming with intrigue, dry humor, and the city's infamous *Berliner Schnauze*.

The postwar proliferation of filmic ruins stands in contrast to movies of the Nazi era, where urban destruction rarely appeared onscreen. Instead, the ruined body symbolized the sacrifices of the people's community. In

Figure 4.7. The organist plays a chorale without a congregation. *Germany, Year Zero* (1:05:39).

Figure 4.8. Edmund and passersby pause to listen to the music. *Germany, Year Zero* (1:05:49).

the brief 1942 documentary depicting the Berlin Philharmonic's birthday concert for the führer, close-ups of audience members form a significant part of the footage. Soldiers in uniform are among those prominently featured, and their injuries and eye patches are on prominent display as Furtwängler conducts Beethoven's Ninth Symphony for a packed house. At the fourth movement's conclusion, the orchestra's dramatically descending thirty-second notes coincide with the image of two wounded soldiers sitting in a box, gauze bandages covering one's nose and the other's cheek. The chorus proclaims for the final time "Freude, schöner Götterfunken! Götterfunken!" ("Joy, beautiful spark of divinity!"), and the audience bursts into applause. Similarly, at the end of *The Great Love* (the most commercially successful film of the Nazi era), injured Luftwaffe pilot Paul Wendlandt convalesces in a beautiful alpine spa town, where, sunning himself on a terrace, he is reunited with singer Hanna Holberg (played by Zarah Leander). Hanna's voice and presence heal all, validating Paul's sacrifice for the national community. These staged displays of emotion are difficult to reconcile with our postwar sensibilities. The German ruined body was but one form of destruction; the Nazi regime, however, would eventually annihilate entire peoples and cultures.

Jewish Ruins

Ruin music making was not strictly a German gentile phenomenon. Jewish ruins, typically synagogues, also hosted performances and religious services in 1945. As Eric Langenbacher writes, "Memory is contested and almost always previously or potentially occupied terrain."[66] In Berlin, the terrain was occupied not only by the Germans but also by the four Allied powers and Jewish survivors. The city was a teeming hub for the displaced Jews of Europe, most of whom were living in one of the city's three displaced persons camps: the American sector's Mariendorf Bialik-Center and Düppel-Center at Schlachtensee, or a smaller, French-controlled Wittenau camp. The Düppel-Center was the largest, and by September 1946, it was home to just over five thousand Jewish refugees, most of whom were from Eastern Europe. These Allied-administered camps, and those like them across postwar Germany, functioned as essential waiting rooms until the displaced could secure permission to emigrate, typically to the United States, Palestine, Canada, or South Africa. After giving a July 1945 concert with Benjamin Britten for displaced persons at Bergen-Belsen, violinist Yehudi Menuhin called the camp "the saddest ruins of the Third Reich."[67]

Even the Hebrew term that the survivors adopted for themselves, *She'erith Hapletah* (surviving remnant), gestured toward the fractured landscape. For some refugees, their experience in displaced person camps would last longer than their Nazi internment, as the last camp did not close until 1952.

Aside from Jewish refugees who were passing through the city, Berlin's surviving Jewish community (*Jüdische Gemeinde*) began talks in May 1945 to discuss their future prospects. Founded in 1829, the community had 160,564 registered Jewish civilians in 1933; by 1945, that number hovered around 7,000, still the largest number of Jews anywhere in postwar Europe.[68] Religious services for survivors and refugees began on May 11, 1945, led by Rabbi Martin Riesenburger at the vandalized Weißensee Jewish cemetery. Carefully placing new glass in the small synagogue adjacent to the cemetery, Riesenburger gave a short sermon as "tears and sobbing filled the room."[69] Most of those present were Jews who had spent the war years hiding in Berlin or living under assumed names. For Riesenburger, the service was about not only who was present but also who had perished in the intervening years. Heinz Galinski, another leading figure in the reconstitution of the Jüdische Gemeinde and the organization's leader between 1949 and 1992, returned from Bergen-Belsen to find the Jewish community "consisted only of rubble."[70]

Six synagogues across Berlin reopened during summer 1945. The first memorial service expressly for the victims of fascism took place in the ruins of Berlin's Pestalozzistrasse Synagogue, in the British sector, in July.[71] That same month at the Rykestrasse Synagogue in Soviet-controlled Prenzlauer Berg, services resumed despite the lack of benches and smashed windows, spearheaded by Erich Nehlhans, the first postwar president of Berlin's Jüdische Gemeinde. The Fraenkelufer Synagogue in the American sector of Kreuzberg reopened with a Rosh Hashanah sundown service on September 7. Photographer Robert Capa was on hand to document the event (fig. 4.9). His photographs show the hard work of the American troops who had repaired structural damage. Even though the walls appear freshly repainted and windows intact, the gaunt look of the worshippers betray their recent traumas. The accompanying article asserts that the survivor audience, exclusively male, were "all over 45-years-old," though it was much more plausible that horrific conditions in the camps prematurely aged the attendees.[72] Less formal events honoring Jews in Germany took place across the occupied country. Jewish American soldiers visiting Worms made their way to the destroyed synagogue, where they sang liturgical music.[73]

Figure 4.9. Rosh Hashanah service, Fraenkelufer Synagogue, Berlin 1945. © Robert Capa/Magnum Photos.

Using Jewish ruins for services and performances held rich symbolic meaning, though these events left radically different resonances than their counterparts for German civilians. In a city like Berlin, where Jewish life had not been confined or restricted to one district or quarter, the community returned to spaces alongside German, non-Jewish civilians, fully integrated into the ruined landscape of the capital. Furthermore, the ruined churches and rubbled synagogues held radically divergent meanings. Churches throughout the country, typically located in old town city centers and towering above other timber-framed buildings, were frequent targets for Allied bombers. Jewish sites, however, such as the Fraenkelufer and Rykestrasse Synagogues, had been the targets of state-sponsored violence, not collateral damage of the air war. After the war's end, performing in these Jewish remnants asserted the community's survival despite Nazi persecution.

Even though the synagogue services and concerts were certainly acts of resilience, the ground on which they took place no longer belonged to the city's Jewish community. As Atina Grossmann and Michael Meng have noted, there were numerous difficulties facing Jewish organizations and individuals who wanted to reclaim their prewar property amid postwar hostility. The four Allies had separate policies on restitution, and navigating these rules and restrictions proved difficult for many. In the west, policies generally favored returning the properties to survivors. But without the large congregations many of these spaces had been designed for, the Jewish community sometimes decided to sell their property. In the east, these debates were avoided, and even suppressed, because the Communists took ownership of all property, whether formerly owned by Jewish citizens or not. In 1945, Erich Nehlhans complained to Soviet authorities about their treatment of Jewish property, noting that the Weißensee Cemetery was being used as a horse stable. In the end, it was often local German government officials, and not Jewish leaders, who decided the fate of postwar Jewish ruins.[74]

Despite a proliferation of Jewish ruin events in 1945, by the late 1940s, these stagings were largely a thing of the past. There are several reasons why this might have been—namely, many survivors and displaced had been granted permission to emigrate. Second, as reconstruction efforts continued, Jewish ruins were often built over to accommodate the demands of the German population. The synagogue on Berlin's Passauer Street was torn down to make way for KaDeWe's parking garage, while other religious sites became the grounds for the modern apartment complexes of the *Wirtschaftswunder*.[75] As Michael Meng noted of the destroyed synagogue, "Berliners did not perceive it as a valuable ruin that had to be saved; they saw it as rubble that could be erased for the building of something better."[76] For many Germans, Jewish rubble conveyed the accusations and unprocessed guilt of the Holocaust, while destroyed German spaces symbolized civilian sacrifice and victimhood. Consequently, the stagings of German and Jewish ruin landscapes could not easily coexist, and ruined Jewish spaces were more often than not subsumed under the mantle of German postwar reconstruction.

Conclusions

If Jewish ruin concerts represented continuity, resilience, and survival, German performances emphasized a kind of aestheticized victimhood, staging the rubble sublime. By using the ruins to give concerts, German musicians were among the first group of artists to interrogate, exploit, and delight in staging the destruction for their own purposes. What could draw attention more clearly to the air war's toll than to play among, around, and inside the rubble? In both East and West Berlin and across occupied Germany, ruin concerts were erected as a kind of sonic memorial to German victims—not to victims of the Germans. As historian Toby Thacker notes, "Photographs of pensive listeners in shattered buildings listening to Beethoven have taken on an iconic status in representations of post-war German cultural history."[77] And yet, was there not something macabre about these performances, with musicians and audience members alike reveling in their own wretchedness? As Sebald unequivocally notes of postwar concertgoers, "We may also wonder whether their breasts did not swell with perverse pride to think that no one in human history had ever played such overwhelming tunes or endured such suffering as the Germans."[78] It was no coincidence that concerts in the ruins almost exclusively featured German composers, not music the Nazis banned on religious or political grounds. It was Beethoven, and not Mendelssohn, whose music formed a counterpoint to the destruction.

The deliberate choice to play in bombed shells was rendered all the more dramatic considering there were other places in which German ensembles could and did perform, such as movie theaters and surviving concert halls. Ensembles (and audiences, for that matter) made the decision to play in partially and completely destroyed venues because they did not have to concede these spaces to the Allies. The occupiers did not requisition ruins for military use. None of the victors wanted them, for the ruins belonged solely to the Germans.

Ruin performances enabled German ensembles to engage with victimhood and suffering despite Allied reeducation efforts. By revisiting sites destroyed by the air war—namely halls and churches that were once symbols of great national pride—musicians recast the traumatic experiences of wartime bombing into a postwar commentary of survival. In Munich, Nuremberg, Dresden, and Berlin, instrumentalists returned to sites loaded with prewar meaning. Musicalizing in the ruins meant ensembles could show the devastating toll of the air war while avoiding more difficult questions of complicity and guilt.

Ruin concerts persisted well after Nazi Germany's surrender, firmly etched in German cultural memory. In July 2015, Nuremberg's Teacher Choral Association and the Nuremberg Symphony staged a performance of *The Creation* to commemorate the seventieth anniversary of the war's end. The purple poster advertising the concert featured a sketch of the ruined St. Sebald as its background. Similarly, each February 13 in Dresden, performances of Mauersberger's *Dresdner Requiem* commemorate the city's firebombing.[79] The entrance of Berlin's Kaiser Wilhelm Memorial Church has been left a ruin, though a new church to host services and concerts was built on the ruins in 1963. The vicissitudes of the postwar period can be heard in these performances, containing the remnants, both musical and physical, of the Allied air war.

Notes

1. Henry Gluski, telephone interview by the author, July 1, 2010.
2. Monica Black, *Death in Berlin: From Weimar to Divided Germany* (Cambridge: Cambridge University Press, 2010), 180.
3. George Clare, *Before the Wall: Berlin Days, 1946–1948* (New York: E. P. Dutton, 1990), 18. See also R. Murray Schafer, "The Music of the Environment," in *Audio Culture: Readings in Modern Music*, ed. Christoph Cox and Daniel Werner (New York: Bloomsbury, 2017), 36; and Georgina Born, ed., *Music, Sound, and Space: Transformations of Public and Private Experience* (Cambridge: Cambridge University Press, 2013), 24–31.
4. Richard Brett-Smith, *Berlin '45: The Grey City* (London: Macmillan, 1967), 107.
5. Georgina Born, "Afterword: Music Policy, Aesthetic and Social Difference," in *Rock and Popular Music*, ed. Tony Bennett, Simon Frith, and Lawrence Grossberg (London: Routledge, 1993), 266–92.
6. Benedict Anderson, *Imagined Communities: Reflections on the Origin and Spread of Nationalism* (London: Verso, 1983), 149.
7. Adolph Hitler, *Manual of the German Radio*, 1938–39, quoted in Schafer, "The Music of the Environment," 37. See also Christopher Hailey, "Rethinking Sound: Music and Radio in Weimar Germany," in *Music and Performance during the Weimar Republic*, ed. Bryan Gilliam (Cambridge: Cambridge University Press, 1994), 13–36; and Andrew Oster, "Rubble, Radio, and Reconstruction: The Genre of Funkoper in Postwar Occupied Germany and the Federal Republic, 1946–1957" (PhD diss., Princeton University, 2010), 1–35.
8. For more on Heldengedenktag celebrations, see Black, *Death in Berlin*, 101, and for more information about the Request Concert radio program and film, see Marc Silberman,

German Cinema: Texts in Context (Detroit: Wayne State University Press, 1995), 66–80; Brian Currid, *A National Acoustics: Music and Mass Publicity in Weimar and Nazi Germany* (Minneapolis: University of Minnesota Press, 2006), 54–58; Peter Fritzsche, *Life and Death in the Third Reich* (Cambridge, MA: Belknap Press of Harvard University Press, 2008), 71–75; Nanny Drechsler, *Die Funktion der Musik im deutschen Rundfunk, 1933–1945* (Pfaffenweiler: Centaurus-Verlagsgesellschaft, 1988), 131–34; and Heinz Goedecke and Wilhelm Krug, eds. (1942) 2002, *Wunschkonzerte für die Wehrmacht*. Reprint, Emmelshausen: Condo, 122.

9. Joseph Goebbels, *Tagebücher von Joseph Goebbels*, Teil II, Diktate 1941–1945, vol. 15, ed. Maximilian Gschaid (Munich: K. G. Saur Verlag, 1995), 180.

10. Annegret Fauser, *Sounds of War: Music in the United States during World War II* (Oxford: Oxford University Press, 2013), 9.

11. Dietmar Arnold and Reiner Janick, *Sirenen und gepackte Koffer: Bunkeralltag in Berlin* (Berlin: Ch. Links, 2003), 13. Concerning the Kuckuck-Ruf and stages of an air raid, see Jörg Friedrich, *The Fire: The Bombing of Germany*, trans. Allison Brown (New York: Columbia University Press, 2006), 328; and Horst Götsch, "Man konnte die Bomben zählen," in *Wie Silberfische flimmerten Bomber am Himmel: Erinnerungen an das Inferno des Krieges in Berlin-Lichtenberg, 1940–1945*, ed. Christine Steer and Dietmar Arnold (Berlin: Edition Berliner Unterwelten, 2004), 48–51. For an account of radio listening in a bunker, see Helmut Altner, *Berlin Dance of Death*, trans. Tony Le Tissier (Havertown, PA: Casemate, 2002), 126.

12. Quoted in Carolyn Birdsall, *Nazi Soundscapes: Sound, Technology and Urban Space in Germany, 1933–1945* (Amsterdam: Amsterdam University Press, 2012), 11. Around 250 cases where an individual listened to a foreign radio station resulted in a death sentence. These individuals were punished so severely because they had passed along the information they obtained to a third party. For more, see Birdsall, *Nazi Soundscapes*, 131–39; Currid, *A National Acoustics*, 49; Hailey, "Rethinking Sound," in Gilliam, *Music and Performance*, 13–14; Oster, "Rubble, Radio, and Reconstruction," 59; and Erik Levi, *Music in the Third Reich* (New York: St. Martin's, 1994), 124.

13. The quotations are from Currid, *A National Acoustics*, 1; Joseph Sauer quoted in Friedrich, *The Fire*, 266, and Brett-Smith, *Berlin '45*, 75, respectively. For more on radio and Hitler's death, see Esteban Buch, *Beethoven's Ninth: A Political History* (Chicago: University of Chicago Press, 2003), 219.

14. Radio Usage Report, February 17, 1947, RG 260, Box 34, Radio Control, Radio Policy File (1945–1949), NARA II; and Gerth-Wolfgang Baruch, "Der deutsche Rundfunk," *Melos*, January 1947, 69–72. Radio Luxembourg served as the main US propaganda station from September 1944 until November 1945, before the creation of stations throughout Germany. Larry Hartenian, *Controlling Information in U.S. Occupied Germany, 1945–49: Media and Manipulation and Propaganda* (Lewistown, NY: Edwin Mellen, 2003), 52–54; Gesa Kordes, "Darmstadt, Postwar Experimentation, and the West German Search for a New Musical Identity," in Pamela Potter and Celia Applegate, eds., *Music and German National Identity* (Chicago: University of Chicago Press, 2002), 212; and Florian Weiß, Sedjro Mensah, and Thomas P. Strauss, *The Link with Home—And the Germans Listened In: The Radio Stations of the Western Powers from 1945 to 1994* (Berlin: Ruksaldruck, 2001), 10.

15. Paddy Scannell and David Cardiff, *A Social History of British Broadcasting, 1922–1939: Serving the Nation* (Oxford: Basil Blackwell, 1991), xiii.

16. Josephine Dolan, "The Voice That Cannot Be Heard: Radio/Broadcasting and the 'Archive,'" *The Radio Journal* 1, no. 1 (2003): 71.

17. Jonathan Sterne, *The Audible Past: Cultural Origins of Sound Reproduction* (Durham, NC: Duke University Press, 2003), 13.

18. Michael Bohnen, "Bericht über den Aufbau der Städtischen Oper in der Zeit vom 1.Mai 1945 bis 30. April 1946," May 6, 1946, C Rep. 120, Nr. 1484, Landesarchiv; "Hört den Rundfunksender Berlin," *Tägliche Rundschau*, May 20, 1945; "Hier spricht Berlin," *Tägliche Rundschau*, May 27, 1945; and Toby Thacker, *Music after Hitler, 1945–1955* (Farnham, UK: Ashgate, 2007), 34. The British would later fine Ludwig 10,000 DM in lieu of an 18-month jail term for failing to declare his Nazi Party membership.

19. Rundfunk Programme vom 23. Mai 1945 bis 5. Februar 1946, Deutsches Rundfunk Archiv, Potsdam, Germany; and Baruch, "Der deutsche Rundfunk," 69–72.

20. Ribbentrop was tried at Nuremberg and executed for war crimes in 1946. Weiß, Mensah, and Strauss, *The Link with Home*, 25–26.

21. Charles S. Lewis, "Music Programming," August 23, 1946, RG 260, Box 134, Records of the Information Control Division: Central Decimal File of the Executive Office, 1944–49, NARA II. When the DIAS first aired, it was broadcast by *Drahtfunk*, a wired radio service that Berliners could get when they attached their telephone wires to a radio set. *Drahtfunk* broadcasting is of a poorer quality than *Rundfunk*. For more on DIAS, see Donald Roger Browne, "The History and Programming Policies of RIAS: Radio in the American Sector (of Berlin)" (PhD diss., University of Michigan, 1961), viii, 355; and Hartenian, *Controlling Information in U.S. Occupied Germany*, 54.

22. Browne, "The History and Programming Policies of RIAS," 227.

23. The RIAS Symphony Orchestra became the German Symphony Orchestra in 1993. Amy C. Beal, "The Army, the Airwaves, and the Avant-Garde: American Classical Music in Postwar West Germany," *American Music* 21, no. 4 (Winter 2003): 485–86; H. W. Heinsheimer, "Musik im amerikanischen Rundfunk," *Melos* 14, no. 12 (October 1947): 332–35.

24. "6871st District Information Services Control Command: Newsletter," August 28, 1945, Records of the Information Control Division: Records of Information Services Division Staff Advisor, 1945–49, RG 260, Box 63, NARA II. For more on reeducation, see Toby Thacker, "Playing Beethoven like an Indian," in *The Postwar Challenge: Cultural, Social, and Political Change in Western Europe, 1945–58*, ed. Dominick Geppert (Oxford: Oxford University Press, 2003), 369–71; and Alex Ross, *The Rest Is Noise: Listening to the Twentieth Century* (New York: Farrar, Straus and Giroux, 2007), 349. On Taylor's role in postwar Germany, see David Monod, *Settling Scores: German Music, Denazification, and the Americans, 1945–1953* (Chapel Hill: University of North Carolina Press, 2005), 18, 22; and Davidson Taylor, "We Are All Grateful," May 23, 1945, RG 260, Box 237, Records of the Education and Cultural Affairs Division: Records Relating to Music and Theater, NARA II.

25. Radio Usage Report, February 17, 1947, RG 260, Box 34, Radio Control, Radio Policy File (1945–1949), NARA II.

26. The quotations are from "Draft Guidance on the Control of Music," June 8, 1945, RG 260, Box 134, Records of the Information Control Division: Central Decimal File of the Executive Office, 1944–49, NARA II.

27. Quoted in Michael Kater, *The Twisted Muse: Musicians and Their Music in the Third Reich* (Oxford: Oxford University Press, 1997), 178. While the War Department suspected Hindemith had been more compliant with the Nazi regime than he admitted, music officers were unaware of this fact. Monod, *Settling Scores*, 115–26.

28. For more on twelve-tone music in Nazi Germany, see Joan Evans, "Stravinsky's Music in Hitler's Germany," *Journal of the American Musicological Society* 56 (Fall 2003): 525–94; Michael Kater, *Composers of the Nazi Era: Eight Portraits* (New York: Oxford

University Press, 2000), 31–56, 111–43; Kater, *The Twisted Muse*, 73, 177–241; Levi, *Music in the Third Reich*, 92, 112–13. After surviving the war, Webern had the misfortune of being shot by an intoxicated American Army cook who mistakenly believed the composer was trying to foil his lucrative black market deal. For more details surrounding Webern's death, see Hans Moldenhauer, *The Death of Anton Webern: A Drama in Documents* (New York: Philosophical Library, 1961); Hans Moldenhauer, "Webern's Death," *Musical Times* 111, no. 1531 (September 1970): 877–81; and Ross, *The Rest Is Noise*, 348–52.

29. Hans Heinz Stuckenschmidt, *Zum Hören geboren: Ein Leben mit der Musik unserer Zeit* (Munich: Deutscher Taschen Verlag, 1982), 141.

30. Cultural officers in all media fields relied a great deal upon political reliable German civilians, for, as ICD Chief Robert McClure noted, "it is believed that the outward and visible aspects of the work should be entrusted entirely to Germans of proper background and qualifications." McClure, "Suggested Information Control Program for the Reorientation of German Youth," August 22, 1945, Records of the Information Control Division: Central Decimal File of the Executive Office, 1944–49. RG 260, Box 134. NARA II. For more on Stuckenschmidt's work, see Hans Heinz Stuckenschmidt, "Vorträge in Attichy, Mai-July 1945," Folder 2444, Stuckenschmidt Papers, AdK. Stuckenschmidt was a prolific writer, and in addition to writing several books on twentieth-century music, he also authored texts on composers Blacher, Ravel, Schoenberg, and Stravinsky, among others. See Hans Heinz Stuckenschmidt, *Twentieth Century Music* (London: World University, 1969); Stuckenschmidt, *Boris Blacher* (Berlin: Bote & Bock, 1985); Stuckenschmidt, *Maurice Ravel: Variationen über Person und Werk* (Frankfurt: Suhrkamp, 1966); Stuckenschmidt, *Schönberg: Leben, Umwelt, Werk* (Zürich: Atlantis, 1974); and Stuckenschmidt, *Strawinsky und sein Jahrhundert* (Berlin: Piper, 1957).

31. "Erstes Gespräch zwischen Musiker und Musikfreund," *Studio für Neue Musik*, September 3, 1946, Stuckenschmidt Papers, Folder 2571, AdK.

32. Ibid.

33. "Felix Mendelssohn Bartholdy, Gedenkwoche," November 4, 1947, Folder: E-Musik, Musiksendungen, B 104-00-24, German Radio Archive, Potsdam, Germany.

34. Radio Usage Report, February 17, 1947, RG 260, Box 34, Radio Control, Radio Policy File (1945–1949), NARA II.

35. Nicolas Nabokov, "Boris Blacher," in *Boris Blacher*, ed. Heribert Henrich and Thomas Eickhoff (Berlin: Fuldaer, 2003), 9. See also Thomas Eickhoff and Werner Grünzweig, "Gerty Herzog–Blacher im Gespräch," in *Boris Blacher*, ed. Heribert Henrich and Thomas Eickhoff (Berlin: Fuldaer, 2003), 33, 66–69; and Stuckenschmidt, *Boris Blacher*, 29.

36. Mathias Lehmann, "Musik über den Holocaust," in *Das Unbehagen in der "dritten Generation": Reflexionen des Holocausts, Antisemitismus und Nationalsozialismus*, ed. Klaus Holz and Sven Wende (Muenster: Lit, 2004), 47–48; and Oster, "Rubble, Radio, and Reconstruction," 12, 33, 141.

37. Dr. Wilhelm Hoffmann, "Die letzten Tage von Berlin," *Der Rundfunk* 30, April 28–May 4, 1946. For more on Wilhelm Hoffmann, see Francis R. Nicosia, "Introduction: Resistance to National Socialism in the Work of Peter Hoffmann," in *Germans against Nazism: Nonconformity, Opposition and Resistance in the Third Reich*, ed. Francis R. Nicosia and Lawrence D. Stokes (New York: Berghahn Books, 2015), 6–7.

38. Hoffmann, "Die letzten Tage von Berlin," 30.

39. Boris Blacher, *Die letzten Tage von Berlin*, score, 1946, Folder 1.75.142, Boris Blacher Papers, AdK.

40. Max Butting, *Musikgeschichte, die ich miterlebte* (Berlin: Henschel, 1955), 237.
41. Folder 908, Max Butting Papers, AdK. "Seit 1933, galt er als unerwünscht, öffentlich und private Behinderungen verursachten eine Schaffenspause."
42. Max Butting, *Nach dem Kriege: Vier Cantaten für gemischten Chor und Kammerorchester*, Op. 59, score, 1948, Max Butting Papers, Folder 89, AdK. ". . . vor erst zehn Jahren bauten wir die Zwingburg, in deren Schutt und Trümmern wir heute kriechen."
43. Max Butting, *Nach dem Kriege: Vier Cantaten für Gemischten Chor und Kammerorchester*, Op. 59, score, 1948, Max Butting Papers, Folder 89, AdK. "Gib uns Frieden, gib uns Frieden, gib uns Frieden, gib uns Frieden, gib uns Frieden, daß der neue Frühling Kräfte in uns findet aus dem Trümmerelend aufzuwachen in die Freude, die der Mensch zu seinem Leben braucht."
44. Henry Gluski, telephone interview by the author, July 1, 2010.
45. Bitter, *What Dreams May Come* (Miami: Charlton, 1999), 65.
46. Winthrop Sargeant, "Europe's Culture," *Time*, November 4, 1946, 51.
47. Eric Rentschler, "The Place of Rubble in the Trümmerfilm," in *The Ruins of Modernity*, ed. Julia Hell and Andreas Schönle (Durham, NC: Duke University Press, 2010), 418.
48. The quotations are from Svetlana Boym, *The Future of Nostalgia* (New York: Basic Books, 2001), 211; Alexander Mitscherlich and Margarete Mitscherlich, *The Inability to Mourn: Principles of Collective Behavior*, trans. Beverly R. Placzek (New York: Grove, 1975), 4; Hannah Arendt, "The Aftermath of Nazi Rule: Report from Germany," *Commentary*, October 1, 1950, 342; and W. G. Sebald, "Air War and Literature," in *On the Natural History of Destruction*, trans. Anthea Bell (New York: Random House, 2004), 46. For more on the air war, see Robert G. Moeller, "Germans as Victims? Thoughts on a Post-Cold War History of WWII's Legacies," *History and Memory* 17, no. 1/2 (Spring/Summer 2005): 151.
49. Moeller, "Germans as Victims?" 147–94; Moeller, *War Stories: The Search for a Usable Past in the Federal Republic of Germany* (Berkeley: University of California Press, 2003), 1–20; Eric Langenbacher, "Changing Memory Regimes in Contemporary Germany?" *German Politics and Society* 21, no. 2 (Summer 2003): 52–53; and Anna Parkinson, *An Emotional State: The Politics of Emotion in Postwar West German Culture* (Ann Arbor: University of Michigan Press, 2015), 113–45.
50. Allgemeiner Deutscher Nachrichtendienst, March 1952.
51. For further reading, see Shirli Gilbert, *Music and the Holocaust: Confronting Life in the Nazi Ghettos and Camps* (Oxford: Oxford University Press, 2005); Guido Fackler, "Music in Concentration Camps," *Music and Politics* 1, no. 1 (Winter 2007); Wolfgang Benz, *Dachau and the Nazi Terror: 1933-1945*, vol. 1 (Dachau: Dachauer Hefte, 2002); and Joseph Toltz, "Hidden Testimony: Musical Experience and Memory in Jewish Holocaust Survivors" (PhD diss., Sydney Conservatorium of Music, 2011).
52. Michael Meng, *Shattered Spaces: Encountering Jewish Ruins in Postwar Germany and Poland* (Cambridge, MA: Harvard University Press, 2011), 86.
53. Clemens Wachter, *Kultur in Nürnberg 1945-1950: Kulturpolitik, kulturelles Leben und Bild der Stadt zwischen dem Ende der NS-Diktatur und der Prosperität der fünfziger Jahre* (Nuremberg: Stadtarchiv, 1999), 139–40.
54. Quoted in Heinrich Weber, *Die Geschichte des Lehrergesangvereins Nürnberg e.V., 1878-2003* (Nuremberg: LGV, 2003), 117. See also "Karl Demmer," in Manfred K. Grieb, ed., *Nürnberger Künstlerlexikon* (Munich: K. G. Saur, 2007), 250.
55. Quoted in Karl Foesel, "Wiederaufbau einer Musik-Stadt," in *Städtische Bühnen Nürnberg: 50 Jahre Opernhaus*, ed. Friedrich Bröger (Nuremberg: Städtische Bühnen

Nürnberg-Fürth, 1955), n.p. See also Rolf Agop, *Lex mihi ars: Nachdenkliche und kuriose Begegnungen mit großen Musikern* (Siegen, Germany: Kalliope, 1985), 27.

56. Virgil Thomson, "German Culture and Army Rule," *Herald Tribune*, Paris Edition, September 22, 1946. For more on Munich's postwar musical culture, see Ulrich J. Blomann, "A Semblance of Freedom: Karl Amadeus Hartmann Between Democratic Renewal and Cold War, 1945–47," translated by Jürgen Thym, *Twentieth-Century Music* 9/1-2 (March 2012): 143–159; and Alexander Rothe, "Rethinking Postwar History: Munich's *Musica Viva* during the Karl Amadeus Hartmann Years (1945–63)," *Musical Quarterly* 90/2 (2007): 230–74.

57. Martha Sprigge, "Abilities to Mourn: Musical Commemoration in the German Democratic Republic, 1945–1989" (PhD diss., University of Chicago, 2013), 130–32, and 138 (quotation on p. 138). For more on Mauersberger's work with the Kreuzchor and subsequent performances of the motets within his *Dresden Cycle*, see pp. 102–84. Concerning Dresden's bombing, see Friedrich, *The Fire*, 12, 16, 310–15.

58. Brett-Smith, *Berlin '45*, 135.

59. Rudolf Elver and Karl Hochreither, eds., *Bach-Kantaten in Berlin: Eine Jubiläumsschrift im Auftrag des Bach-Chores und der Kaiser-Wilhelm-Gedächtnis-Kirche* (Berlin: CZV-Verlag, 1991), 32.

60. Memorandum from the Abteilungen Finanzen, Wirtschaft und Volksbildung, October 18, 1950, B Rep. 014, Nr. 2178, Landesarchiv.

61. Meeting at the Schloß-Hotel, October 29, 1950, B Rep. 014, Nr. 2178, Landesarchiv, Berlin; Hans Heinz Stuckenschmidt, "Die Filmharmoniker im Marmorhaus," *Die Neue Zeitung* (Berlin), January 8, 1952.

62. Michael P. Steinberg, "Afterword: Whose Culture? Whose History? Whose Music?" in *The Oxford Handbook of the New Cultural History of Music*, ed. Jane F. Fulcher (Oxford: Oxford University Press, 2011), 555.

63. Wigand Lange, *Theater in Deutschland nach 1945: Zur Theaterpolitik der amerikanischen Besatzungsbehörden* (Frankfurt: Peter Lang, 1980), 322.

64. Hans Heinz Stuckenschmidt, "Die Filmharmoniker im Marmorhaus," *Die Neue Zeitung* (Berlin), January 8, 1952.

65. Robert Shandley, *Rubble Films: German Cinema in the Shadow of the Third Reich* (Philadelphia: Temple University Press, 2001), 2.

66. Langenbacher, "Changing Memory Regimes in Contemporary Germany?" 50.

67. Yehudi Menuhin, *Unfinished Journey* (New York: Fromm International, 1997), 186. See also Shirli Gilbert, "We Long for a Home," in *"We Are Here": New Approaches to Jewish Displaced Persons in Postwar Germany*, ed. Avinoam Patt and Michael Berkowitz (Detroit: Wayne University Press, 2010), 291.

68. Tina Frühauf, "'Five Days in Berlin: The 'Menuhin Affair' of 1947 and the Politics of Jewish Post-Holocaust National Identity," *Musical Quarterly* 96, no. 1 (Spring 2013): 14–49; Atina Grossmann, *Germans, Jews, and Allies: Close Encounters in Occupied Germany* (Princeton, NJ: Princeton University Press, 2007), 120; and Jay Howard Geller, *Jews in Post-Holocaust Germany, 1945–1953* (Cambridge: Cambridge University Press, 2005), 95.

69. Martin Riesenburger, *Das Licht verlöschte nicht: ein Zeugnis aus der Nacht des Faschismus* (Berlin: Union, 1960), 53–54.

70. Heinz Galinski, "New Beginning of Jewish Life in Berlin," in *After the Holocaust: Rebuilding Jewish Lives in Postwar Germany*, ed. Michael Brenner (Princeton, NJ: Princeton University Press, 1999), 100–2. For a broader history of postwar German Jewish relations,

see Andreas Nachama and Julius H. Schoeps, eds., *Aufbau nach dem Untergang: Deutschjüdische Geschichte nach 1945* (Berlin: Argon, 1992).

71. Meng, *Shattered Spaces*, 64, 90; and Angelika Königseder, *Flucht nach Berlin: Jüdische Displaced Persons, 1945–1948* (Berlin: Metropol, 1998), 175. I am also appreciative of Tina Frühauf's observations on this concert, which I heard in her 2014 lecture, "What Comes after Revival? The Louis Lewandowski Festival in Berlin and The Temporality of (Post-)Revival," City University of New York, Graduate Center.

72. James Baaden, "Cantor Jakob Dymont and His Friday Night Service, Berlin 1934: Part I—A Rabbi's Observations," *Journal of Synagogue Music* 31 (Fall 2016): 95–96; Hermann Simon, ed., *Die Synagoge Rykestrasse, 1904–2004* (Berlin: Hentrich and Hentrich, 2004), 38–50; and "Jewish New Year: American Army Helps Berlin Jews Restore Their Sacred Services," *Life*, October 8, 1945, 49–50, 52.

73. For more on the interactions between Germans and Jews post-1945 in relation to music, see Tina Frühauf and Lily Hirsch, eds., *Dislocated Memories: Jews, Music, and Postwar German Culture* (Oxford: Oxford University Press, 2014), and most especially Philip Bohlman's Afterward, "The Beginning of the End: Moments of Represcence in Post-Holocaust Germany," 265–276. For more on Jewish ruins, see Nils Roemer, *German City, Jewish Memory: The Story of Worms* (Waltham, MA: Brandeis University Press, 2010), 156.

74. Geller, *Jews in Post-Holocaust Germany*, 94; Baaden, "Cantor Jakob Dymont and His Friday Night Service," 95–96; Simon, *Die Synagoge Rykestrasse*, 47–53; "Rykestrasse Synagogue," http://www.jg-berlin.org/en/judaism/synagogues/rykestrasse.html; Meng, *Shattered Spaces*, 5, 31–38, 97; and Grossmann, *Jews, Germans, and Allies*, 109–14.

75. KaDeWe is the abbreviation for *Kaufhaus des Westens*, an upscale department store in Schöneberg. The *Wirtschaftswunder*, or economic miracle, refers to the prosperity enjoyed by West Germany after World War II.

76. Meng, *Shattered Spaces*, 108. For more on the Jewish community in the wake of National Socialism, see Hagit Lavsky, *New Beginnings: Holocaust Survivors in Bergen-Belsen and the British Zone in Germany, 1945–1950* (Detroit: Wayne State University Press, 2002).

77. Thacker, *Music after Hitler*, 75.

78. Sebald, "Air War and Literature," in *On the Natural History of Destruction*, 44.

79. For more information about the Nuremberg concert, see Konzert und Aufführungen des LGV, http://www.lehrergesangverein-nbg.de; for more information about the Dresden concerts, see Tony Joel, *The Dresden Firebombing: Memory and the Politics of Commemoration Destruction* (London: I. B. Tauris, 2013), 95.

5

BERLIN 1945

Toward a Ruin Aesthetic in Music

Rubble, Ruins, and Romanticism

Eberhard Schmidt, political prisoner number 39341, returned to Berlin in May 1945. On his registration form for Soviet authorities, he listed Sachsenhausen Concentration Camp as his only previous address and "dissident" as his religious affiliation. A cellist and composer, Schmidt soon found work by cofounding the Broom (*Der Besen*), one of the city's first antifascist cabaret troupes. The group was aptly named; as both a cleaning implement and a tool to sweep misdeeds under the rug, Schmidt's Broom aimed to "hold up a mirror"[1] to its audiences, exposing German complicity with Nazi war crimes. The composer knew it would not be easy to create a community of listeners where Allied soldiers, civilians, war criminals, and camp inmates now sat side by side, so he organized the Broom's early performances with a unifying theme in mind: the rubble (*die Trümmer*) and its resonance in postwar culture.

Aside from providing an unintended performance space, the ruin also functioned as a catalyst for the composition of new music in Berlin. This chapter considers compositions that owe their existence to the destruction of the country and to the demise of National Socialism, as rubble music openly engaged with suffering and trauma, sounding the earliest expressions of German victimhood. Whether they had spent April 1945 in a cellar or on a death march, the city's composers were committed to rendering their wartime experiences in their postwar musical scores. Eberhard Schmidt, Max Butting, Paul Höffer, and Heinz Tiessen, among others, addressed the regime's collapse, the Allied air war, and subsequent four-power occupation in their early postwar work.

Hearing music as a rubble form is a departure from the discipline's treatment in previous cultural histories that largely focus on the logistical challenges of making music in a destroyed city. Scholars have documented cultural reconstruction largely in regard to material devastation, denazification, and Allied rivalries—topics that do not represent the vanquished German perspective, and for good reason.[2] Rubble music was the messy sound of 1945, as former party members and political prisoners composed pieces about their suffering under the Nazi regime. Composers living in the rubble portrayed this time just as astutely as visual artists, photographers, writers, and filmmakers. When Lyotard discusses what he calls "a writing of the ruins," whereby "this writing preserves the forgotten,"[3] the philosopher's charge could also be extended to music. A composing of the ruins was exactly the task that Berlin's musicians anxiously undertook. From 1945 to 1950, rubble music was written during the liminal space between war and peace, the intervening years of German reconstruction, and the ensuing period of Cold War escalation between the American and Russian occupiers. These works aimed to re-create in music what was bombed into oblivion, a sonic reconstruction made possible both in spite of and because of the occupation, as rubble Lieder became a popular genre in both East and West Berlin. Much like urban planners and architects, Berlin's composers turned to reliable structures. As historian Jeffry Diefendorf notes in his work on German city planning in 1945, "However total the destruction appeared, however much there seemed to be a tabula rasa upon which to rebuild, the intellectual and emotional investments in the former structures remained."[4] Rubble Lieder reconstructed a musical architecture on top of the ruins, a facade on the bombed crater of urban Germany.

The practical aspects of the Lied, its small performing forces, its potential for amateur singers, and its textual possibilities as an expressive outlet made the genre an excellent fit for rubble music. As a genre that took its cues from both twentieth-century cabaret culture and the nineteenth-century German Romantics, Lieder promoted a certain kind of nostalgia, one that did not acknowledge 1945 as a rupture, nor the zero hour as a new beginning, but rather sought sonic continuity with Germany's musical past. This harkening back to the past served the political aims of these musicians in several ways. In the postwar period, cabaret was considered antifascist in its orientation, a liminal space where social and political borders did not necessarily apply, where critique had its place but not censorship. Cabaret was perceived as a return to Weimar, and the lure of reclaiming a genre supposedly untarnished by the Nazi years held great appeal for the city's composers.[5]

Furthermore, as if to combat the monolithic stereotype of Nazi music as Beethoven or Bruckner symphonies, Berlin's composers also emphasized the connection between Lieder and the Romanticism. The Romantics were fascinated by ruins, not just in musical form but also in architecture, visual art, and literature, as seen in paintings from Caspar David Friedrich to newly constructed ruin follies for nineteenth-century country estates. Romantic ruins, as Andrew Davis reminds us, were "wrecked not literally by the forces of nature but by the forces of the Romantic artistic spirit."[6] Even the Nazis were not immune to indulging in a kind of ruin sublime, especially when it fit their own political purposes. From the confines of his prison cell in 1969, architect Albert Speer famously posited his Theory of Ruin Value (*Ruinenwerttheorie*), claiming he designed Berlin's buildings to look like spectacular, monumental ruins a thousand years hence to evoke the crumbling grandeur of ancient Rome and Greece. As Lydia Goehr points out, Speer conveniently wrote this theory only in the postwar period, not during the war, despite his claims to the contrary.[7] Ruins, as a constant reminder of the past embedded in the present, are "an especially powerful trigger for nostalgia,"[8] Andreas Huyssen writes, and by combining warfare's debris with the ruin's romantic elements, the city's postwar artists created their own kind of rubble sublime. Similarly, if we think of the "ruin gaze" to borrow Svetlana Boym's term, where such a perspective encourages "the type of nostalgia that is reflective rather than restorative,"[9] the links between the postwar period and Romanticism come into sharper relief. By reclaiming the Romantics' penchant for destruction and fragmentation in the postwar period, musicians could recast the haphazard rubble of aerial warfare into a deliberate product of aesthetic contemplation, and the romantic fragment provided these composers with yet another link to Germany's nineteenth-century musical traditions. In Schlegel's 1798 volume *Athenaeum*, published by the philosopher and his brother, he writes, "A fragment should be like a little work of art, complete in itself and separated from the rest of the universe like a hedgehog."[10] Schlegel believed that the Romantic fragment resulted from the deterioration of Classical forms, a withering away of balance and proportion in favor of ambiguity and imperfection, for "many of the works of the Ancients have become fragments. Many of the Moderns are fragments the moment they come into being."[11] Schlegel plays on the tension between authentic versus constructed ruin

134 | Rubble Music

Figure 5.1. Alexanderplatz, August 1945. ©Robert Capa/Magnum Photos.

forms, a favorite theme of Romantic artists and a topos to which postwar artists also returned.

Rubble Lieder and rubble song cycles emphasized romantic narrative elements such as alienation and moral ambiguity, referencing earlier works like Schubert's *Winterreise*. The postwar "Hurdy-Gurdy Man" ("Der Leiermann") (fig. 5.1), is reminiscent of the lonely figure in *Winterreise*, presciently described by Wilhelm Müller's lyrics, "No one wants to hear him, no one looks at him."[12] With numb fingers in the middle of Alexanderplatz, he performs as two Soviet soldiers stare past him to the ruined cityscape beyond. It was no coincidence that *Winterreise* would prove to be a favorite of postwar audiences; shortly after Dietrich Fischer-Dieskau's release from an American prisoner-of-war camp, he sang the song cycle for his 1947 RIAS debut.[13]

Not only did the city's destruction enable rubble music; so, too, did the composers who worked within these reconstructed institutions. The following section discusses the work of four East and West Berlin musicians. The immense pressure to define their compositions against "Nazi music" was never far from their minds nor the minds of the Allies. A sense of German victimhood certainly united both east and west, and rubble music was a shared thread between the sectors. Berliners had more in common with one another than with their respective occupiers, and on both sides of the city, composers shared a common project: writing rubble music to express the suffering of a defeated people.

Berlin's cultural reconstruction occurred not over, but rather *within*, the rubble of the cityscape, transforming the ruin from a passive site to one of negotiation, renegotiation, and even transgression. Considering Walter Benjamin's charge that "allegories are, in the realm of thoughts, what ruins are in the realm of things,"[14] it is not surprising that Berlin's composers reimagined the debris in musical terms, using the destroyed landscape as an allegory for German suffering.

Rubble Lieder: Butting, Schmidt, Tiessen, and Höffer

Max Butting (1888–1976)

Max Butting felt relieved the war was over, if for no other reason than to stop hearing the low din of bombers overhead and to finally emerge from his cellar. As Berliners "starved and suffered psychologically," Butting was convinced "they were not sure if their hate was mainly directed against the dictatorship or the enemy."[15] By summer 1945, the composer had "suffered under the shame" of the Nazi regime, writing in his memoir about the paradox of being both "liberated and defeated"[16] with the arrival of the Allies.

An active participant in Weimar's musical life, Butting had been a member of the November Group (*Novembergruppe*), a socialist-leaning arts organization founded in 1918. Exploring the relationship between politics and art in the wake of World War I, the November Group's music branch staged performances of new chamber music, counting composer Heinz Tiessen and Hans Heinz Stuckenschmidt among its members. Since taking over his family's ironmongery in the early 1930s, however, Butting had devoted little time to composition. By 1941, when Butting's wife tried to purchase a copy of her husband's work from a local music store, the owner replied that he had scarcely any of Butting's scores left, concluding that the composer "must be a Jew or dead."[17]

In reality, Butting was a Nazi Party member and very much alive. Having joined the party in 1940, the composer had to pass Soviet denazification in 1945 as a resident of Prenzlauer Berg. In support of the composer's innocence, his friends and family members wrote short testimonials (*Erklärungen*) arguing that Butting became a member for his safety, rather than according to his ideological leanings. Their well-worn zero hour phrases ("If he joined the party, then only due to the pressure of the external circumstances")[18] expressed the paradox of party membership, as the Allies struggled to separate "nominal" Nazi members from those who had taken on leadership roles.

Like many of his contemporaries, joining the Nazi Party did little to impede Butting's postwar reentry into Berlin's musical institutions, and in 1947, he became director of Radio Berlin's Music Section. He worked tirelessly to rectify what he perceived to be shortcomings in radio production and the management of other city institutions. Butting began campaigning for a new composers' union in Berlin, admitting that since the dissolution of the Reichsmusikkammer (RMK), "colleagues no longer had an organization through which they could mutually help one another."[19] As Pamela Potter notes, contrary to the chamber's postwar reputation as a repressive censorship organization, the RMK had actually improved some conditions for its members, including the standardization of wages and benefits. Butting's newly formed composers' section, as part of the Free Federation of Unions (*Freier Deutscher Gewerkschaftsbund* or FDGW) aimed to unite musicians across Germany, although the composer soon found little consensus regarding his plan. Potential members in Munich did not want to participate in a Berlin-based organization, especially one created in the east. Even within the capital, musicians in each sector heard the reconstruction of musical life differently, an indication of the growing ideological confrontation between not only the Allies but also within the German musical establishment. Butting believed musicians in the west were more interested in the commercial possibilities of their work, while those in the east wanted to write music that aligned with the goals of the state. The composers' section gained little traction, and Butting became involved instead with the Soviet organization Club der Kulturschaffenden.

His composers' section would have to wait until 1951 when the Central Committee approved the Union of German Composers and Musicologists (VDKM), with membership limited to musicians residing in Soviet-occupied areas. Butting served on the board, as did Hanns Eisler and Georg Knepler, both newly returned from exile. The union sought to inflect socialist ideology into the work of Germany's musicologists and composers, and eleven branch offices across the country worked in tandem with a central committee in Berlin.[20]

Aside from his work reconstituting Berlin's music organizations, Butting experienced the most productive compositional period of his career. As he admitted in his memoirs, "I cannot deny, that for me even my compositions between 1945 and 1949 meant mainly clarification, confession or exoneration."[21] Butting's works are remarkable for the breadth of topics they attempt to cover: the air war, Allied invasion, civilian suffering, and German culpability for Nazi crimes. Already during summer 1945, the composer began working on *The Guilt* (*Die Schuld*), a Lehrstück scored for two choirs, orchestra, and soloists simply known as "woman," "brother," and "man." Poet Walter Stehr, a former colleague of Butting's from their time working at STAGMA, the RMK sponsored music copyright agency, wrote the libretto. The Soviets had recently liberated Stehr from the Gestapo's Brandenburg-Görden Prison where he was being held on treason charges.[22]

Butting's *The Guilt* was not without precedent; philosopher Karl Jaspers was at work on the same question, albeit in a different form. A former professor at the University of Heidelberg whom the Nazis had forced to step down in 1937, Jaspers and his Jewish wife, Gertrud, lived under constant threat of deportation. They survived by keeping a low profile, and after the war, Jaspers returned to his post at Heidelberg. Between 1945 and 1946, he delivered a series of lectures to his students that would become *The Question of German Guilt* (*Die Schuldfrage*), his book entreating the German people to examine their conduct under National Socialism. Jaspers encouraged his listening audiences and readership to stifle strong emotions such as outrage, revenge, and despair by "putting these feelings on ice"[23] and instead turn to rationality. He argued that there were four types of German guilt: political, criminal, moral, and metaphysical. Jaspers's conception of moral guilt, or duty to oneself and to the collective regardless of the reigning political system, is most clearly the version represented in Butting and Stehr's Lehrstück.

Yet for a work titled *The Guilt*, designed to be a teaching piece, Butting's composition had much more to do with German suffering than culpability. The characters blame one another for the war, and after trading heated accusations, the man and brother conclude that everyone must simply accept responsibility for him- or herself. The composer feared he would be accused of opportunism by writing *The Guilt* so soon after the fall of National Socialism, and he decided to suppress the work himself, concluding that "perhaps this piece is aesthetically a mixture of poor German and banal music."[24] Butting's concerns were not without cause; Jaspers would leave Heidelberg shortly after publishing *The Question of German Guilt*, accepting the philosophy department chair at the University of Basel in 1948.[25]

Butting was most prolific in miniature, however, composing nearly fifty songs for voice and piano about postwar life under the title, *Songs from Berlin (Lieder aus Berlin)*. In a series of evocative fragments he wrote between 1945 and 1947, the composer covered topics from air raid sirens to the black market to the zoo.[26] Each piece is a window into the insanity, irony, and suffering of the rubbled city as Butting wrote the lyrics, even employing Berliner dialect when necessary. In "Three Satirical Lieder," op. 49, from *Songs from Berlin*, an unemployed cynic muses, "If you pick up your flask to get back your clear head, you've quickly boozed away your life's twilight instead,"[27] while another op. 49 song ("The Rage") sardonically concludes, "And the people? Shut the hell up, shut the hell up, in the best case they clear away rubble."[28] In "18 Days," from op. 48, rather than scoring the humor or irony of postwar life, the composer recalled the gory fall of the city. Using expressionist language to describe the street fighting during the Battle of Berlin, Butting writes, "Bodies lay on the street,—under ruins,—swimming in the subway tunnels, hanging in the trees like holiday decorations, like the moon and sun hang in the clouds as gloomy red, dirty lanterns."[29]

"18 Days" was performed at the Theater am Kurfürstendamm as part of a concert sponsored by the Berliner Magistrate, but Butting's music found few supporters. As the composer himself admitted, "The public in 1946 was not interested in being reminded of those 18 days in May 1945, and I was not satisfied with the music."[30] Butting was jaded enough to realize his work might provoke little or no reaction; even before the war, the composer complained of Berlin's conservative musical tastes, "the public here is . . . suspicious of any music written by a composer who is not dead yet."[31]

In 1949, Middle-German Press published five of Butting's 1946 pieces under the title *Songs from Berlin: Five Serious Songs*, op. 47. The composer dedicated the collection to Grete and Siegfried Ostrowski, Jewish friends he had known since childhood who had fled to Palestine with the outbreak of the war.[32] Although the collection is labeled "Part One," none of the composer's other Berlin songs appeared in print. The song cycle follows a narrator who wanders aimlessly while searching for the Berlin of his past, finding only rubble instead. Much like the disillusioned figure in Schubert's *Winterreise*, Butting's protagonist remains unfulfilled and alienated throughout the five fragments: 1. The Curse, 2. Tiergarten, 3. The Tree (At Lustgarten), 4. One Night, and 5. Peace (At Hundekehler Lake). *Five Serious Songs* makes use of two primary visual and narrative romantic tropes—namely, the ruin and the uncanny (*das Unheimliche*), while harmonically the songs are extremely chromatic and often resist identifying a tonic; instead, they are unified by motivic fragments and tonality by assertion. In "1. The Curse," the piano repeats a dotted rhythm rubble motif ten times, mimicking the narrator's amblings through the destruction: "Helpless we are walking down the streets, through rubble and ruins, decay and death" (ex. 5.1).

As a sonic device, the motif transports us through the rubble until the song's conclusion (ex. 5.2), when Butting switches to a chorale texture (m. 64) interrupting the motive with a perfect authentic cadence in E-Major (mm. 79–80). The narrator ponders what would happen if the city's rubble were to vanish but resignedly admits, "Who of us will be so lucky?"[33]

With rubble taking on the gravitas of ruins and the narrator trudging through the destroyed cityscape, Butting depicts the uncanny in the song cycle through the destruction of romantic imagery. He dashes any sense of closure in *Five Serious Songs* by constantly turning the city's idyllic landscapes on their head. In "3. The Tree (At Lustgarten)," grenades have blown apart the idyllic park in front of the Berlin Cathedral as a final tree lies bleeding. (We might hear the song as a counterpoint to Schubert's "Der Lindenbaum" in which a solitary tree contains "many a word of love" carved into its bark.)[34] A peaceful stroll around the bucolic Hundekehler Lake (no. 5) is disrupted by the reappearance of decayed, burned-out ruins in the distance as the narrator concludes, "the truth appears unspeakably evil."[35]

Butting also uses sonic and musical devices to evoke the uncanny. In "2. The Tiergarten," a sparse piano waltz accompanies the narrator's haunting memories of the once idyllic park, sounding in stark contrast to the rubbled present. In "4. One Night" the narrator anxiously ponders who could be knocking at the door at such a late hour, as the pianist plays octaves

Example 5.1. Max Butting, "The Curse" (mm. 1–8), from *Songs from Berlin*, Op. 47.

Example 5.2. Max Butting, "The Curse" (mm. 77–80), from *Songs from Berlin*, Op. 47.

Example 5.3. Max Butting, "A Night" (mm. 24–34), from *Songs from Berlin*, Op. 47.

ominously underneath the tentative musings: "Did a human being knock? Did fate pound? Or did the spirits of the dead reach out?" (ex. 5.3). Butting's text continues, "My heart beats very loudly, because the uncanniness of the hours is almost too heavy to bear,"[36] as the singer and piano trace minor seconds (D–C#–B#) over a C# in the bass. The suspensions and ties create an atmosphere of tonal ambiguity, as the left hand now mimics both the knocking at the door and the beating of the narrator's heart. Butting was recording the rubble landscape outside his front door, working with the musical forms of the German romantics while concerning himself with the problems of the present. The composer bemoaned what he perceived as the German musical establishment's lack of interest in new music that dealt with contemporary issues, evoking one of his Romantic idols: "One just has to read the writings of Robert Schumann, in which he critically engages with and criticizes his present. Where does this happen today in a remotely similar and similarly comprehensive manner?" as Butting castigated musicologists and composers alike for failing to engage with "the burning questions of our times."[37] For Butting, the way forward was to rebuild the city's ensembles, organizations, and institutions, and there could be no question that Berlin's musicians would create a new musical culture from the bombed fragments of the old.

Eberhard Schmidt (1906–96)

Sitting in the Jägerstraße clubhouse of the Club der Kulturschaffenden, Max Butting soon befriended Eberhard Schmidt, a rising star of the East Berlin cabaret scene. Schmidt found Butting to be well-versed in the city's musical culture and "a loveable, helpful person" who had "suffered deeply from the question of German guilt during National Socialism."[38] The elder composer offered Schmidt helpful advice on his compositions and listened attentively to stories of Schmidt's concentration camp internment. Although their war experiences varied greatly, the two composers spent hours at the clubhouse discussing the city's reconstruction, becoming fast, if unlikely, friends. Schmidt could not help but feel that spring 1945 "was the most beautiful May that I ever experienced."[39] While on a death march from Sachsenhausen, he was liberated by American troops near Schwerin. Still dressed in his prison uniform and wearing two different shoes, the composer walked two hundred kilometers back to the capital.

It was Schmidt's second time living in the city. In 1927, he had moved from upper Silesia to Berlin to study law at Friedrich-Wilhelm-Universität, taking lessons in cello and music theory at the Stern Conservatory in his spare time. After realizing he had little interest in law and even less interest in becoming a lawyer, he left the university in 1929 to focus on his music career. He soon joined the Communist Party and married an activist in the leftist student movement, Jewish singer Cora Eppstein. With the Nazis' rise to power, the couple fled to Paris in 1935, where Eppstein died of typhus in 1939. Schmidt volunteered to fight in the Spanish Civil War, joining Republican forces against General Francisco Franco's Nationalists. He was soon captured and held in three different French prisoner-of-war camps before being sent back to Nazi Germany.

Imprisoned in Sachsenhausen between 1941 and 1945, Schmidt was initially assigned to hard labor, but his living conditions improved once he was transferred to the camp's warehouse and put in charge of tools. Internment did not keep Schmidt from his musical activities, and he founded a singing group and joined a string quartet, even finding time to compose.[40] One of the few songs he saved from Sachsenhausen, "Muselman," was about the camp's weakest and most vulnerable inmates; a song that survived longer than its subjects.

After the war, Schmidt began working at the Volksbildungsamt in Pankow (located in northeast Berlin) registering artists with Soviet authorities. After he met artist Eva Fritzsche at the Volksbildungsamt, they decided to found the Broom. Ruin became the theme of the troupe, and by the second performance, "Man, now you are standing before the ruins" ("Mensch, nu stehste vor die Trümmer"), Schmidt penned a number of satirical songs about life during the war, including the tongue-in-cheek, "But you had a private bunker!" The brief program notes reminded audiences that "without this time and its evil masters, we would have no ruins today."[41]

Schmidt also wrote rubble songs about the pains and ironies of postwar life. His first, "Look Ahead" ("Nach vorne den Blick"), encouraged rapid rebuilding in the manner of a socialist worker's song, while "We Play in Ruins" ("Wir spielen in Ruinen") described children searching for food while being admonished by Russian soldiers. Schmidt's largest scale work completed in 1945 was *The War Was Over* (*Aus war der Krieg*), scored for choir and orchestra, with a text written by Fritzsche.[42] The choir opens with the words, "The war was over! We crawled out of the basements, and felt our wounds and counted our dead, and around us the rubble!"[43] as the bassoons imitated a march beneath. In January 1946, the Staatsoper's opera chorus and the Rundfunk Symphony Orchestra performed the work at Masurenallee. Ultimately, burdened by the financial toll of running their own cabaret troupe, Fritzsche and Schmidt had to abandon the venture in early 1946. A few months later, under Soviet auspices, they opened Fresh Wind (*Frischer Wind*), a second cabaret on Friedrichstraße. This venture was similarly short-lived, however, as members of the troupe realized they had irreconcilable ideas about postwar politics, the Nazi past, and divided Germany's future.[44]

Schmidt, the former concentration camp inmate, and Butting, the former party member, both depicted German suffering in their rubble Lieder. They were ideologically motivated to write pieces that aligned with the interests of the burgeoning East German state, cultivating an accessible populism that would be encouraged by the Socialist Unity Part (SED). But as the work of Heinz Tiessen and Paul Höffer showed, rubble music was one of the few commonalities between east and west, often crossing the city's borders more easily than the musicians who played it.

Heinz Tiessen (1887–1971)

In Tiessen's autobiography, *My Life until 1945* (*Mein Leben bis 1945*), the composer presents a brief but finessed picture of his activities under the Third Reich. He taught at the Hochschule für Musik between 1929 and 1945 but was frustrated by the deteriorating living conditions. Classes could not be held regularly for the last year and a half of the war due to frequent bombings, and many of the students had been drafted, making it difficult for professors to continue their courses. Tiessen's concerns about Jewish friends hardly enters the narrative, though he does concede, "Through the departure of the Jews I lost—as did new music as such—around two-thirds of the interested parties,"[45] grievously minimizing the devastating effects of Nazi war crimes. In order to continue living and working in Berlin, the composer made certain accommodations to the regime, serving as a censor for the Propaganda Ministry in addition to his teaching position.[46]

Even though the collapse of the Third Reich gave Tiessen "freedom from spiritual pressure and the long missed vital air,"[47] the Soviets would not allow him to resume the same position at the Hochschule. Tiessen's case illustrates the utter arbitrariness of denazification decisions, as well as the Soviets' preferential treatment reserved for star performers. Instead, he began working to rebuild choral organizations (*Chorgemeinschaft*) in Zehlendorf and took over the directorship of the former Stern Conservatory in 1946, where he had been a student forty years earlier.[48] Named for its German Jewish cofounder Julius Stern, the conservatory was renamed by the Nazis and operated in the Berlin Philharmonic on Bernburgerstraße until its 1944 bombing. Plagued by difficulties managing the conservatory from the beginning, Tiessen admitted of his tenure in a 1946 interview, "The last six months have shown me that my idealistic zest for action in the rubble city of Berlin has only limited starting points: The most important conditions must be created first!"[49] These "most important conditions" included heated rooms, qualified teachers, and securing the funding necessary to operate. Separated sectors made hiring faculty more challenging.

Aside from his duties at the conservatory and his work with Berlin's amateur choirs, Tiessen concentrated renewed energy on composition. Like Butting and Schmidt, Tiessen turned to lieder, completing his three op. 53 songs ("Heimkehr," "Zwiegespräch," "Die holde Katherine") during summer 1945. All three pieces feature a text by Klabund, the pen name of Jewish German poet Alfred Henschke, who suffered from recurring bouts of tuberculosis and died in 1928 at the untimely age of 37.[50] Tiessen's sudden turn to the text of a Jewish poet stood in stark contrast to his former work for the Propaganda Ministry. He completed the most self-confessional of the songs, "Homecoming" (*Heimkehr*), on July 11. The text comes from Klabund's *Irene or, A Conviction: A Song from Klabund* (*Irene oder, die Gesinnung: Ein Gesang von Klabund*), and features a narrator who returns home to find it, and himself, unrecognizable:[51]

Ich suche die Heimat: zerrissen, zertreten,	I search for home: torn, trodden,
Ich suche mich selber und finde mich nicht.	I search for myself and cannot find me.

Throughout the piece, Tiessen makes use of *Heimat*'s double meaning: both a physical place and a sensibility, as the protagonist in the poem finds neither. In stark contrast to Butting's *Songs from Berlin*, which explicitly describe the ruins, this narrator does not see the landscape as it is but as it is frozen in his memories. Although he looks for familiar signs of his small village—the pond, the well, and the beautiful house—they are absent. Tiessen's setting makes ample use of diminished harmonies, deceptive cadences, and shifts between groupings of two-, three-, and four-beat units, resisting regular metrical underpinnings. The piece is constructed in two parts connected by a D-minor motive in octaves (ex. 5.4).

Over the line, "I search for home," Tiessen writes "with greatest expression" (*mit größtem Ausdruck*) as he cycles rapidly through different key areas, obscuring any sense of tonic. The song concludes with a recitativo-like texture as the piano sustains diminished chords over which the singer despairs, "I search for myself and cannot find me" (ex. 5.5). The sudden shift in dynamics from *sF* to *pp* in the accompaniment indicates the jarring, uncertain world to which the narrator returns.

In Tiessen's following three op. 55 songs—"Weltlauf," "Dies Irae," "Prolog zur Harzreise" (1945–47)—scored for soprano and piano, the composer set two poems by German Jewish poet Heinrich Heine and one by Julius Bab, a prominent theater critic and founder of Berlin's Jüdischer Kulturbund.[52] The composer's song cycle uses Heine's and Bab's texts to explore death, thwarted homecoming, and a solo journey into nature by using

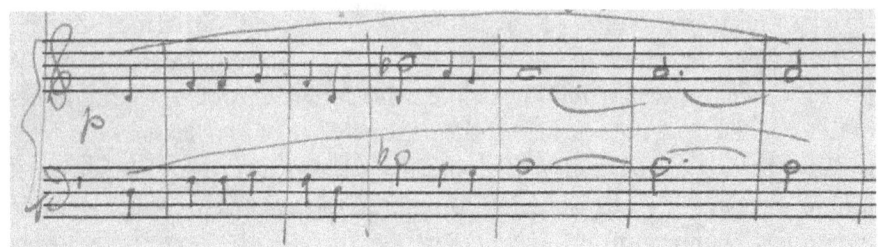

Example 5.4. Heinz Tiessen, "Heimkehr" (mm. 1–7), Op. 53. Courtesy of Andreas Meurer, Musikverlag Ries & Erler, and Akademie der Künste.

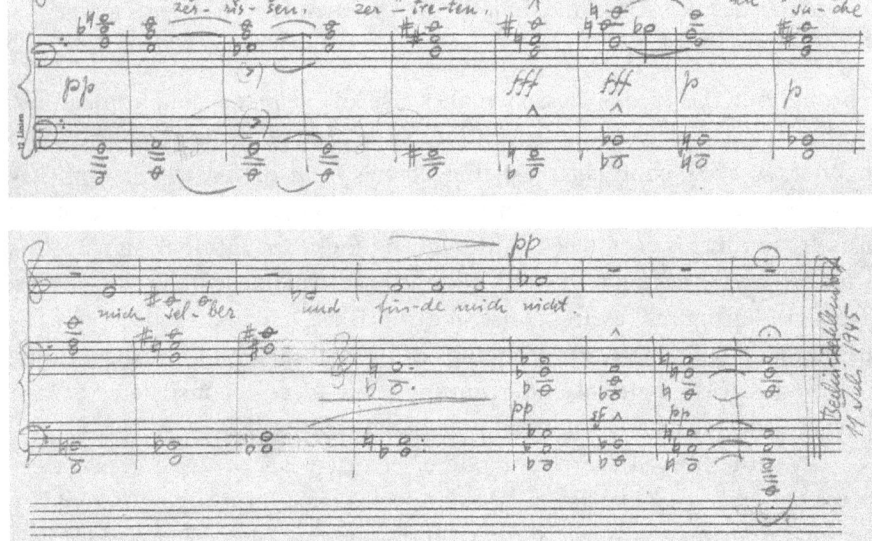

Example 5.5. Heinz Tiessen, "Heimkehr" (mm. 96–112), Op. 53. Courtesy of Andreas Meurer, Musikverlag Ries & Erler, and Akademie der Künste.

romantic themes and narrative devices that speak to postwar alienation and disillusionment.

Song no. 1 features Heine's poem *Weltlauf* ("The Way of the World"), a Hegelian term describing the tension between everyday, prosaic experience and the longing for a higher, sublime ideal. For Adorno, the notion of *Weltlauf* was the late-Romantic frame through which to hear Mahler's first four symphonies as a "breakthrough to something better, the closeness to

Example 5.6. Heinz Tiessen, "Weltlauf" (mm. 14–18), Op. 55. Courtesy of Andreas Meurer, Musikverlag Ries & Erler, and Akademie der Künste.

dialect and the discontinuities full of inner torment."[53] Tiessen also heard the "inner torment" in the notion of *Weltlauf*, embracing Heine's bitter irony in his setting of the poem, using primarily homophonic textures and sparse, parallel octaves within the standard modulations of a Lutheran chorale. The concluding lines of Heine's poem, "If you have absolutely nothing then you may as well give up the ghost, because a right to live, *Lump*, belongs only to those who have something,"[54] which Tiessen sets bombastically over E-Major chords that resolve to A minor, take on an especially stark connotation in their postwar context. Klabund's phrase, "the right to live," eerily echoed the Nazi phrase, "life unworthy of life" ("lebensunwertes Leben"), which the National Socialists used to justify the Aktion T4 program, or state-sponsored murder of individuals with disabilities.[55] After the final line of "Weltlauf," Tiessen noted the date and his location (Berlin-Schlachtensee, October 4, 1945) on his personal copy of the sheet music (fig. 5.6) Schlachtensee was both an idyllic lake southwest of the city center and the future site of the largest displaced persons camp in Berlin, as the contradiction between picnicking Berliners and displaced Jews embodied its own kind of postwar *Weltlauf*.

For his second song, "Dies Irae" of op. 55, Tiessen selected the poetry of Julius Bab, the German Jewish playwright who fled Nazi Germany and his work with the Kulturbund in 1938, settling in New York. Bab's text was written in 1918 and describes Judgment Day as trumpets sound and we are called to answer for that "through which we came into being."[56] Tiessen scores the text in a highly dissonant setting, neglecting to identify a tonic and denying any sense of closure. Song no. 3 in the cycle features another Heine poem, "Prolog zur Harzreise." The *Harzreise* collection was a travel report Heine wrote in 1824 as he slowly made his way from Göttingen to the Harz Mountains; Heine himself referred to the writings as "literary fragments" as his poems were interspersed with prose observations of the journey. At the end of "Prolog zur Harzreise," the narrator eschews worldly goods for a mountainous sublime as the literary fragments of Heine's youth correspond with the fractured reality of Tiessen's Berlin:

> Fare ye well, ye polished salons,
> Polished men and women too,
> For the mountain heights I leave you,
> Thence to look in mirth on you.[57]

In the composer's setting, the soprano voice ascends with each reiteration of "higher" (*steigen*), ending the piece with an octave vocal slide from a″ to a′ as the piano gives a fanfare in D Major.

In 1949, Tiessen returned to the Hochschule as its director, and he enjoyed a successful career as a pedagogue and composer. Although Tiessen maintained that the National Socialists had completely and then partially boycotted his work, there is no evidence to substantiate his claims.[58] In a 1957 letter to Joachim Tiburtius, the famed cultural senator of West Berlin, Tiessen thanked Tiburtius for his help in staging a recent performance of the composer's work, noting "My boycott during the years of Hitler's Reich," as well as "the loss of virtually all of my printed works through aerial bombs dropped on the Leipzig and Berlin publishing houses," meant "that after 1945 only a few, scattered pieces could be played for the public."[59] Tiessen's revisionist history was a common refrain echoed by composers in the postwar period who were anxious to establish postwar, antifascist credentials. Furthermore, his work was frequently conducted after 1945 by his former student, Sergiu Celibidache, and performed by the Berlin Philharmonic (*Vorspiel zu einem Revolutionsdrama*, op. 33) and RIAS Symphony Orchestra (*Hamlet* Suite, op. 30, *Salambo* Suite, op. 34a, Symphony no. 2, op. 17). Dietrich Fischer-Dieskau also took a liking to Tiessen's music, eventually recording "Vöglein Schwermut," op. 23, no. 3.[60] As Tiessen's case shows, victimhood, whether real or constructed, was a central element of rubble music.

Paul Höffer (1895–1949)

Among Tiessen's closest allies and colleagues was Paul Höffer, a fellow West Berlin composer who taught with Tiessen at the Hochschule before the war. A professor of composition and theory since 1933, Höffer had been an active and lauded member of the Third Reich's musical culture. With stylistic influences that included Mahler and Hindemith as well as Schumann and Schubert, Höffer aligned himself with the interests of the RMK when it suited him, accepting various commissions from Nazi officials, the Luftwaffe, and the Wehrmacht. He won a gold medal at the 1936 Olympics for his cantata *Olympic Vow* (*Olympischer Schwur*), and in 1944, he was included on a preferential list of contemporary composers for radio broadcast in Nazi Germany.[61]

By the middle of April 1945, Höffer knew the Russians had surrounded Berlin. He sought to distract himself by working on a toccata for solo piano at his home in Charlottenburg. Extremely chromatic and filled with syncopations, Höffer wrote beneath the toccata's final fermata, "born under pain, April 15, 1945."[62] On April 22, the composer mused in his diary that of an estimated 480 Berlin air raids, he had personally experienced about 460.[63] Now all he had to do was survive a few more weeks.

The first works Höffer wrote after the cease-fire were rubble lieder that vacillated between hope for the future and despair over the traumatic memories of the past. He finished *Song of the New Youth* (*Lied der neuen Jugend*) in October 1945, which featured a text by poet Walter Dehmel. Over a triumphant G-major march, singers proclaim, "We are the youth who want to rebuild what surrounds us crumbled in ruins."[64] The promise of rebuilding is nowhere to be heard, however, in his next song, "Fire in the Night," written in December 1945. Trapped among flames caused by aerial bombing, the narrator calls for help until the fire has extinguished itself at daybreak.[65] In looking both forward and backward, Höffer was caught between reliving the horror of the air war and his impetus to rebuild the fallen city.

Due to his activities under National Socialism, the Soviets barred the composer from returning to his position at the Hochschule. Along with musicologist Josef Rufer, Höffer decided instead to found the International Music Institute in Berlin Zehlendorf. The International Music Institute's main source of income was student tuition, although the Kunstamt-Zehlendorf and the American military government also contributed funds, sanctioning the institute because it promoted modern music supposedly free from the trappings of fascism and militarism. The institute aimed to support young composers, and the curriculum focused on modernists such as Bartók, Schoenberg, and Hindemith. In keeping with the postwar consensus that Nazi music was a quantifiable entity, Höffer and Rufer omitted music composed in fascist Germany from their courses, and students refrained from asking their teachers about their activities under National Socialism.

In 1948 when Hochschule director Bernhard Bennedik left Berlin, Höffer was offered the position and a chance to return to his former employer. Although the Hochschule was in the British sector, the Soviets had appointed Bennedik in 1945 before the other Allies had arrived. A founder of the Kulturbund, Bennedik soon proved immensely unpopular. Before Höffer accepted the directorship, however, the British military government asked him to stop participating in Kulturbund events, an indication of the increasing tension between the eastern and western sectors of the city. Shortly after assuming his new post, Höffer died unexpectedly in August 1949.[66]

Despite the number of composers who were writing rubble music, their contributions were not always well received by Berlin audiences. The 1947 festival, "Berlin Music Days" (*Berliner Musiktage*), featured works by Butting, Höffer, and Tiessen. Cosponsored by the Department of Volksbildung and the composer's section of the Freier Deutscher Gewerkschaftsbund (FDGW), the festival's aim was to unite composers across the city, bridging east-west and generational divides. Unfortunately for festival organizers, Berlin Music Days coincided with Wilhelm Furtwängler's first postwar performances in Berlin. The fledgling festival could not compete with the return of the city's most controversial musical personality, and the Berlin Music Days were terribly attended, doomed for oblivion. Furtwängler, meanwhile, had to return to the stage for seventeen curtain calls.[67]

In 1945, musical life was rubbled; by 1950, it was fragmented; and by 1961, it was divided. As Tiessen would note of East and West Berlin, "It's like living in foreign countries that are close together."[68] Negotiating the pitfalls of Allied cultural policies and the logistics of a divided city, Berlin's musicians found it impossible to create a cohesive musical culture that involved all sectors. With each superpower vying for the support of the city's musicians, their competition calcified the ideological leanings of Berlin's artists. While Tiessen and Höffer remained in the west, Butting and Schmidt became decorated composers of the German Democratic Republic. Each side of the city developed its own, distinct musical culture, fueled not only by the doctrines and policies of their respective occupiers but also by the musicians who resided there.

A genre that romanticized the ruins by recasting them as monuments to natural decay, this music was the controversial and conflicted sound of early postfascist Germany. Instead of the romantic artist-hero, then the postwar subject was the Brechtian antihero, the victim-perpetrator wondering through the ruined city. This music had often uncomfortable and competing aims: to document and to dramatize the final days of the war, to re-create in music the breadth of lived experience, and to give sonic space to German suffering that neither the Nazi regime nor the Cold War occupiers could permit. In a continuum of loss and death, it was Berliners who would emerge from the rubbled haze of Nazism and air raids. Rubble music could proclaim that it was the Germans who had suffered most of all. And who was left to contradict them?

Notes

1. Eberhard Schmidt Papers, Folder 513, "Mensch, nu stehste vor die Trümmer," Program Text by Otto Meyer, AdK.

2. For accounts that focus on denazification and reeducation, see in particular David Monod, *Settling Scores: German Music, Denazification, and the Americans, 1945–1953* (Chapel Hill: University of North Carolina Press, 2005); and Toby Thacker, *Music after Hitler, 1945–1955* (Farnham, UK: Ashgate, 2007). For more on the difficulties of ruin music making, see Brewster S. Chamberlin, *Kultur auf Trümmern: Berliner Berichte der amerikanischen Information Control Section Juli-Dezember 1945* (Stuttgart: Deutsche Verlags-Anstalt, 1979), 1–20; and Harald Kunz, ed., *Musikstadt Berlin zwischen Krieg und Frieden: Musikalische Bilanz einer Viermächtestadt* (Wiesbaden: Bote and Bock, 1956), 7–90.

3. Jean François Lyotard, *Heidegger and "the Jews,"* trans. Andreas Michel and Mark S. Roberts (Minneapolis: University of Minnesota Press, 1990), 43.

4. Jeffry Diefendorf, "The New City: German Urban Planning and the Zero Hour," in Geoffrey J. Giles, ed., *Stunde Null: The End and the Beginning Fifty Years Ago* (Washington, DC: German Historical Institute, 1997), 90.

5. Peter Jelavich, *Berlin Cabaret* (Cambridge, MA: Harvard University Press, 1993), 228–57.

6. Andrew Davis, *Sonata Fragments: Romantic Narratives in Chopin, Schumann, and Brahms* (Bloomington: Indiana University Press, 2017), 28.

7. Lydia Goehr, *Elective Affinities: Musical Essays on the History of Aesthetic Theory* (New York: Columbia University Press, 2008), 145–46. For more on *Ruinenwerttheorie*, see Albert Speer, *Erinnerungen* (Berlin: Propyläen, 1969), 55–56; and Benedict Anderson, *Buried City, Unearthing Teufelsberg: Berlin and Its Geography of Forgetting* (London: Routledge, 2017), 37–41.

8. Andreas Huyssen, "Nostalgia for Ruins," *Grey Room* 23 (Spring 2006): 6.

9. Svetlana Boym, "Ruinophilia: Appreciation of Ruins," http://monumenttotransformation.org/atlas-of-transformation/html/r/ruinophilia/ruinophilia-appreciation-of-ruins-svetlana-boym.html.

10. Quoted in Charles Rosen, *The Romantic Generation* (Cambridge, MA: Harvard University Press, 1995), 48.

11. Quoted in Michael S. Roth, ed., *Irresistible Decay: Ruins Reclaimed* (Los Angeles: Getty Research Institute for the History of Art and the Humanities, 1997), 72. For a further discussion of Schlegel's notion of the romantic fragment, see Davis, *Sonata Fragments*, 28.

12. Franz Schubert and Wilhelm Müller, "Der Leiermann," *Die Winterreise* (Leipzig: Breitkopf & Härtel, 1895). "Keiner mag ihn hören, keiner sieht ihn an."

13. Kenneth S. Whitton, *Dietrich Fischer-Dieskau Mastersinger: A Documented Study* (New York: Holmes and Meier, 1981), 27–31.

14. Walter Benjamin, *The Origins of German Tragic Drama*, trans. John Osborne (London: Verso, 1998), 178.

15. Max Butting, *Musikgeschichte, die ich miterlebte* (Berlin: Henschel, 1955), 265.

16. Ibid., 225–26.

17. Ibid., 225. For more on the November Group, see Elizabeth Janik, *Recomposing German Music: Politics and Musical Tradition in Cold War Berlin* (Leiden, the Netherlands: Brill, 2005), 50–51, 154.

18. Max Butting Papers, Folder 817, Joseph Haas Memorandum, December 12, 1945, AdK. See also Michael Kater, *The Twisted Muse: Musicians and Their Music in the Third Reich* (Oxford: Oxford University Press, 1997), 223.

19. Ibid., 231.

20. For more on the RMK, see Pamela M. Potter, *Art of Suppression: Confronting the Nazi Past in Histories of the Visual and Performing Arts* (Berkeley: University of California Press, 2016), 12. Concerning the FDGW, see Janik, *Recomposing German Music*, 105, 176, 237. Information on the Composer's Union can be found in Butting, *Musikgeschichte*, 232–33, and Elaine Kelly, *Composing the Canon in the German Democratic Republic: Narratives of Nineteenth-Century Music* (Oxford: Oxford University Press, 2014), 33. For more on Knepler and musicology in east and west Berlin, see Anne C. Shreffler, "Berlin Walls: Dalhaus, Knepler, and Ideologies of Music History," in *The Journal of Musicology* 20/4 (Fall 2003): 498–525.

21. Butting, *Musikgeschichte*, 230.

22. Max Butting Papers, Folder 817, Walter Stehr Memorandum, September 28, 1945, AdK. See also Butting, *Musikgeschichte*, 227–28; and Kater, *Twisted Muse*, 91.

23. Quoted in Anna Parkinson, *An Emotional State: The Politics of Emotion in Postwar West German Culture* (Ann Arbor: University of Michigan Press, 2015), 38. See also p. 56.

24. Dietrich Brennecke, *Das Lebenswerk Max Buttings* (Leipzig: VEB Deutscher Verlag, 1973), 138. See also Butting, *Musikgeschichte*, 228. The unpublished score for Butting's *The Guilt* can be found in the Max Butting Papers, Folder 117, AdK.

25. Parkinson, *An Emotional State*, 56–57. Although Jaspers claimed he and Gertrud immigrated in opposition to postwar anti-Semitism, there is little doubt his public stance on German guilt had made his continued presence in Heidelberg untenable.

26. Brennecke, *Das Lebenswerk Max Buttings*, 137.

27. Max Butting, "Der dumme Luda," op. 49, no. 2, from *Drei Spottlieder*, score, 1946, Max Butting Papers, Folder 115, AdK. "Trinkt man Schnaps nun wieda klar zu sein, hat man schnell versauft den lebten Schein."

28. Max Butting, "Die Wut," op. 49, no. 1, from *Drei Spottlieder*, score, 1946, Max Butting Papers, Folder 115, AdK. "Und das Volk? Es halt die Schnauze, halt die Schnauze, bestenfalls enttrümmert es."

29. Max Butting, "Die 18 Tage," score, 1946, Max Butting Papers, Folder 116, AdK. "Leichen liegen auf der Straße, – unter Trümmern, – schwimmen in den U-Bahn-Schächten,

hängen an den Bäumen als ein Festschmuck, so wie Mond und Sonne in den Wolken stehn als düster-rote, schmutzige Lampions." See also Butting, *Musikgeschichte*, 228.

30. Quoted in Brennecke, *Das Lebenswerk Max Buttings*, 139.

31. Quoted in Ronald Taylor, *Berlin and Its Culture: A Historical Portrait* (New Haven, CT: Yale University Press, 1997), 204.

32. Siegfried was the former chief of surgery at the Municipal Hospital in central Berlin (Mitte). "Siegfried Ostrowski," http://aerzte.erez-israel.de/ostrowski/; Sigfried Ostrowski, "Vom Schicksal jüdischer Ärzte im Dritten Reich," *Bulletin of the Leo Baeck Institute* 6, no. 24 (1963): 313–51.

33. Max Butting, "Der Fluch," *Lieder aus Berlin: Fünf ernste Lieder* (Halle: Mitteldeutscher Verlag, 1949). "Verschwinden die Trümmer, der Fluch kann nicht bleiben, in die neuen Häuser geht er nicht ein."

34. Franz Schubert and Wilhelm Müller, "Der Lindenbaum," in *Die Winterreise* (Leipzig: Breitkopf & Härtel, 1895). For more on the concept of memory in *der Lindenbaum*, see Jürgen Thym, "Song as Memory, Memory as Song," *Archiv für Musikwissenschaft* 69 (2012): 263–73. (*Der Lindenbaum* is discussed on pages 266–68.)

35. Butting, "Der Friede (am Hundekehler See)," in *Lieder aus Berlin*. "Die Wahrheit schien so unsagbar gemein."

36. Max Butting, "Eine Nacht," *Lieder aus Berlin*. "Mein Herz hat wohl sehr laut geschlagen, weil das Unheimliche der Stunde fast zu schwer ist, um es zu tragen."

37. Butting, *Musikgeschichte*, 260.

38. Eberhard Schmidt, *Ein Lied—ein Atemzug: Erinnerungen und Dokumente*, ed. Manfred Machlitt (Berlin: Verlag Neue Musik, 1987), 167, 169.

39. Ibid., 138.

40. "Fragen zur Zeit nach 1945," Eberhard Schmidt Papers, Folder 457, and Folder 560, AdK. See also Schmidt, *Ein Lied—ein Atemzug*, 106–14, 124–26, 131–33, and 141. For more on both Schmidt and Eppstein, see Juliane Brauer, "Eberhard Schmidt" and "Cora Eppstein," *Lexikon verfolgter Musiker und Musikerinnen der NS-Zeit*, University of Hamburg. Concerning Eppstein's death, see "Cora-Eppstein-Platz: Stadt Saarbrücken würdigt Nazi-Gegnerin," May 24, 2016, http://www.saarbruecker-zeitung.de.

41. Eberhard Schmidt Papers, Folder 513, AdK.

42. For more on Eva Fritzsche, see Ines Walk, "Eva Fritzsche," *DEFA Stiftung*, http://www.defa-stiftung.de/DesktopDefault.aspx?TabID=852.

43. Eberhard Schmidt, "Erinnerung 1945: Aus war der Krieg," score, 1945, text by Eva Fritzsche, Eberhard Schmidt Papers, Folder 79, AdK; and Schmidt, *Ein Lied—ein Atemzug*, 146.

44. Schmidt, *Ein Lied—ein Atemzug*, 147–52. In 1947, Fritzsche accepted a position with the DEFA, while Schmidt focused on his freelance career. The couple married in 1950.

45. Heinz Tiessen, *Mein Leben bis 1945*, Heinz Tiessen Papers, Folder 1568, AdK, 28.

46. Harry Waibel, *Diener vieler Herren: Ehemalige NS-Funktionäre in der SBZ/DDR* (Frankfurt: Peter Lang, 2011), 341.

47. Tiessen, *Mein Leben bis 1945*, 30.

48. "Wie sollen wir aufbauen?," Interview with Professor Heinz Tiessen, *Melos: Zeitschrift für neue Musik*, November 1946, 16; Wallner-Basté, "Betrifft: Musikabteilung: Aus den Akten des Kulturamts Zehlendorf," *Musikstadt Berlin zwischen Krieg und Frieden*, 18; and Wallner-Basté to Tiessen, July 19, 1945, Heinz Tiessen Papers, Folder 3.1.1498, AdK. In the 1960s, the Stern Conservatory merged with Hochschule für Musik (West Berlin) to create the Berlin State School of Music and the Performing Arts and was eventually renamed the Berlin University of the Arts (Universität der Künste) in 2001.

49. "Wie sollen wir aufbauen?," 16.

50. Rebecca Rovit, *The Jewish Kulturbund Theatre Company in Nazi Berlin: Studies in Theatre History and Culture* (Iowa City: University of Iowa Press, 2012), 24.

51. Klabund, *Irene oder die Gesinnung, Ein Gesang von Klabund* (Berlin: Eric Reiss, 1918), 24–25; Matthias Konzett, *Encyclopedia of German Literature* (Chicago: Routledge, 2000), 585–86; Heinz Tiessen, "Heimkehr," 1945, score, Heinz Tiessen Papers, Folder 1.85.223, AdK.

52. Tiessen's op. 54, no. 1, *Do It Today* ("Tue es noch heut") with a text by Walter Dehmel, and "The Way of the World," *Weltlauf*, op. 54, no. 2 with a text by Heine, are both four-part choral settings.

53. Theodor Adorno, "Mahler," in *Quasi una Fantasia: Essays on Modern Music*, trans. Rodney Livingstone (London: Verso, 1998), 89.

54. Heinz Tiessen, "Weltlauf," *Drei Lieder nach Gedichten von Heinrich Heine und Julius Bab für Sopran und Klavier*, op. 55 (Dresden: Dresdener Verlagsgesellschaft, 1950). "Wenn du gar nichts hast, ach so lasse dich begraben – Denn dein Recht zum Leben, Lump, haben nur die etwas haben." Translation from Jay Howard Geller, *The Other Jewish Question: Identifying the Jew and Making Sense of Modernity* (New York: Fordham University Press, 2011), 382.

55. See Henry Friedlander, *The Origins of Nazi Genocide: From Euthanasia to the Final Solution* (Chapel Hill: University of North Carolina Press, 1995), 111–50, 216.

56. Julius Bab, *Menschenstimme: Gedichte aus der Kriegszeit, 1914–1918* (Stettin: Norddeutscher Verlag für Literatur und Kunst, 1920), 71. ". . . durch die wir wurden und sind."

57. Henrich Heine, "Prolog," in *Anthea: Poems and Translations*, trans. William Stigand (London: Kegan Paul, Trench, Trübner, 1907), 304.

58. Janik, *Recomposing German Music*, 204; and Heinz Tiessen to Herr Schermall, October 10, 1950, Heinz Tiessen Papers, Folder 1493, AdK.

59. Heinz Tiessen to Joachim Tiburtius, March 20, 1957, Heinz Tiessen Papers, Folder 1491, AdK.

60. Sergiu Celibidache, *Complete RIAS Recordings* (1948–1957), Audite, 2011, compact disc; Celibidache, *The Berlin Recordings* (1945–47), Audite, 2013, compact disc; and Dietrich Fischer-Dieskau, *Stilwandlungen des Klavierliedes (1850–1950)*, EMI Classics, 2000, compact disc.

61. Kater, *Twisted Muse*, 187; and Stefan Jena, "Dabeisein ist Alles: Die Musik zu den Olympischen Spielen 1936 in Berlin," *Studien zur Musikwissenschaft* 56 (2010): 282.

62. Paul Höffer, "Toccata," score, 1945, Paul Höffer Papers, Carton 21, Folder 5, Staatsbibliothek, Berlin. "Unter Schmerzen geboren, 15.4.45."

63. "Aus den Tägebüchern, 1933–1945," April 22, 1945, Heinz Tiessen Papers, Folder 3166, AdK.

64. Paul Höffer, "Lied der neuen Jugend," score, 1945, Paul Höffer Papers, Carton 21, Folder 2, Staatsbibliothek, Berlin. "Wir sind die Jungend, die aufbauen wollen, was uns in Trümmer zerfallen umringt."

65. Paul Höffer, "Feuer in der Nacht," score, 1945, Paul Höffer Papers, Carton 21, Folder 7, Staatsbibliothek, Berlin.

66. Janik, *Recomposing German Music*, 124, 174, 204; David Pike, *The Politics of Culture in Soviet Occupied Germany, 1945–1949* (Stanford, CA: Stanford University Press, 1992), 324; Thacker, *Music after Hitler*, 35; Amy C. Beal, *New Music, New Allies: American Experimental Music from the Zero Hour to Reunification* (Berkeley: University of California Press, 2006), 38–41; and Christine Fischer-Defoy, ed., *Kunst, im Aufbau ein Stein: Die Westberliner*

Kunst- und Musikhochschulen im Spannungsfeld der Nachkriegszeit (Berlin: Hochschule der Künste, 2001), 309–18.

    67. Janik, *Recomposing German Music*, 153; Hans Heinz Stuckenschmidt, "Spieler oder Werk? Zweites Furtwängler-Konzert und Neue Musik," *Neue Zeitung*, June 3, 1947; and "Furtwängler wieder in Berlin," *Frankfurter Neue Presse* May 5, 1947.

    68. Quoted in Janik, *Recomposing German Music*, 209.

CONCLUSION

In the end, musicians and composers were not unlike the urban planners and architects who worked to find a cohesive narrative of German reconstruction. In a 1946 Berlin lecture, Hans Scharoun, future architect of the Philharmonic's new concert hall at Potsdamer Platz (completed in 1963), discussed Germany's urban destruction. Scharoun noted that the "ruptured city form," ultimately "gives us the possibility to design an urban landscape" to "compose that which is overwhelming and scaleless into manageable and proportional parts."[1] Scharoun's emphasis on the possibilities of form and structure, and the ability "to compose," literally, a postwar cityscape, overtly links the *Stadtlandschaft* (urban landscape) and *Kulturlandschaft* (cultural landscape). Across Germany, musicians and architects reconstructed musical and structural forms over the rubble of the old. As Emily Richmond Pollock notes in her work on the meticulous reconstruction of Munich's National Theater, bombed in 1943 but painstakingly rebuilt in 1959 to look like its nineteenth-century predecessor, German officials opted for a return to, rather than a break from, tradition. These decisions had far-reaching implications for the city's conservative musical culture and its relationship to National Socialism, raising difficult questions concerning cultural amnesia and civilian suffering.[2]

The legacies of rubble music did not end in 1950s Germany. With Allied funding and vested ideological interests in all four sectors of Berlin, the politicization of musical organizations only intensified. By 1949, all large-scale musical institutions were firmly entrenched geographically and, by default, along occupation borders. Despite these divisions, in East and West Berlin, notions about German victimhood and civilian suffering persisted in both private and public spheres. Just as Robert G. Moeller and Frank Biess have shown that notions of German victimhood shaped the fledgling Federal Republic and German Democratic Republic, so, too, did these narratives leave an audible mark on the musical cultures of East and West Germany.[3] Institutional programming and leadership decisions reflected the difficult compromises that the Berlin Philharmonic, Städtische Oper, and Staatsoper made within their ranks and with the occupiers to continue performing.

The shortcomings of the denazification process plagued the Philharmonic in the ensuing postwar years. In 1952, Wilhelm Furtwängler was renamed the Philharmonic's director for life, a position he held until his death two years later. Even though Herbert von Karajan had performed with the orchestra a total of only four times, in December 1954 the ensemble voted to appoint Karajan to be their new conductor, effectively terminating Sergiu Celibidache's contract. A former Nazi Party member (in fact, the conductor had joined twice, once in Salzburg and again in Ulm during the 1930s), Karajan's selection was riddled with controversy.[4] The orchestra was only six weeks away from embarking on a concert tour of the United States, meant to be a show of gratitude for the Americans' efforts during the Berlin Blockade. The Philharmonic's Intendant, Gerhart von Westerman, believed the orchestra's new conductor would have to be someone of whom Columbia Artists Management, the ensemble's New York presenter, would approve. Because the agency, in Westerman's estimation, "expects us to appear with a German conductor at the helm,"[5] he felt Karajan was a better choice than Celibidache. Karajan's presence drew protests and controversy in New York outside of Carnegie Hall, but his performances were praised for their artistry by critics and audiences. He remained the Philharmonic's chief conductor and artistic director until 1989.[6]

As the city's sectors moved further apart politically, the opera houses of East and West also had little choice but to make their respective compromises. While the Communist Party believed the Staatsoper to be a vital cultural institution for the burgeoning East German state, the Städtische Oper aimed to resurrect the country's musical traditions from the ruins of the Third Reich. Even though both opera houses sought to produce antifascist operas, they pursued this goal by radically different and often contradictory means. In West Berlin, this meant premiering new work by German composers, such as Werner Egk, even if they had already been highly successful under National Socialism, or staging prewar repertory to maintain links with the German musical past. Beethoven's *Fidelio* became a signature of the Städtische Oper.

In the East, the struggle for operatic socialist realism dominated critical and popular discourses, as tensions came to a head between artists who had spent the war years in Moscow, a concentration camp, or the West.[7] Most East German Communist Party leaders (Sozialistische Einheitspartei Deutschlands, SED) were prewar KPD members (German Communist Party), newly returned to Berlin from Russia, with little sympathy for artists like Bertolt Brecht, Hanns Eisler, Paul Dessau, or Staatsoper intendant Ernst Legal, who had spent the war years either in the United States or in Nazi Germany. Tägliche Rundschau, the party organ of the SED, criticized the Staatsoper and Legal in a blistering 1950 article, deeming the house's productions to be "alien to the Volk" and calling on authorities "to stop the reign of shadows on the stage of the Berlin Staatsoper," due to "a handful of untalented mystics and formalists that have crept into the management."[8]

The conflict culminated in a scandal over the premiere of Brecht and Dessau's 1951 opera, *Das Verhör des Lukullus* (The Trial of Lucullus), as SED leaders suppressed the work for what they perceived as its formalist tendencies and inaccessibility. Ernst Legal would be forced to resign at the Staatsoper shortly thereafter for his support of the contentious *Lukullus* premiere, and that same year, Frida Leider resigned to focus on her teaching at the Hochschule für Musik.[9]

Aside from institutional reconstruction, programming, and personnel decisions of the city's ensembles, the complex legacies of rubble music were also heard in compositional choices and alternative performance practices across postwar Germany. These aesthetic decisions reflected the disillusionment of a postwar period bereft of redemption and closure, and drew attention to the lingering resonances of war's trauma as a younger generation of musicians came of age. In selected works of these avant-garde composers, we can hear traces of the ruin musical aesthetic instead of the Darmstadt School's insistence on a bold, uncompromising new start.[10]

These pieces directly reference the air war and bodily infirmity. A teenaged Karlheinz Stockhausen spent the war working at a Wehrmacht field hospital, tending to soldiers struck by Allied incendiary bombs. This grisly, grim work left a marked impression on him, and a number of his postwar compositions make direct reference to the composer's wartime traumas. As Jane Fulcher has compellingly demonstrated, Stockhausen's seminal electronic work, *Gesang der Jünglinge* (Song of the Youths) (1955–56), was the composer's response to these experiences. With a narrative from the Book of Daniel, which describes three Jewish men surviving trial by fire, Stockhausen later wrote that he was himself "a youth in the fiery furnace."[11] Yet the enigmatic composer did not elaborate on the obvious and troubling parallels between this furnace and death camp crematoriums. Was he fashioning himself as a victim, equating his suffering with those who had perished in the Holocaust? Or was the furnace an allegory for urban Germany in flames from Allied bombs? The cacophony of sonic wartime experience is also heard in Stockhausen's 1968 *Short Waves* (*Kurzwellen*) and the "Oktophonie" of the composer's monumental opera cycle *Licht* (1977–2003), which featured an 8-track tape simulating the explosions, crashes, and bombs of the air war.[12]

Alexander Kluge and Ben Lerner have argued the air war also informs a contemporary performance of John Cage's *As Slow as Possible* in Halberstadt, Germany. American bombers leveled Halberstadt in April 1945, leaving behind some 1.5 million cubic meters of rubble.[13] The city's St. Burchardi Church, itself a ruin, has hosted a performance of Cage's piece since 2001 when a specially installed organ began the composition with a rest of seventeen months. With *As Slow as Possible* set to conclude in 2640, its tones are reminiscent of the once ubiquitous sound of the air raid siren in Nazi Germany, a warning signal that vibrated between 300 and 400 Hz.

Suffering and bodily ruin can be heard in the work of still other postwar composers. Bernd Alois Zimmermann's service on the Eastern Front as a reluctant Wehrmacht soldier informed his opera *Die Soldaten* (The Soldiers) (1957–64), which combines diverse influences from Germany's rich musical past, such as Bach chorales and twelve-tone rows. Iannis Xenakis's experiences as a member of the Greek Resistance and bodily injuries sustained during the ensuing Greek Civil War can be heard through the jet engines and crashes of *Diamorphoses* (1957).[14] Whether these works by Stockhausen, Zimmermann, Xenakis, and Cage serve as first- or secondhand witness to aerial bombing or armed combat, they are united by their explorations of physical and psychological trauma—the unresolved rubble of the war's violence and destruction.

Aside from these musical scores, performances in Germany from the latter twentieth- and beginning of the twenty-first century also made use of urban ruin and decay, ruminating on the legacies of the Allied air war in myriad ways. Thousands of bunkers and air raid shelters remained after World War II, and across urban Germany, these spaces were repurposed because the cost and time to destroy them exceeded available material resources. More recently, these spaces have become music venues, such as Berlin's Artist Homes initiative, a Hohenzollerndamm bunker converted to gallery space, a concert hall, and practice rooms.[15] One tower of Hamburg's Heiligengeistfeld bunker serves as a popular music venue for bands (Übel und Gefährlich); in Aachen, the Goffartstraße bunker became a music club; and in Cologne, the massive bunker on Berliner Straße is now known as Culture Bunker Cologne, staging dance, music, theater, and comedy events.[16] Structures once used to shelter and defend the people's community are now the repurposed spaces of the air war—their permanent concrete walls standing in stark contrast to the ephemerality of musical performance.

In the postwar period, institutions, musicians, and composers blurred the distinctions between the romantic sublime and the ruinous terrain of aerial warfare by transforming rubble into ruins. The rubble wanderer and the ruin flaneur became one and the same, traversing the capital in contemplation of German suffering, however self-inflicted, however self-imposed. As eyewitness and "earwitness"[17] accounts, musical scores, and archival documents reveal, music, as "the most German of the arts,"[18] played an indispensable part of this narrative. The uniquely sonic possibilities of wartime rubble, in both the acoustic and performative senses, resonated for decades to come.

Notes

1. Hans Scharoun, lecture, September 5, 1946, in *Hans Scharoun: Bauten, Entwürfe, Texte*, ed. P. Pfankuch (Berlin: Akademie der Künste, 1974), 158. See also Francesca Rogier, "The Monumentality of Rhetoric," in Sarah Williams Goldhagen and Réjean Legault, eds., *Anxious Modernisms: Experimentation in Postwar Architectural Culture* (Cambridge, MA: MIT Press, 2000), 167.

2. Emily Richmond Pollock, "Pride of Place: The 1963 Rebuilding of the Munich Nationaltheater," in *Dreams of Germany: Music and (Trans)national Imaginaries*, ed. Neil Gregor and Tom Irvine (New York: Berghahn Books, 2019), 145–68.

3. See Robert G. Moeller, *War Stories: The Search for a Usable Past in the Federal Republic of Germany* (Berkeley: University of California Press, 2003); Robert G. Moeller, "Germans as Victims? Thoughts on a Post–Cold War History of WWII's Legacies," *History and Memory* 17, no. 1/2 (Spring/Summer 2005): 147–94; and Frank Biess, *Homecomings: Returning POWs and the Legacies of Defeat in Postwar Germany* (Princeton, NJ: Princeton University Press, 2006), 1–16, 43–69.

4. Klaus Lang, *Celibidache und Furtwängler: Der große philharmonische Konflikt in der Berliner Nachkriegszeit* (Munich: Wissner, 2010), 389; and Michael Kater, *The Twisted Muse: Musicians and Their Music in the Third Reich* (Oxford: Oxford University Press, 1997), 58–64. Karajan joined the Nazi Party in 1933 while living in Salzburg, where he quickly became a rising star. When he relocated to Ulm in 1935, he joined the party once again.

5. Quoted in Susanne Stähr, "Epochenwechsel mit Herbert von Karajan," in *Variationen mit Orchester: 125 Jahre Berliner Philharmoniker*, ed. Gerhard Forck (Berlin: Henschel, 2007), 1:269.

6. See "Musicians Oppose Concert Here by 'Nazi-Led' Berlin Orchestra," *New York Times*, 20 February 1955; and Howard Taubman, "Touchy Problem: Question of Art and Politics is Raised anew by Berlin Philharmonic Visit," *New York Times*, March 6, 1955.

7. Elaine Kelly, *Composing the Canon in the German Democratic Republic: Narratives of Nineteenth-Century Music* (Oxford: Oxford University Press, 2014), 3–17; and Joy H. Calico,

"The Politics of Opera in the German Democratic Republic, 1945–1961" (PhD diss., Duke University, 1999), 1–47.

8. Quoted in Calico, "The Politics of Opera," 34. From "Das Reich der Schatten auf der Bühne," *Tägliche Rundschau*, November 19, 1950.

9. Frida Leider, *Playing My Part, 1888–1975* (New York: Da Capo, 1959), 209–10; Joy H. Calico, *Brecht at the Opera* (Berkeley: University of California Press, 2008), 109–22; Calico, "The Politics of Opera," 29–36. The opera was renamed *Die Verurteilung des Lukullus* (The Condemnation of Lucullus).

10. My thanks to Annegret Fauser for a recent conversation at the 2016 American Musicological Society in which we discussed Darmstadt's relation to rubble music.

11. Quoted in John Smalley, "Gesang der Jünglinge: History and Analysis," Program Notes, Masterpieces of 20th-Century Electronic Music, Lincoln Center, New York, 2000. See also Jane F. Fulcher, "From 'The Voice of the Maréchal' to Musique Concrète: Pierre Schaeffer and the Case for Cultural History," in *The Oxford Handbook of the New Cultural History of Music*, ed. Jane F. Fulcher (Oxford: Oxford University Press, 2011), 381–402.

12. Alex Ross, *The Rest Is Noise: Listening to the Twentieth Century* (New York: Farrar, Straus and Giroux, 2007), 344; and Robin Maconie, *Other Planets: The Complete Works of Karlheinz Stockhausen* (Lanham, MD: Rowman and Littlefield, 2016), 374.

13. To listen to Cage's *As Slow as Possible*, visit "Organ^2/ASLSP," at http://www.aslsp.org/de/. Kluge and Lerner discussed Cage's piece at a joint lecture at Princeton University: "The Sky Stops Painting and Turns to Criticism," Lecture and Reading, Princeton, NJ, October 21, 2016. For more on Halberstadt's destruction, see Alexander Kluge, *Air Raid* (London: UK Seagull Books, 2012) and Helmut Puff, *Miniature Monuments: Modeling German History* (Berlin: de Gruyter, 2014), 223–28. Concerning air raid sirens more generally, see Jörg Friedrich, *The Fire: The Bombing of Germany*, trans. Allison Brown (New York: Columbia University Press, 2006), 328.

14. Richard Taruskin, *Music in the Late Twentieth Century: The Oxford History of Western Music* (Oxford: Oxford University Press, 2005), 189.

15. For more on the bunker, see "Artist Homes: Der Bunker," http://www.artist-homes.com/; "Der Kulturbunker vom Roseneck," *Der Tagesspiegel*, February 17, 2017, http://www.tagesspiegel.de/berlin/bezirke/charlottenburg-wilmersdorf/berlin-schmargendorf-der-kulturbunker-vom-roseneck/19404612.html.

16. Concerning acoustic memories of the air war, see Robert Maier's edited volume, *Akustisches Gedächtnis und Zweiter Weltkrieg* (Göttingen: V&R Unipress, 2011). For further information concerning bunkers and their postwar afterlives, see Elke Purpus, Günther B. Sellen, Walter Geis, and Helmut Buchen, eds., *Bunker in Köln—Versuche einer Sichtbar-Machung* (Essen, Germany: Klartext, 2006); Michael Foedrowitz, *Bunkerwelten: Luftschutzanlagen in Norddeutschland* (Berlin: Ch. Links Verlag, 1998); and Helga Schmal and Tobias Selke, *Bunker: Luftschutz und Luftschutzbau in Hamburg* (Hamburg: Christians, 2001).

17. Carolyn Birdsall uses "earwitness" to write about civilians whose accounts of fascism are marked by the sonoric experience of sirens and bombings rather than visual destruction. Birdsall's term comes, in part, from the Elias Canetti short story, *Der Ohrenzeuge* (The Earwitness), in which the title character wants to indict individuals with sonic, rather than visual, evidence. Carolyn Birdsall, *Nazi Soundscapes: Sound, Technology and Urban Space in Germany, 1933–1945* (Amsterdam: Amsterdam University Press, 2012), 11.

18. Thomas Mann, *The Story of a Novel: The Genesis of Doctor Faustus*, trans. Richard Winston and Clara Winston (New York: Knopf, 1961), 123.

BIBLIOGRAPHY

Adorno, Theodor. *Essays on Music.* Edited by Richard Leppert. Translated by Susan Gillespie. Berkeley: University of California Press, 2002.
———. "Mahler." In *Quasi una Fantasia: Essays on Modern Music*, translated by Rodney Livingstone, 81–110. London: Verso, 1998.
———. "Wagner's Relevance for Today." Translated by Susan Gillespie. In *Grand Street* no. 44 (1993): 32–59.
———. "What National Socialism Has Done to the Arts." In Leppert, *Essays on Music*, 373–390.
Agop, Rolf. *Lex mihi ars: Nachdenkliche und kuriose Begegnungen mit großen Musikern.* Siegen, Germany: Kalliope, 1985.
Allied Forces, Supreme Headquarters. *Manual for the Control of German Information Service.* May 12, 1945.
Altner, Helmut. *Berlin Dance of Death.* Translated by Tony Le Tissier. Havertown, PA: Casemate, 2002.
Anderson, Benedict. *Buried City, Unearthing Teufelsberg: Berlin and Its Geography of Forgetting.* London: Routledge, 2017.
———. *Imagined Communities: Reflections on the Origin and Spread of Nationalism.* London: Verso, 1983.
Andreas-Friedrich, Ruth. *Battleground Berlin: Diaries, 1945–1948.* New York: Paragon House, 1984.
———. *Berlin Underground, 1938–1945.* Translated by Barrow Mussey. New York: Henry Holt, 1947.
Anonymous. *A Woman in Berlin: Eight Weeks in the Conquered City.* Translated by Philip Boehm. New York: Metropolitan Books, 2005.
Apel, Dora. *Beautiful Terrible Ruins: Detroit and the Anxiety of Decline.* New Brunswick, NJ: Rutgers University Press, 2015.
"Arche Nora läuft vom Stapel." *Der Spiegel*, July 19, 1947.
Arendt, Hannah. "The Aftermath of Nazi Rule: Report from Germany." *Commentary*, October 1, 1950.
Arnold, Dietmar, and Reiner Janick, eds. *Sirenen und gepackte Koffer: Bunkeralltag in Berlin.* Berlin: Ch. Links, 2003.
Aster, Misha. *Das Reichsorchester: Die Berliner Philharmoniker und der Nationalsozialismus.* Munich: Siedler, 2007.
Baaden, James. "Cantor Jakob Dymont and His Friday Night Service, Berlin 1934: Part I—A Rabbi's Observations." *Journal of Synagogue Music* 31 (Fall 2016): 95–96.
Bab, Julius. *Menschenstimme: Gedichte aus der Kriegszeit, 1914–1918.* Stettin: Norddeutscher Verlag für Literatur und Kunst, 1920.
Bance, Alan, ed. *The Cultural Legacy of the British Occupation in Germany.* The London Symposium. Stuttgarter Arbeiten zur Germanistik. Stuttgart: Hans-Dieter Heinz, 1997.
Baruch, Gerth-Wolfgang. "Der deutsche Rundfunk." *Melos*, January 1947, 69–72.

Baruma, Ian. *Zero Hour: A History of 1945*. New York: Penguin, 2013.
Beal, Amy C. *New Music, New Allies: American Experimental Music from the Zero Hour to Reunification*. Berkeley: University of California Press, 2006.
———. "The Army, the Airwaves, and the Avant-Garde: American Classical Music in Postwar West Germany." *American Music* 21, no. 4 (Winter 2003): 474–513.
Becher, Johannes R. "Ansprache von Johannes R. Becher." In *Gründungskundgebung des Kulturbundes zur demokratischen Erneuerung Deutschlands*, 32–40. Berlin: Aufbau, 1945.
Beevor, Anthony. *The Fall of Berlin 1945*. New York: Penguin, 2003.
Below, Nicolaus von. *At Hitler's Side: The Memoirs of Hitler's Luftwaffe Adjutant, 1937–1945*. London: Greenhill Books, 2001.
Benda, Hans von. "Phoenix aus der Asche." *Tagesspiegel*, May 16, 1965.
Benjamin, Walter. *The Origins of German Tragic Drama*. Translated by John Osborne. London: Verso, 1998.
Benz, Wolfgang. *Dachau and the Nazi Terror, 1933–1945*, vol. 1. Dachau: Dachauer Hefte, 2002.
Berger, Erna. *Auf Flügeln des Gesanges: Erinnerungen einer Sängerin*. Zurich: Atlantis, 1998.
Berghahn, Volker R. *America and the Intellectual Cold Wars in Europe: Shepard Stone between Philanthropy, Academy, and Diplomacy*. Princeton, NJ: Princeton University Press, 2001.
Beveridge, William Henry. *An Urgent Message from Germany*. London: Pilot Press, 1946.
Biess, Frank. *Homecomings: Returning POWs and the Legacies of Defeat in Postwar Germany*. Princeton, NJ: Princeton University Press, 2006.
Birdsall, Carolyn. *Nazi Soundscapes: Sound, Technology and Urban Space in Germany, 1933–1945*. Amsterdam: Amsterdam University Press, 2012.
Bitter, John. *What Dreams May Come*. Miami: Charlton, 1999.
Black, Monica. *Death in Berlin: From Weimar to Divided Germany*. Cambridge: Cambridge University Press, 2010.
"Blick in die Zeit." *Melos*, April 1947: 175.
Blomann, Ulrich J. "A Semblance of Freedom: Karl Amadeus Hartmann Between Democratic Renewal and Cold War, 1945-47." Translated by Jürgen Thym. *Twentieth-Century Music* 9/1-2 (March 2012): 143–159.
Böll, Heinrich. "In Defense of 'Rubble Literature' (1952)." In *Missing Persons and Other Essays*. Translated by Leila Vennewitz. Evanston, IL: Northwestern University Press, 1994.
Bohlman, Philip. "Afterward: The Beginning of the End: Moments of Represence in Post-Holocaust Germany," in *Dislocated Memories: Jews, Music, and Postwar German Culture*, edited by Tina Frühauf and Lily Hirsch, 265–276. Oxford: Oxford University Press, 2014.
Born, Georgina. "Afterword: Music Policy, Aesthetic and Social Difference." In *Rock and Popular Music: Politics, Policies, Institutions*, edited by Tony Bennett, Simon Frith, and Lawrence Grossberg, 265–290. London: Routledge, 1993.
———, ed. *Music, Sound, and Space: Transformations of Public and Private Experience*. Cambridge: Cambridge University Press, 2013.
Borris, Siegfried. *Über Wesen und Werden der neuen Musik in Deutschland: Vom Expressionismus zum Vitalismus. Beiträge zu einer neuen Musikkunde*. Berlin: A. Steffan, 1948.
Botstein, Leon. "After Fifty Years: Thoughts on Music and the End of World War II." *The Musical Quarterly* 79/2 (Summer 1995): 225–30.

Boym, Svetlana. *The Future of Nostalgia*. New York: Basic Books, 2001.
Brennecke, Dietrich. *Das Lebenswerk Max Buttings*. Akademie der Künste der DDR. Leipzig: VEB, 1973.
Brenner, Michael. *After the Holocaust: Rebuilding Jewish Lives in Postwar Germany*. Princeton, NJ: Princeton University Press, 1999.
Brett-Smith, Richard. *Berlin '45: The Grey City*. London: Macmillan, 1967.
Brockmann, Stephen. *A Critical History of German Film*. Rochester, NY: Camden House, 2011.
———. *German Literary Culture at the Zero Hour*. Rochester, NY: Camden House, 2004.
———. "German Literature, Year Zero: Writers and Politics, 1945–1953." In *Stunde Null: The End and the Beginning Fifty Years Ago*, edited by Geoffrey J. Giles, 59–74. Washington, DC: German Historical Institute, 1997.
Bröger, Friedrich, ed. *Städtische Bühnen Nürnberg: 50 Jahre Opernhaus*. Nuremberg: Städtische Bühnen Nürnberg-Fürth, 1955.
Browne, Donald Roger. "The History and Programming Policies of RIAS: Radio in the American Sector (of Berlin)." PhD Diss., University of Michigan, 1961.
Buch, Esteban. *Beethoven's Ninth: A Political History*. Chicago: University of Chicago Press, 2003.
Burton, Humphrey. *Menuhin: A Life*. London: Faber and Faber, 2000.
Busch, Fritz. *Pages from a Musician's Life*. Westport, CT: Greenwood, 1971.
Butting, Max. *Lieder aus Berlin: Fünf ernste Lieder*. Halle: Mitteldeutscher, 1949.
———. *Musikgeschichte, die ich miterlebte*. Berlin: Henschel, 1955.
Byford-Jones, W. *Berlin Twilight*. London: Hutchinson, 1947.
Calico, Joy H. *Arnold Schoenberg's* A Survivor from Warsaw *in Postwar Europe*. Berkeley: University of California Press, 2014.
———. *Brecht at the Opera*. Berkeley: University of California Press, 2008.
———. "*Jüdische Chronik*: The Third Space of Commemoration between East and West Germany." *Musical Quarterly* 88, no. 1 (Spring 2005): 95–122.
———. "The Politics of Opera in the German Democratic Republic, 1945–1961," PhD diss., Duke University, 1999.
Campion, Corey J. "Negotiating Difference: French and American Cultural Occupation Policies and German Expectations, 1945–1949." PhD diss., Georgetown University, 2010.
Cannon, Alex. "Tradition, Still Remains: Sustainability through Ruin in Vietnamese Music for Diversion." *Ethnomusicology Forum* 25/2 (2016): 146–171.
Carnegy, Patrick. *Wagner and the Art of the Theatre*. New Haven, CT: Yale University Press, 2006.
Celibidache, Sergiu. *The Berlin Recordings, 1945–47*. Audite, 2013.
Chamberlin, Brewster S. *Kultur auf Trümmern: Berliner Berichte der amerikanischen Information Control Section Juli-Dezember 1945*. Stuttgart: Deutsche Verlags-Anstalt, 1979.
Clare, George. *Before the Wall: Berlin Days, 1946–1948*. New York: E. P. Dutton, 1990.
———. *Berlin Days*. London: Papermac, 1994.
Clemens, Gabriele. *Britische Kulturpolitik in Deutschland 1945–1949: Literatur, Film, Musik und Theater*. Stuttgart: Franz Steiner, 1997.
Cox, Christoph, and Daniel Warner, eds. *Audio Culture: Readings in Modern Music*. New York: Bloomsbury, 2017.

Cramer, Heinz von. "John Bitter im Haus der Kultur." *Berlin am Mittag*, July 12, 1947.
Crew, David F. *Bodies and Ruins: Imaging the Bombing of Germany, 1945 to the Present.* Ann Arbor: University of Michigan Press, 2017.
Currid, Brian. *A National Acoustics: Music and Mass Publicity in Weimar and Nazi Germany.* Minneapolis: University of Minnesota Press, 2006.
Cuomo, Glenn, ed. *National Socialist Cultural Policy.* New York: St. Martin's Press, 1995.
Dallas, Gregor. *1945: The War that Never Ended.* New Haven, CT: Yale University Press, 2005.
"Das Reich der Schatten auf der Bühne." *Tägliche Rundschau*, November 19, 1950.
Davidson, Eugene. *The Death and Life of Germany: An Account of the American Occupation.* New York: Knopf, 1959.
Davis, Andrew. *Sonata Fragments: Romantic Narratives in Chopin, Schumann, and Brahms.* Bloomington: Indiana University Press, 2017.
Davison, W. Phillips. *A Personal History of WWII: How a Pacifist Draftee Accidentally became a Military Government Official in Postwar Germany.* Lincoln, NE: iUniverse, 2006.
"Der Kulturbunker vom Roseneck." *Der Tagesspiegel*, February 17, 2017. http://www.tagesspiegel.de/berlin/bezirke/charlottenburg-wilmersdorf/berlin-schmargendorf-der-kulturbunker-vom-roseneck/19404612.html.
Dibelius, Ulrich. *Moderne Musik, 1945–1965.* Munich: R. Piper, 1966.
Diefendorf, Jeffry. "The New City: German Urban Planning and the Zero Hour." In *Stunde Null: The End and the Beginning Fifty Years Ago*, edited by Geoffrey J. Giles, 89–104. Washington, DC: German Historical Institute, 1997.
Dolan, Josephine. "The Voice that Cannot Be Heard: Radio/Broadcasting and the 'Archive.'" *The Radio Journal* 1, no. 1 (2003): 63–72.
Drechsler, Nanny. *Die Funktion der Musik im deutschen Rundfunk, 1933–1945.* Musikwissenschaftliche Studien, vol. 3. Pfaffenweiler: Centaurus, 1988.
Dymschitz, Alexander. *Ein unvergeßlicher Frühling.* Berlin: Dietz, 1970.
Egk, Werner. *Die Zeit Wartet Nicht: Künstlerisches, Zeitgeschichtliches, Privates aus meinem Leben.* Mainz: Schott, 2001.
Eickhoff, Thomas. *Politische Dimensionen einer Komponisten-Biographie im 20.Jahrhundert: Gottfried von Einem.* Stuttgart: Steiner, 1998.
Eickhoff, Thomas, and Werner Grünzweig. "Gerty Herzog–Blacher im Gespräch." In *Boris Blacher*, edited by Heribert Henrich and Thomas Eickhoff, 23–36. Berlin: Fuldaer, 2003.
Eley, Geoff, and Jan Palmowski, eds. *Citizenship and National Identity in Twentieth-Century Germany.* Stanford, CA: Stanford University Press, 2008.
Elver, Rudolf, and Karl Hochreither, eds. *Bach-Kantaten in Berlin: Eine Jubiläumsschrift im Auftrag des Bach-Chores und der Kaiser-Wilhelm-Gedächtnis-Kirche.* Berlin: CZV, 1991.
Evans, Jennifer. *Life in the Ruins: Cityscape and Sexuality in Cold War in Berlin.* New York: Palgrave, 2011.
Evans, Joan. "Stravinsky's Music in Hitler's Germany." *Journal of the American Musicological Society* 56 (Fall 2003): 525–94.
Fackler, Guido. "Music in Concentration Camps." Translated by Peter Logan. *Music and Politics* 1, no. 1 (Winter 2007). doi: 10.3998/mp.9460447.0001.102.
Fauser, Annegret. *Sounds of War: Music in the United States during World War II.* Oxford: Oxford University Press, 2013.
Fehrenbach, Heide. *Cinema in Democratizing Germany: Reconstructing National Identity after Hitler.* Chapel Hill: University of North Carolina Press, 1999.

———. *Race after Hitler: Black Occupation Children in Postwar Germany and America.* Princeton, NJ: Princeton University Press, 2005.
Fischer-Defoy, Christine, ed. *Kunst, im Aufbau ein Stein: Die Westberliner Kunst- und Musikhochschulen im Spannungsfeld der Nachkriegszeit.* Berlin: Hochschule der Künste, 2001.
Fisher, Jaimey. "Who's Watching the Rubble-Kids? Youth, Pedagogy, and Politics in Early DEFA Films." *New German Critique* 82 (Winter 2001): 91–125.
"500 Mark für Furtwängler-Karte." *Der Spiegel*, May 31, 1947.
Foedrowitz, Michael. *Bunkerwelten: Luftschutzanlagen in Norddeutschland.* Berlin: Ch. Links, 1998.
Forck, Gerhard, ed. *Variationen mit Orchester: 125 Jahre Berliner Philharmoniker*, vol. 1. Berlin: Henschel, 2007.
Fosler-Lussier, Danielle. *Music in America's Cold War Diplomacy.* Berkeley: University of California Press, 2015.
Foundation for Research in the Afro-American Creative Arts. "W. Rudolph Dunbar: Pioneering Orchestra Conductor." *The Black Perspective in Music* 9/2 (Autumn 1981): 193–225.
Frei, Norbert. *Adenauer's Germany and the Nazi Past: The Politics of Amnesty and Integration.* New York: Columbia University Press, 2002.
Friedlander, Henry. *The Origins of Nazi Genocide: From Euthanasia to the Final Solution.* Chapel Hill: University of North Carolina Press, 1995.
Friedrich, Jörg. *The Fire: The Bombing of Germany.* Translated by Allison Brown. New York: Columbia University Press, 2006.
Fritzsche, Peter. *Life and Death in the Third Reich.* Cambridge, MA: Belknap Press of Harvard University Press, 2008.
Frühauf, Tina. "Five Days in Berlin: The 'Menuhin Affair' of 1947 and the Politics of Jewish Post-Holocaust National Identity." *Musical Quarterly* 96, no. 1 (Spring 2013): 14–49.
Frühauf, Tina, and Lily Hirsch, eds. *Dislocated Memories: Jews, Music, and Postwar German Culture.* Oxford: Oxford University Press, 2014.
Fuchs, Anne. "The Bombing of Dresden and the Idea of Cultural Impact." In *Cultural Impact in the German Context: Studies in Transmission, Reception, and Influence*, edited by Rebecca Braun and Lynn Marven, 36–57. Rochester, NY: Camden House, 2010.
Führe, Dorothea. *Die französische Besatzungspolitik in Berlin von 1945 bis 1949: Deprussianisation und Decentralisation.* Berlin: Weißensee, 2001.
Fulcher, Jane F. "From 'The Voice of the Maréchal' to Musique Concrète: Pierre Schaeffer and the Case for Cultural History." In *The Oxford Handbook of the New Cultural History of Music*, edited by Jane F. Fulcher, 381–402. Oxford: Oxford University Press, 2011.
———, ed. *The Oxford Handbook of the New Cultural History of Music.* Oxford: Oxford University Press, 2011.
"Furtwängler wieder in Berlin." *Frankfurter Neue Presse*, May 5, 1947.
Furtwängler, Wilhelm. *Notebooks, 1924–1954.* Translated by Shaun Whiteside. London: Quartet Books, 1989.
Geller, Jay Howard. *Jews in Post-Holocaust Germany, 1945–1953.* Cambridge: Cambridge University Press, 2005.
———. *The Other Jewish Question: Identifying the Jew and Making Sense of Modernity.* New York: Fordham University Press, 2011.

Geppert, Dominick, ed. *The Postwar Challenge: Cultural, Social, and Political Change in Western Europe, 1945–58*. Oxford: Oxford University Press, 2003.

Geuen, Heinz, and Anno Mungen, eds. *Kontinuitäten | Diskontinuitäten: Musik und Politik in Deutschland zwischen 1920 und 1970*. Schliengen, Germany: Argus Editions, 2006.

Giesen, Rolf. *Nazi Propaganda Films: A History of Filmography*. Jefferson, NC: McFarland, 2003.

Gilbert, Shirli. *Music and the Holocaust: Confronting Life in the Nazi Ghettos and Camps* Oxford: Oxford University Press, 2005.

Giles, Geoffrey J., ed. *Stunde Null: The End and the Beginning Fifty Years Ago*. Washington, DC: German Historical Institute, 1997.

Gilliam, Bryan, ed. *Music and Performance during the Weimar Republic*. Cambridge: Cambridge University Press, 1994.

Gilmore, Roger. "France's Postwar Policies and Activities in Germany, 1945–1956." PhD diss., University of Geneva, 1973.

Giroud, Vincent. *Nicolas Nabokov: A Life in Freedom and Music*. Oxford: Oxford University Press, 2015.

Glaser, Hermann. *The Rubble Years: The Cultural Roots of Postwar Germany*. New York: Paragon House, 1986.

Glaser, Hermann, Lutz von Pufendorf, and Michael Schöneich, eds. *So viel Anfang war nie: Deutsche Städte, 1945–1949*. Berlin: Siedler, 1989.

Goebbels, Joseph. *Tagebücher von Joseph Goebbels, Teil II, Diktate 1941–1945*, vol. 15. Edited by Maximilian Gschaid. Munich: K. G. Saur, 1995.

Goedecke, Heinz and Wilhelm Krug, eds. *Wunschkonzerte für die Wehrmacht*. Emmelshausen: Condo, 1942. Reprinted 2002.

Goehr, Lydia. *Elective Affinities: Musical Essays on the History of Aesthetic Theory*. New York: Columbia University Press, 2008.

Goldhagen, Sarah Williams, and Réjean Legault, eds. *Anxious Modernisms: Experimentation in Postwar Architectural Culture*. Cambridge, MA: MIT Press, 2000.

Goldstein, Cora Sol. *Capturing the German Eye: American Visual Propaganda in Occupied Germany*. Chicago: University of Chicago Press, 2009.

———. *Purges, Exclusions, and Limits: Art Policies in Germany, 1933–1949*. Chicago: Cultural Policy Center, University of Chicago.

Grieb, Manfred K., ed. *Nürnberger Künstlerlexikon*. Munich: K. G. Saur, 2007.

Grossmann, Atina. *Jews, Germans, and Allies: Close Encounters in Occupied Germany*. Princeton, NJ: Princeton University Press, 2007.

Hartenian, Larry. *Controlling Information in U.S. Occupied Germany, 1945–49: Media and Manipulation and Propaganda*. Lewistown, NY: Edwin Mellen, 2003.

Hartmann, Erich. *Die Berliner Philharmoniker in der Stunde Null: Erinnerungen an die Zeit des Untergangs der alten Philharmonie vor 50 Jahren*. Berlin: Werner Feja, 1996.

Heine, Henrich. *Anthea: Poems and Translations*. Translated by William Stigand. London: Kegan Paul, Trench, Trübner, 1907.

Heinsheimer, H. W. "Musik im amerikanischen Rundfunk." *Melos* 14, no. 12 (October 1947): 332–35.

Hell, Julia, and Andreas Schönle, eds. *The Ruins of Modernity*. Durham, NC: Duke University Press, 2010.

Henrich, Heribert, and Thomas Eickhoff, eds. *Boris Blacher: Archiv zur Musik des 20. Jahrhunderts*, Vol. 7. Berlin: Fuldaer, 2003.
"Hier spricht Berlin." *Tägliche Rundschau*, May 27, 1945.
Höckner, Karla. *Beschreibung eines Jahres: Berliner Notizen*. Berlin: Arani, 1984.
Hoffmann, Wilhelm. "Die letzten Tage von Berlin." *Der Rundfunk* 30, April 28–May 4, 1946.
Holz, Klaus, and Sven Wende, eds. *Das Unbehagen in der "dritten Generation": Reflexionen des Holocausts, Antisemitismus und Nationalsozialismus*. Muenster: Lit, 2004.
"Hört den Rundfunksender Berlin." *Tägliche Rundschau*, May 20, 1945.
Hutcheon, Linda, and Michael Hutcheon. *Four Last Songs: Aging and Creativity in Verdi, Strauss, Messiaen, and Britten*. Chicago: University of Chicago Press, 2015.
———. *Opera: The Art of Dying*. Cambridge, MA: Harvard University Press, 2004.
Huyssen, Andreas. "Nostalgia for Ruins." *Grey Room* 23 (Spring 2006): 6–21.
———. *Present Pasts: Urban Palimpsests and the Politics of Memory*. Stanford, CA: Stanford University Press, 2003.
Janik, Elizabeth. *Recomposing German Music: Politics and Musical Tradition in Cold War Berlin*. Leiden, the Netherlands: Brill, 2005.
Jelavich, Peter. *Berlin Cabaret*. Cambridge, MA: Harvard University Press, 1993.
Jena, Stefan. "Dabeisein ist Alles: Die Musik zu den Olympischen Spielen 1936 in Berlin." *Studien zur Musikwissenschaft* 56 (2010): 265–85.
"Jewish New Year: American Army Helps Berlin Jews Restore Their Sacred Services." *Life*, October 8, 1945.
Joel, Tony. *The Dresden Firebombing: Memory and the Politics of Commemoration Destruction* London: I. B. Tauris, 2013.
Johnson, Edward N. *Fünf Monate in Berlin: Briefe von Edward N. Johnson aus dem Jahre 1946*. Edited by Werner Breunig and Jürgen Wetzel. Munich: de Gruyter, 2014.
Judt, Tony. *Postwar: A History of Europe since 1945*. New York: Penguin, 2005.
Junker, Detlef, ed. *The United States and Germany in the Era of the Cold War*. Cambridge: Cambridge University Press, 2004.
Kardorff, Ursula von. *Diary of a Nightmare: Berlin 1942–45*. New York: John Day, 1966.
Kater, Michael. *Composers of the Nazi Era: Eight Portraits*. New York: Oxford University Press, 2000.
———. *The Twisted Muse: Musicians and Their Music in the Third Reich*. Oxford: Oxford University Press, 1997.
Kellermann, Bernhard, Eduard Spangler, Paul Wegener, and Johannes R. Becher. "Manifest und Ansprachen." In *Gründungskundgebung des Kulturbundes*. Berlin: Aufbau, 1945.
Kelly, Elaine. *Composing the Canon in the German Democratic Republic: Narratives of Nineteenth-Century Music*. Oxford: Oxford University Press, 2014.
Kershaw, Ian. *The End: The Defiance and Destruction of Hitler's Germany, 1944–1945*. New York: Penguin, 2011.
Kinderman, William. *Beethoven*. Oxford: Oxford University Press, 2009.
Klabund. *Irene oder die Gesinnung, Ein Gesang von Klabund*. Berlin: Eric Reiss, 1918.
Kluge, Alexander. *Air Raid*. London: UK Seagull Books, 2012.
Königseder, Angelika. *Flucht nach Berlin: Jüdische Displaced Persons, 1945–1948*. Berlin: Metropol, 1998.
Konzett, Matthias. *Encyclopedia of German Literature*. Chicago: Routledge, 2000.

Kroll, Ernst. "Berliner Opern-Chronik in drei Teilen." In *Musikstadt Berlin zwischen Krieg und Frieden: Musikalische Bilanz einer Viermächtestadt*, edited by Harald Kunz, 62–67. Wiesbaden: Bote & Bock, 1956.
Kulenkampff, H. W. "Auf dem Weg zur englischen Oper." *Melos*, April 1947: 176–78.
Kunz, Harald, ed. *Musikstadt Berlin zwischen Krieg und Frieden: Musikalische Bilanz einer Viermächtestadt*. Wiesbaden: Bote and Bock, 1956.
Lang, Klaus. *Celibidache und Furtwängler: Der große philharmonische Konflikt in der Berliner Nachkriegszeit*. Munich: Wissner, 2010.
Lange, Wigand. *Theater in Deutschland nach 1945: Zur Theaterpolitik der amerikanischen Besatzungsbehörden*. Frankfurt: Peter Lang, 1980.
Langenbacher, Eric. "Changing Memory Regimes in Contemporary Germany?" *German Politics and Society* 21, no. 2 (Summer 2003): 46–68.
Latshaw, Charles William. "William Grant Still's Afro-American Symphony: A Critical Edition." PhD diss., Indiana University, 2014.
Lavsky, Hagit. *New Beginnings: Holocaust Survivors in Bergen-Belsen and the British Zone in Germany, 1945–1950*. Detroit: Wayne State University Press, 2002.
Lawford-Hinrichsen, Irene. *Music Publishing and Patronage: C. F. Peters*. Kenton, UK: Edition Press, 2000.
Leider, Frida. *Playing My Part, 1888–1975*. New York: Da Capo, 1959.
Levi, Erik. *Music in the Third Reich*. New York: St. Martin's Press, 1994.
Lyotard, Jean François. *Heidegger and 'the Jews.'* Translated by Andreas Michel and Mark S. Roberts. Minneapolis: University of Minnesota Press, 1990.
MacDonogh, Giles. *After the Reich: The Brutal History of the Allied Occupation*. New York: Basic Books, 2009.
Maconie, Robin. *Other Planets: The Complete Works of Karlheinz Stockhausen*. Lanham, MD: Rowman and Littlefield, 2016.
Maier, Robert, ed. *Akustisches Gedächtnis und Zweiter Weltkrieg*. Göttingen: V and R Unipress, 2011.
Mann, Thomas. *Briefe, 1937–1947*, vol. 2. Edited by Erika Mann. Frankfurt: Fischer, 1961.
———. "Germany Today: A Famous Exile's Impression of a Ruined, Vanquished Land and an Unchanging People." *New York Times Magazine*, September 25, 1949.
———. *The Story of a Novel: The Genesis of Doctor Faustus*. Translated by Richard Winston and Clara Winston. New York: Knopf, 1961.
Marein, Josef. "Brittens *Peter Grimes*." *Die Welt*, March 27, 1947, http://www.zeit.de/1947/13/brittens-peter-grimes.
Martin, Douglas. "Henry Ries, 86, Photographer who Captured Berlin Airlift." *New York Times*, May 26, 2004. https://www.nytimes.com/2004/05/26/business/henry-ries-86-photographer-who-captured-berlin-airlift.html.
McAlister, Elizabeth. "Soundscapes of Disaster and Humanitarianism: Survival Singing, Relief Telethons, and the Haiti Earthquake." *Small Axe: A Caribbean Platform for Criticism* 39 (November 2012): 22–38.
Melrose, Georgiana. *A Strange Occupation*. Elms Court, UK: Arthur H. Stockwell, 1988.
Meng, Michael. *Shattered Spaces: Encountering Jewish Ruins in Postwar Germany and Poland*. Cambridge, MA: Harvard University Press, 2011.
Menuhin, Yehudi. *Unfinished Journey*. New York: Fromm International, 1997.
Mitscherlich, Alexander, and Margarete Mitscherlich. *The Inability to Mourn: Principles of Collective Behavior*. Translated by Beverly R. Placzek. New York: Grove, 1975.

Moeller, Robert G. "Germans as Victims? Thoughts on a Post–Cold War History of WWII's Legacies." *History and Memory* 17, no. 1/2 (Spring/Summer 2005): 147–94.

———. "On the History of Man-Made Destruction: Loss, Death, Memory, and Germany in the Bombing War." *History Workshop Journal* 61 (Spring 2006): 103–34.

———. *Protecting Motherhood: Women and the Family in the Politics of Postwar West Germany*. Berkeley: University of California Press, 1993.

———. *War Stories: The Search for a Usable Past in the Federal Republic of Germany*. Berkeley: University of California Press, 2003.

Moldenhauer, Hans. *The Death of Anton Webern: A Drama in Documents*. New York: Philosophical Library, 1961.

———. "Webern's Death." *Musical Times* 111, no. 1531 (September 1970): 877–81.

Moltke, Johannes von. "Ruin Cinema." In *Ruins of Modernity*, edited Julia Hell and Andreas Schönle, 395–417. Durham, NC: Duke University Press, 2010.

Monod, David. "Internationalism, Regionalism, and National Culture: Music Control in Bavaria, 1945–1948." *Central European History* 33, no. 3 (2000): 339–68.

———. *Settling Scores: German Music, Denazification, and the Americans, 1945–1953*. Chapel Hill: University of North Carolina Press, 2005.

Moore, Deborah Dash. *GI Jews: How World War II Changed a Generation*. Cambridge, MA: Belknap Press of Harvard University Press, 2004.

Muck, Peter, ed. *Einhundert Jahre Berliner Philharmonisches Orchester*, vol. 2. Tutzing, Germany: H. Schneider, 1982.

"Musicians Oppose Concert Here by 'Nazi-Led' Berlin Orchestra." *New York Times*, February 20, 1955.

"Music: Rhythm in Berlin." *Time*, September 10, 1945.

Nabokov, Nicolas. "Boris Blacher." In *Boris Blacher: Archiv zur Musik des 20.Jahrhundert*, vol. 7, edited by Henrich Heribert and Thomas Eickhoff, 11–21. Berlin: Fuldaer, 2003.

———. *Old Friends and New Music*. Boston: Little, Brown, 1951.

Nachama, Andreas, and Julius H. Schoeps, eds. *Aufbau nach dem Untergang: Deutsch-jüdische Geschichte nach 1945*. Berlin: Argon, 1992.

Naimark, Norman M. *The Russians in Germany: A History of the Soviet Zone of Occupation, 1945–1949*. Cambridge, MA: Harvard University Press, 1995.

"National Socialists Oust Busch as Orchestra Conductor of Dresden Opera House." *New York Times*, March 7, 1933.

"Negro Wins Plaudits Conducting in Berlin." *New York Times*, September 3, 1945.

"Neues Leben—neue Klänge: Gespräch mit Hans von Benda." *Berliner Zeitung*, May 21, 1945.

Nicholas, Lynn. *The Rape of Europa*. New York: Vintage Books, 1995.

Nicosia, Francis R., and Lawrence D. Stokes, eds. *Germans against Nazism: Nonconformity, Opposition and Resistance in the Third Reich*. New York: Berghahn Books, 2015.

Nieden, Susanne zur, ed. *Alltag im Ausnahmezustand: Frauentagebücher im zerstörten Deutschland 1943 bis 1945*. Berlin: Orlanda Frauenverlag, 1993.

Nossack, Hans Erich. *The End: Hamburg, 1943*. Translated by Joel Agee. Chicago: University of Chicago Press, 2004.

"One Man Can Save German Music: Leo Borchard." *Newsweek*, August 27, 1945, 62–64.

Oster, Andrew. "Rubble, Radio, and Reconstruction: The Genre of Funkoper in Postwar Occupied Germany and the Federal Republic, 1946–1957." PhD diss., Princeton University, 2010.

Ostrowski, Sigfried. "Vom Schicksal Jüdische Ärzte im Dritten Reich." *Bulletin of the Leo Baeck Institute* 6, no. 24 (1963): 313–51.
Paddock, Alfred. *U.S. Army Special Warfare: Its Origins.* Lawrence: University Press of Kansas, 2002.
Parkinson, Anna. *An Emotional State: The Politics of Emotion in Postwar West German Culture.* Ann Arbor: University of Michigan Press, 2015.
Patt, Avinoam J., and Michael Berkowitz, eds. *"We Are Here": New Approaches to Jewish Displaced Persons in Postwar Germany.* Detroit: Wayne University Press, 2010.
Pike, David. *The Politics of Culture in Soviet Occupied Germany, 1945–1949.* Stanford, CA: Stanford University Press, 1992.
Pollock, Emily Richmond. "Pride of Place: The 1963 Rebuilding of the Munich Nationaltheater." In *Dreams of Germany: Music and (Trans)national Imaginaries*, edited by Neil Gregor and Tom Irvine, 145–68. New York: Berghahn Books, 2019.
Pommerin, Reiner. *Culture in the Federal Republic of Germany, 1945–1995.* Oxford: Berg, 1996.
Potter, Pamela M. *Art of Suppression: Confronting the Nazi Past in Histories of the Visual and Performing Arts.* Berkeley: University of California Press, 2016.
———. *The Most German of the Arts: Musicology and Society from the Weimar Republic to the End of Hitler's Reich.* New Haven, CT: Yale University Press, 1998.
———. "The Nazi 'Seizure' of the Berlin Philharmonic." In *National Socialist Cultural Policy.* Edited by Glen Cuomo, 39–66. *National Socialist Cultural Policy.* New York: St. Martin's Press, 1995.
———. "What Is 'Nazi Music'?" *The Musical Quarterly* 88, no. 3 (2005): 428–55.
Potter, Pamela, and Celia Applegate, eds. *Music and German National Identity.* Chicago: University of Chicago Press, 2002.
Prinz, Friedrich. *Trümmerzeit in München: Kultur und Gesellschaft einer deutschen Großstadt im Aufbruch 1945–1949.* Munich: Prinz, 1984.
Puff, Helmut. *Miniature Monuments: Modeling German History.* Berlin: de Gruyter, 2014.
Purpus, Elke, Günther B. Sellen, Walter Geis, and Helmut Buchen, eds. *Bunker in Köln—Versuche einer Sichtbar-Machung.* Essen: Klartext, 2006.
Randall, Amanda Z. "Austrian Trümmerfilm? What a Genre's Absence Reveals about National Postwar Cinema and Film Studies." *German Studies Review* 38, no. 3 (October 2015): 573–95.
Rasche, Stefan. *Das Stilleben in der westdeutschen Malerei der Nachkriegzeit: Gegenständliche Positionen zwischen 1945 und 1963.* Muenster: Lit, 1995.
Rauh-Kühne, Cornelia. "Life Rewarded the Latecomers." In *The United States and Germany in the Era of the Cold War*, edited by Detlef Junker, 65–72. Cambridge: Cambridge University Press, 2004.
Rentschler, Eric. "The Place of Rubble in the Trümmerfilm." In *Ruins of Modernity*, edited by Julia Hell and Andreas Schönle, 418–38. Durham, NC: Duke University Press, 2010.
Richmond Pollock, Emily. "Pride of Place: The 1963 Rebuilding of the Munich Nationaltheater." In *Dreams of Germany: Music and (Trans)national Imaginaries*, edited by Neil Gregor and Tom Irvine, 145–68. New York: Berghahn Books, 2019.
Richter, Hans Werner. "Literatur im Interregnum." *Der Ruf* 15, March 1947.
Riesenburger, Martin. *Das Licht verlöschte nicht: ein Zeugnis aus der Nacht des Faschismus.* Berlin: Union, 1960.
Riethmüller, Albrecht, ed. *Deutsche Leitkultur Musik?: Zur Musikgeschichte nach dem Holocaust.* Stuttgart: Franz Steiner, 2006.

Roemer, Nils. *German City, Jewish Memory: The Story of Worms.* Waltham, MA: Brandeis University Press, 2010.
Rogier, Francesca. "The Monumentality of Rhetoric." In *Anxious Modernisms: Experimentation in Postwar Architectural Culture,* edited by Sarah Williams Goldhagen and Réjean Legault, 165–90. Cambridge, MA: MIT Press, 2000.
Rosen, Charles. *The Romantic Generation.* Cambridge, MA: Harvard University Press, 1995.
Ross, Alex. "Monument Man." *New Yorker,* July 24, 2014. https://www.newyorker.com/culture/cultural-comment/richard-strauss-and-the-american-army
———. *The Rest Is Noise: Listening to the Twentieth Century.* New York: Farrar, Straus and Giroux, 2007.
Roth, Michael S., ed. *Irresistible Decay: Ruins Reclaimed.* Los Angeles: Getty Research Institute for the History of Art and the Humanities, 1997.
Rothe, Alexander. "Rethinking Postwar History: Munich's *Musica Viva* during the Karl Amadeus Hartmann Years (1945–63)." *Musical Quarterly* 90/2 (2007): 230–74.
Rovit, Rebecca. *The Jewish Kulturbund Theatre Company in Nazi Berlin: Studies in Theatre History and Culture.* Iowa City: University of Iowa Press, 2012.
Ryzewski, Krysta. "Making Music in Detroit: Archaeology, Popular Music, and Post-Industrial Heritage." In *Contemporary Archeology and the City,* edited by Laura McAtackney and Krysta Ryzewski, 69–90. Oxford: Oxford University Press, 2017.
Sargeant, Winthrop. "Europe's Culture." *Time,* November 4, 1946.
Scannell, Paddy, and David Cardiff. *A Social History of British Broadcasting, 1922–1939: Serving the Nation.* Oxford: Basil Blackwell, 1991.
Schafer, R. Murray. "The Music of the Environment." In *Audio Culture: Readings in Modern Music,* edited by Christoph Cox and Daniel Werner, 29–39. New York: Bloomsbury, 2017.
Scharf, Claus, and Hans-Jürgen Schröder. *Die Deutschlandpolitik Frankreichs und die Französische Zone 1945–1949.* Wiesbaden: Franz Steiner, 1979.
Scharoun, Hans. *Hans Scharoun: Bauten, Entwürfe, Texte.* Edited by P. Pfankuch. Berlin: Akademie der Künste, 1974.
Schivelbusch, Wolfgang. *In a Cold Crater: Cultural and Intellectual Life in Berlin, 1945–1948.* Translated by Kelly Barry. Berkeley: University of California Press, 1998.
Scherliess, Volker, ed. *"Stunde Null": Zur Musik um 1945: Bericht über das Symposion der Gesellschaft für Musikforschung an der Musikhochschule Lübeck 24–27. September 2003.* Kassel: Bärenreiter, 2014.
Schmal, Helga, and Tobias Selke. *Bunker: Luftschutz und Luftschutzbau in Hamburg.* Hamburg: Christians, 2001.
Schmidt, Eberhard. *Ein Lied—ein Atemzug: Erinnerungen und Dokumente.* Edited by Manfred Machlitt. Berlin: Verlag Neue Musik, 1987.
Schmitz, Helmut, and Annette Seidel-Arpaci, eds. *Narratives of Trauma: Discourses of German Wartime Suffering in National and International Perspective.* Amsterdam: Rodopi, 2011.
Schubert, Franz, and Wilhelm Müller. "Der Lindenbaum." In *Die Winterreise.* Leipzig: Breitkopf & Härtel, 1895.
Schulmeister, Karl-Heinz. *Auf dem Wege zu einer neuen Kultur: Der Kulturbund in den Jahren 1945–1949.* Berlin: Dietz, 1977.
Schwartz, Jessica A. "A 'Voice to Sing': Rongelapese Musical Activism and the Production of Nuclear Knowledge." *Music and Politics* 6, no. 1 (Winter 2012). https://quod.lib.umich

.edu/m/mp/9460447.0006.101/--voice-to-sing-rongelapese-musical-activism?rgn=main;view=fulltext.

Sebald, W. G. *On the Natural History of Destruction*. Translated by Anthea Bell. New York: Random House, 2004.

Sederberg, Kathryn. "Writing through Crisis: Time, History, Futurity in German Diaries of the Second World War." *Biography* 40, no. 2 (Spring 2017): 323–41.

Shandley, Robert. *Rubble Films: German Cinema in the Shadow of the Third Reich*. Philadelphia: Temple University Press, 2001.

Shreffler, Anne C. "Berlin Walls: Dalhaus, Knepler, and Ideologies of Music History." In *The Journal of Musicology* 20, no. 4 (Fall 2003): 498–525.

Silberman, Marc. *German Cinema: Texts in Context*. Detroit: Wayne State University Press, 1995.

Simon, Hermann, ed. *Die Synagoge Rykestrasse, 1904–2004*, Jüdische Miniature, Stiftung neue Synagoge Berlin, Centrum Judaicum. Berlin: Hentrich & Hentrich, 2004.

Smalley, John. "Gesang der Jünglinge: History and Analysis." Program notes, Masterpieces of 20th-Century Electronic Music. Lincoln Center, New York, 2000.

Speer, Albert. *Erinnerungen*. Berlin: Propyläen, 1969.

———. *Inside the Third Reich*. Translated by Richard Winston and Clara Winston. Toronto: Macmillan, 1970.

Sprigge, Martha. "Abilities to Mourn: Musical Commemoration in the German Democratic Republic, 1945–1989." PhD diss., University of Chicago, 2013.

———. "Dresden's Musical Ruins." *Journal of the Royal Musical Association* 144, no. 1 (2019): 83–121.

Stähr, Susanne. "Die Ära Furtwängler." In Forck, *Variationen mit Orchester*, 195–96.

Steege, Paul. *Black Market, Cold War: Everyday Life in Berlin, 1946–1949*. Cambridge: Cambridge University Press, 2007.

Steer, Christine, and Dietmar Arnold, eds. *Wie Silberfische flimmerten Bomber am Himmel: Erinnerungen an das Inferno des Krieges in Berlin-Lichtenberg, 1940–1945*. Berlin: Edition Berliner Unterwelten, 2004.

Steinweis, Alan. *Art, Ideology, and Economics: The Reich Chambers of Music, Theater and the Visual Arts*. Chapel Hill: University of North Carolina Press, 1993.

Sterne, Jonathan. *The Audible Past: Cultural Origins of Sound Reproduction*. Durham, NC: Duke University Press, 2003.

Stonor Saunders, Frances. *The Cultural Cold War: The CIA and the World of Arts and Letters*. New York: New Press, 1999.

Strässner, Matthias. *Der Dirigent Leo Borchard: Eine unvollendete Karriere*. Berlin: Transit, 1999.

Strauss, Richard. "The Artistic Testament of Richard Strauss." Translated by Alfred Mann. *Musical Quarterly* 36, no. 1 (January 1950): 1–8.

Stuckenschmidt, Hans Heinz. *Boris Blacher*. Berlin: Bote & Bock, 1985.

———. "Die Filmharmoniker im Marmorhaus." *Die Neue Zeitung*, January 8, 1952.

———. "Leonore 40/45." *Die Neue Zeitung*, March 28, 1952.

———. *Maurice Ravel: Variationen über Person und Werk*. Frankfurt: Suhrkamp, 1966.

———. *Neue Musik in der Bundesrepublik Deutschland: Dokumentation 1957/58*. Frankfurt: C. F. Peters, 1958.

———. *Schönberg: Leben, Umwelt, Werk*. Zurich: Atlantis, 1974.

———. "Spieler oder Werk? Zweites Furtwängler-Konzert und Neue Musik." *Neue Zeitung*, June 3, 1947.

———. *Strawinsky und sein Jahrhundert*. Berlin: Piper, 1957.
———. *Twentieth Century Music*. London: World University, 1969.
———. *Zum Hören geboren: Ein Leben mit der Musik unserer Zeit*. Munich: Deutscher Taschen, 1982.
Süss, Dietmar. *Death from the Skies: How the British and Germans Survived Bombing in World War II*. Translated by Lesley Sharpe and Jeremy Noakes. Oxford: Oxford University Press, 2010.
Taruskin, Richard. *Music in the Late Twentieth Century: The Oxford History of Western Music*. Oxford: Oxford University Press, 2005.
Taubman, Howard. "Touchy Problem: Question of Art and Politics Is Raised Anew by Berlin Philharmonic Visit." *New York Times*, March 6, 1955.
Taylor, Ronald. *Berlin and Its Culture: A Historical Portrait*. New Haven, CT: Yale University Press, 1997.
"Terror gegen die Philharmoniker." *Neues Deutschland*, October 7, 1948.
Thacker, Toby. "'Gesungen oder musiziert wird aber fast in jedem Haus': Representing and Constructing Citizenship through Music in Twentieth-Century Germany." In *Citizenship and National Identity in Twentieth-Century Germany*, edited by Geoff Eley and Jan Palmowski, 164–180. Stanford, CA: Stanford University Press, 2008.
———. *Music after Hitler, 1945–1955*. Farnham, UK: Ashgate, 2007.
Thurman, Kira. "Singing the Civilizing Mission in the Land of Bach, Beethoven, and Brahms: The Fisk Jubilee Singers in Nineteenth-Century Germany." *Journal of World History* 27, no. 3 (September 2016): 443–71.
———. "Black Europe: A Useful Category for Historical Analysis." *Black Perspectives: African American Intellectual History Society Blog* (December 2016).
Thym, Jürgen. "Song as Memory, Memory as Song," *Archiv für Musikwissenschaft* 69 (2012): 263–73.
Toltz, Joseph. "Hidden Testimony: Musical Experience and Memory in Jewish Holocaust Survivors." PhD diss., Sydney Conservatorium of Music, 2011.
Tommasini, Anthony. "Music: A Cultural Disconnect on Wagner." *New York Times*, August 5, 2001.
Trümpi, Fritz. *Politisierte Orchester: Die Wiener Philharmoniker und das Berliner Philharmoniche Orchester im Nationalsozialismus*. Vienna: Böhlau, 2011.
Wachter, Clemens. *Kultur in Nürnberg 1945–1950: Kulturpolitik, kulturelles Leben und Bild der Stadt zwischen dem Ende der NS-Diktatur und der Prosperität der fünfziger Jahre*. Nuremberg: Stadtarchiv, 1999.
Waibel, Harry. *Diener vieler Herren: Ehemalige NS-Funktionäre in der SBZ/DDR*. Frankfurt: Peter Lang, 2011.
"Was geht in der Städtischen Oper vor?" *Neues Deutschland*, October 20, 1946.
Watchorn, Peter. *Isolde Ahlgrimm, Vienna and the Early Music Revival*. Farnham, UK: Ashgate, 2007.
Weber, Heinrich. *Die Geschichte des Lehrergesangvereins Nürnberg e.V., 1878–2003*. Nuremberg: LGV, 2003.
Weiß, Florian, Sedjro Mensah, and Thomas P. Strauss, eds. *The Link with Home—And the Germans Listened In: The Radio Stations of the Western Powers from 1945 to 1994*. Berlin: Ruksaldruck, 2001.
Wellens, Ian. *Music on the Frontline: Nicolas Nabokov's Struggle against Communism and Middlebrow Culture*. Farnham, UK: Ashgate, 2002.

Welz, Wilfried, ed. *Rathaus Schöneberg: Stationen einer politischen Karriere*. Berlin: Spitz, 1995.

Wetzelsberger, Bertil. "Wie sollen wir aufbauen?" *Melos*, November 1946: 15.

Westphal, Kurt. "Internationale neue Musik in Berlin." *Melos*, August/September 1947: 292–94.

Whitton, Kenneth S. *Dietrich Fischer-Dieskau Mastersinger: A Documented Study*. New York: Holmes & Meier, 1981.

"Wiederaufbau der alten Städtischen Oper: Michael Bohnen über seine Pläne." *Der Berliner*, February 2, 1946.

Wilhelm, Kurt. *Richard Strauss Persönlich: Eine Bildbiographie*. Munich: Kindler, 1984.

Willis, F. Roy. *The French in Germany, 1945–1949*. Stanford, CA: Stanford University Press, 1962.

Willson, Flora. "Classic Staging: Pauline Viardot and the 1859 Orphée Revival." *Cambridge Opera Journal* 22, no. 3 (November 2010): 301–26.

Wlodarski, Amy Lynn. *George Rochberg, American Composer: Personal Trauma and Artistic Creativity*. Eastman Studies in Music. Rochester, NY: University of Rochester Press, 2019.

———. *Musical Witness and Holocaust Representation*. Cambridge: Cambridge University Press, 2015.

Woebs, Raphael. *Die Politische Theorie in der Neuen Musik: Karl Amadeus Hartmann und Hannah Arendt*. Munich: Wilhelm Fink, 2010.

Zuckermann, Solly. *From Apes to Warlords: The Autobiography of Solly Zuckermann*. London: Hamilton, 1978.

Archival Resources

Akademie der Künste, Music Archive. Berlin, Germany.
Berlin Philharmonic Archive. Berlin, Germany.
Bitter, John, Dr., Special Collections. University of Miami Library. Coral Gables, Florida.
Center for Anti-Semitic Research. Berlin, Germany.
German Radio Archive. Potsdam, Germany.
Landesarchiv. Berlin, Germany.
National Archives and Records Administration II. College Park, Maryland.
United States Holocaust Memorial Museum Archive, Washington, DC.
YIVO Institute for Jewish Research. New York, New York.

INDEX

Admiralspalast, 68, 72
Adorno, Theodor W.: culture in bombed cities, 8; thoughts on Mahler, 146; thoughts on Nazi musical culture, 37; thoughts on Wagner after WWII, 85, 86
Agop, Rolf, 111
Ahlgrimm, Hans, 46
Airlift, Berlin, 11, 61
Alexanderplatz, 134
Allied air war: Berlin's destruction, 4; communities of listeners created by, 94; devastation wrought by, 5, 67; methods used, 3–4
Allied Kommandatura, 31
Alt, Bernard, 46
Alter, Henry: biography, 25; skepticism of Bitter, 55; thoughts on Furtwänger and von Karajan, 58; thoughts on Soviet policies, 75; work on behalf of Berlin Philharmonic, 47
Ambassadors of Music, 114, 115
American cultural officer, 20–25
American Forces Network (AFN): broadcasting during the Blockade, 106; creation of, 99; Gluski's work for, 93, 106
Anders, Peter, 72, 73
Andreas-Friedrich, Ruth: Account of immediate postwar period, 43–44, 50; thoughts on the Kulturbund, 20
Arendt, Hannah, 107
Audilet, Oskar, 46

Bab, Julius, 147
Bach, J. S.: Bach Choir ruin performances, 114; cantatas, 50; chorale, 102; in postwar Dresden, 112; Zimmermann quotations of in *Die Soldaten*, 159
Bans, 34. *See also* blacklists
Barber, Samuel: *Adagio for Strings*, 55; American music to be promoted in Germany, 35

Bartók, Béla, 36, 55, 102, 149
Bayreuth, 67, 68, 84, 86
Becher, Johannes R., 20
Beethoven, Ludwig van: Allied concerns about, 35; postwar performances of, 19, 35, 73, 106, 117, 123; *Egmont* Overture, 114, 116; *Eroica* Symphony, 35, 51, 96; *Fidelio*, 76, 83–84, 98; Fürtwangler's performances of, 60, 61; in Nazi Germany, 34, 96; Ninth Symphony as Nazi propaganda, 119; radio performances of, 16; *Romanze*, op. 40, 116; Seventh Symphony, 96; symphonies in ruins, 46, 133
Beethovensaal, 45
Benda, Hans von: first postwar conducting appearances, 1, 12, 16; performance in Dahlem, 106
Benjamin, Walter, 135
Bennedik, Bernhard, 150
Berg, Alban, 101, 102
Berger, Erna: last recording under the Third Reich, 1; in *Hansel and Gretel*, 82; operatic reconstruction work, 71–73
Berlin: blockade, 61, 106; currency reform, 61; early division of East and West, 3; map of the sectors, 22
Berlin Chamber Orchestra, 1, 106
Berlin Music Days Festival, 150
Berlin Philharmonic Orchestra: *Ambassadors of Music* documentary film, 114, *115*; concert-goers during the Third Reich, 59; concerts for the Allies, 54; denazification of, 30, 47–48; early postwar concerts, 44–45; final concert during National Socialism, 1; hall on Bernbergerstrasse, 16, 45–46; Nazi propaganda footage, 119; Nazi propaganda tours, 57; work with the American occupiers, 37
Bersarin, Nikolai: cultural work; 18, 43, 44, 68, 69, 73; death of, 19, 72
Bethmann, Hermann, 53

177

Bitter, John: attending concerts in Berlin, 106–107; biography, 24–25; conducting the Berlin Philharmonic, 55–56; friendship with Blacher, 104; work with Berlin Philharmonic, 47, 48, 57, 60, 62

Blacher, Boris: *The Last Days of Berlin*, 104–105; music in postwar Berlin, 36; postwar career and work with the occupiers, 103; premiere of *The Flood*, 81, 104

Blacher, Gerty Herzog, 103

black market, 60

blacklists: conductors banned by Americans, 53, 56; French non-use of, 32; music banned by the Allies, 34; occupier use of, 10, 31

Blues, 53

Bohnen, Michael: Director of the Städtische Oper, 69, 73–74, 80–81; President of the Chamber of Artists, 50

Böll, Heinrich, 7

Borchard, Leo: biography of, 44; death, 50, 54; postwar activities, 43–51

Borries, Siegfried, 116

Brahms, Johannes, 1, 55, 60, 99

Brecht, Bertolt, 151, 158

Brett-Smith, Richard, 33, 94

British Allies: cultural officers, 27; governing of sector in early months, 26–27

Britten, Benjamin, 36, 80–81, 119

Broom, The, 131

Bruckner, Anton, 60, 133

Burgwinkel, Josef, 82

Burkhardt, Arno, 48

Bush, Alan, 36

Busch, Ernst, 18

Busch, Fritz, 53

Butting, Max: biographical information, 135–142; compositions after the war, 105, 131; *The Guilt*, 137; performances of his music in postwar period, 36; postwar work for Radio Berlin, 105; Songs from Berlin (*Lieder aus Berlin*), 138–141; thoughts on postwar German-Allied relations, 55

cabaret, 18, 117, 131–132, 142–143

Cage, John, 159

Carniolus, Jacobus Gallus, 112

Capa, Robert, 120, 134

Celibidache, Sergiu: correspondence with Furtwängler, 61; first concerts with the Berlin Philharmonic, 54; performing in the rubble of the Philharmonic, 114, 115, 116; playing Tiessen's music in the postwar period, 148; termination of Philharmonic contract, 157

Chamber of Artists in the Soviet Sector: building on Schülterstrasse, 26; denazification, 31; founding of, 19; organization, 50

Charlottenburg, 19, 21, 43, 48, 98, 114, 149

Christkaus, Curt, 46

Clare, George, 27, 94

Clarke, Eric, 24, 56, *71*

Clay, Lucius, 51, 82

Clay, Marjorie, 82

Cold War, 11, 17, 69, 132, 151

Copland, Aaron, 35, 36

Creighton, Thomas, 50, 53

Dahlem, 71, 106

Debussy, Claude, 115

Degenerate Music. See *Entartete Musik*

Demmer, Karl, 111

democracy: as opposed to Soviet policies, 62; as related to music, 21, 23, 30

denazification: American ICD personnel, 29–30; Fragebogen, 29–31; Spruchkammern and Prüfungsausschüsse, 31; of music, 33–37; uneven policies across Berlin, 31–32

Dessau, Paul, 158

Deutsches Theater (Berlin), 108

DIAS, 99

Dietrich, Marlene, 117

displaced persons camps, 119–120

Distler, Hugo, 112

Domgraf-Faßbender, Willi, 72, 73

Dresden, 7, 9, 53; rubble concert, 111–112

Dunbar, Rudolph, 48–53; conducting, *49*; program with Berlin Philharmonic, 52

Dymschitz, Alexander, 17–19

Ederer, Alois, 46

Egk, Werner: account of the war's end, 2; music during WWII, 44; opera *die Circe*, 81; postwar commissions, 157

Eisler, Hanns, 137, 158
Electrola, 56
Ellington, Duke, 35
Entartete Musik: Allied understandings of, 35–37, 100; on RIAS, 102
Enzensberger, Hans Magnus, 7
Eppstein, Cora, 142

Fidelio, 76, *78*, 83–84
Fischer-Dieskau, Dietrich: early postwar career, 76, 135; first appearance at the Städtische Oper, 81; recording Tiessen's music, 148
Foreign Affair, A, 7, 117
Fraenkelufer Synagogue, 120, *121*, 122
Frank, Benno, 24, 37, 56
Frauentag, 108, *110*
Frederick, Mellinger, 24
Free Federation of Unions (*Freier Deutscher Gewerkschaftsbund* or FDGW), 136, 150
French Allies: cultural officers, 27; governing of their sector, 27–28; Office of Music and Drama, 27; beaux arts program and other cultural initiatives, 28
Frick, Gottlob, 85
Friedrich, Caspar David, 7, 82, 133
Fritzsche, Eva, 143
Furtwängler, Wilhelm: activities under National Socialism, 56, 114; blacklisting of, 53; comments on *Ambassadors of Music*, 115; conducting Wager in Berlin after the war, 85–86; denazification process, 57–58; Philharmonic Director for life, 157; postwar account, 2; postwar exile in Switzerland, 43; return concerts in Berlin, 58, 60

Galinski, Heinz, 120
German guilt, 137–138
German suffering, 84, 86–87
German victimhood: problematic understandings of, 3; opera as an expression of victimhood, 69
Germany, Year Zero, 7, 117, 118
Gluck, Christoph Willibald, 76, 106
Gluski, Henry, 93, 106
Glyndebourne, 53

Goebbels, Joseph, 19, 35, 95
Göring, Hermann, 36, 68
Goethe, Johann Wolfgang von, 116
Graupner, Alfred, 48
Great Love, The, 119
Greindl, Josef, 72, 73
Grunewald, 50
Gruppe 47, 7

Halberstadt, 159
Hamburg, 4, 55, 67, 80, 101, 159
Handke, Adolph, 48
Harlem Symphony Orchestra, 51
Hartmann, Erich: postwar treatment, 46; thoughts about John Bitter, 56
Hartmann, Fritz, 48
Haydn, Joseph: *The Creation* in Nuremberg, 109; first postwar concert of, 1; on the radio, 99; other early postwar concerts of, 106
Hedler, Georg, 48
Heger, Robert: blacklisting of, 53; conducting at the Städtische Oper, 78, 81; head of Staatskapelle, 69; postwar performances, 50
Heine, Heinrich, 145–148
Heldengedenktag (Heroes Commemoration Day), 35, 95
Heldt, Werner, 7
Hillers, Marta, 75
Hindemith, Paul: Bitter's performances of in postwar Germany, 56; Hindemith Affair, 57; influence on other composers, 149; on the radio, 102; supposed banning in Nazi Germany, 36, 101
Hinrichsen, Walter, 24
Höber, Lorenz, 47, 48, 50
Hochschule für Musik, 20, 54, 76, 103, 144, 158
Hofer, Karl, 7, *8*
Höffer, Paul: biography, 148–151; International Music Institute, 104, 149; RIAS appearances, 102; rubble compositions, 131; *Toccata*, 1; work in postwar Berlin, 36
Hofmann, Ludwig, 73, 82
Horst Wessel Lied, 33, 55, 62
Hutton, Thomas, 61

Information Control Division (ICD): origins of, 22; radio section, 100
Inter-Allied Lending Library (Berlin), 36

Jaspers, Gertrud, 137
Jaspers, Karl, 137, 138
Jewish community (*Jüdische Gemeinde*), 120, 122
Jewish musicians, 44, 60
Jewish ruins, 119–123
Josselson, Michael, 25
Jüdischer Kulturbund, 145, 147

KaDeWe (Kaufhaus des Westens), 122
Kaiser Wilhelm Memorial Church, 113, 114, 124
Karajan, Herbert von, 58, 157
Kardorff, Ursula von, 78
Kerr, Harrison, 35–36
Kleber, Wolfram, 48
Klemperer, Otto, 44
Klose, Margarete, 72, 85
Kluge, Alexander, 159
Knappertsbusch, Hans: blacklisted, 53; propaganda tours, 57, 115
Knef, Hildegard, 76
Knepler, Georg, 83, 137
Kodály, Zoltán, 36, 44
Koussevitzky, Serge, 103
Krenek, Ernst, 102
Kreuzkirche (Dresden), 9, 112
Kroll Opera, 16, 44
Krueger, Alfred, 46
Kulturbund, 19, 20, 26, 150
Kurfürstendamm, 25, 28, 138
Kutz, Karina, 78

Leander, Zarah, 119
Legal, Ernst, 69, 71, 158
Leider, Frida: postwar work with the Staatsoper, 75–76, 82–83; *Tristan and Isolde* direction, 85; resignation at the Staatsoper, 158
Lemnitz, Tiana, 72, 76
Lenz, Willi, 47

Lerner, Ben, 159
Ludwig, Leopold: blacklisting, 53; conducting the Philharmonic in April 1945, 46; early postwar radio concerts, 98
Lyotard, Jean François, 132

Madame Butterfly, 80, 82
Mahler, Gustav, 60, 93, 146, 149
Mann, Thomas, 19, 84
Mauersberger, Rudolf, 112
McClure, Robert, 23, 56
Mendelssohn, Felix: Berlin Philharmonic performances of, 44–45, 47, 54; postwar concerts of, 16, 35, 85, 123; prohibition in Nazi Germany, 5, 35; radio broadcasts of, 93, 102
Mentzel, Ilse, 76
Menuhin, Yehudi, 86, 119
Metropolitan Opera, New York, 24, 53, 56
Meyerbeer, Giacomo, 35
Milhaud, Darius, 102, 104
Mitropoulos, Dmitri, 103
Mitscherlich, Alexander, 107–108
Mitscherlich, Margarete, 107–108
Mozart, Wolfgang Amadeus: music under the Third Reich, 71; on the radio, 98; postwar performances of his music, 16, 45, 55, 68
Müller, Anneliese, 76
Munich: Bavarian State Opera, 85; connection between music and architecture, 9; end of the War, 2; *Fidelio*, 81; Furtwängler's performances in, 61; Munich Staatsoper, 80; music officers, 36; National Theater reconstruction, 156; Prinzregententheater, 67; radio, 97, 99; ruin concerts in, 107, 111–112; Schaubühne, 24; Staatsoper, 80
Murderers are among Us, The, 6
music: as an antifascist symbol, 36; as sabotage, 35; importation of national musics by the Allies, 35

Nabokov, Nicolas: biography, 24; descriptions of Berlin, 45, 85; friendship with Blacher, 104; self-promotion of his music, 54;

thoughts on denazification, 30; work as an intelligence officer, 20–21, 23, 25, 82
Naumann, Rolf, 46
Nazi music, 33, 86
Nazi Party: attempts to define, 33–34; membership in, 136
Nehlhans, Erich, 120, 122
Neukölln, 21, 47
Neumann, Karl August, 72
November Group (*Novembergruppe*), 135
Nuremberg: opera house, 67; ruin music making, 109–110

Offenbach, Jacques, 36, 82
Office of War Information, 11
Onkel Emil, 43
Opera, 67–92
ordinary labor, 48
Orff, Karl, 2
Orpheus and Eurydice, 76–77

Passauer Street Synagogue, 122
Pestalozzistrasse Synagogue, 120
Peter Grimes, 80–81, 83
Pink, Ivor, 34
Piston, Walter, 36
polio epidemic, 11
Political Intelligence Division, 26
Porter, Cole, 35
Potsdam Conference and Agreement, 28, 61, 70
Potsdamer Platz, 84
Prenzlauer Berg, 21, 105, 120, 136
Prohaska, Jaro, 72, 85
Prokofiev, Sergei, 24, 106
propaganda footage, 115
Propaganda Ministry, 29, 30, 31, 144, 145

Quante, Friedrich, 44

radio: Allied Radio efforts in Berlin after the War, 93; American Forces Network, 93, 99, 106; American sector (RIAS), 97, 99–100; Greater German Radio, Masurenallee, 1, 62, 96; patronage of Berlin composers, 103–104; repair shop, *98*; Soviet radio (Radio Berlin), 98, 136; under the Nazi era, 95–96
reeducation program: approaches to, 11, 21–22; American personnel, 23; American justification for, 33; radio programming, 93
Reich Chamber of Culture (RKK): Berlin location of, 19; degenerate music, 36; denazification of members, 31; files hidden in the attic, 26; new historiographies of the RKK, 5
Reich Chamber of Music (RMK), 19; copyright organization, 137; cultural ambassadors of, 44; Effectiveness of, 136; Paul Höffer, 149; in relation to denazification, 30; leadership of, 57, 60, 81
Reichsorchester, 45, 54
Request Concert (film), 95
restitution: of costumes, *71*; of opera holdings, 69–72; of Jewish property, 122
RIAS, 96, 101
Ribbentrop, Joachim von, 99
Richter, Hans Werner, 7
Ries, Henry, 7
Riesenburger, Martin, 120
Rodziński, Artur, 103
Romanticism, 6, 82, 131, 133
Rosenbaum, Samuel, 34
Rosenberg, Alfred, 36
Rossellini, Roberto, 6, 117
Rubble: defining feature of this book, 2; other genres and art forms, 6; rubble sublime, 6, 123, 133; rebuilding with music, *109*, *110*
Rubble films, 6, 117–119
Rubble Lieder, 132–135
Rubble women, 74–80
Rufer, Josef, 149
Ruins: concerts in, 94, *112*, *113*; listening to, 93–94; Romanticized ruin art forms, 133, *134*; ruined bodies, 117, 118; *Ruinenwerttheorie* (Theory of Ruin Value), 133
Ruins at Night, 8
Rundfunkhaus, 47

Russian Allies, 17–20, 35
Rykestrasse Synagogue, 120, 122

Sachsenhausen Concentration Camp, 46, 131, 142, 143
Scharoun, Hans, 156
Schlegel, Friedrich, 133
Schlövogt, Helmut, 46
Schlüter, Erna, 85
Schmidt, Eberhard: compositions, 143; internment in Sachsenhausen, 142–143; survival in Sachsenhausen, 131
Schmidt, Karl, 73
Schoenberg, Arnold, 102
Schöneberg, 1, 12, 21, 114
Schubert, Franz, 99, 134, 139, 149
Schuldes, Anton, 46
Schüler, Johannes, 73
Schumann, Robert, 141, 149
Schütz, Heinrich, 112
Sebald, W. G., 107, 123
segregation, 51
She'erith Hapletah (Surviving Remnant), 120
Soviet Military Administration of Germany (SMAD), 18, 20
Speer, Albert, 84, 133
Staatsoper (Berlin): during the Cold War, 156; finances, 82, 85–86; rebuilding after the war, 67–73; ruin of, 16, 17
Städtische Oper (Deutsche Oper): British supervised, 28; during the Cold War, 156; Intendant of, 50; rebuilding after the war, 67–70, 73–74, 78–83
Stalin, Joseph, 26, 28, 61
Stars and Stripes Forever, The, 55, 62
Staudte, Wolfgang, 6
Steglitz, 21, 44, 46
Stehr, Walter, 138
Stern Conservatory, 144
Still, William Grant, 51, 53
Stockhausen, Karlheinz, 158
Stoehr, Joseph, 47, 48
Stöß, Hermann, 114
Strauss, Richard: Brentano Lieder, 1; Death and Transfiguration, 1, 46; Der Rosenkavalier, 55; Don Juan, 51; Metamorphosen, 2; Music played under the Third Reich, 35; popularity with American occupiers, 2; suggestions for rebuilding opera, 68
Stravinsky, Igor, 24; music in Nazi Germany, 36; in postwar Germany, 101, 102
Stuckenschmidt, Hans Heinz: comments on Ambassadors of Music, 115; membership in the November Group, 135; program notes for the Philharmonic, 60; work for the Americans and RIAS, 101
Stunde Null. See Zero Hour
suicide, 46, 51, 80, 96
Suthaus, Ludwig, 85

Taylor, Davidson, 100
Tchaikovsky, Piotr: Berlin Philharmonic early postwar performances, 45; Eugene Onegin, 81–82; Pathétique Symphony, 115; postwar performances of, 1, 35, 55, 73; Sixth Symphony, 51
Tegel, 47
Tempelhof, 21, 60, 93, 106
Theater des Westens: early postwar performances, 47; philharmonic rehearsals, 46; Städtische Oper relocating to, 68
Thimonnier, René, 34
Thomson, Virgil, 36, 111
Tiburtius, Joachim, 148
Tiessen, Heinz: biography, 144–148; membership in the November Group, 135; Op. 55, Heine and Bab Songs, 145–147; Op. 53, Klabund Songs, 145; rubble compositions, 132
Tietjen, Heinz: early postwar opera reconstruction, 68–69; work with the Städtische Oper, 81
Tippett, Michael, 35
Titania Palast: first postwar concerts, 44, 47; former movie theater, 46; Furtwängler's return concerts, 60; Wagner at the Titania Palast, 85
Treptow, Günter, 78
Trümmer art forms, 6–8
Tulpanov, Sergei, 18–19, 70

Ulrich, Kurt, 46
Union of German Composers and Musicologists (VDKM), 137

Vienna Philharmonic, 47, 61
Vogel, Alex, 57
Volksempfänger, 95, 96
Volksgemeinschaft, 95
Volksoper (Berlin), 68
Volkssturm, 45, 46
von Einem, Gottfried, 44

Wagner, Richard: aesthetic goals in relation to the Nazi Regime, 84–85; Allied evocations of, 27, 35; comparisons of contemporary opera with, 81; music in Nazi Germany, 34; music in postwar Germany, 54, 83, 84–86
Wagner, Wieland, 86
Wagner, Winifred, 67
Walter, Bruno, 114
Weber, Carl Maria von, 51, 73
Webern, Anton, 101
Wehrmacht: administration offices, 44; commissions, 149; non-serving musicians, 54, 103; Philharmonic musicians and military service, 46; radio program, 95; Stockhausen, 158; Stuckenschmidt's service, 101; wearing of uniform at concerts, 111; Zimmermann, 159
Weill, Kurt, 102
Weimar, 18, 26: Kroll opera, 44; musical culture, 135; postwar desire to return to, 133; radio listening, 95
Weißensee Jewish cemetery, 120, 122
Westerman, Gerhart von, 157
Wiesbaden opera house, 67
Wilder, Billy, 6, 117
Wilmersdorf, 21, 44, 104
Winterreise, 134, 135, 139
Wirtschaftswunder, 122
Witte, Erich, 82
Woywoth, Hans, 48

Xenakis, Iannis, 159

Zehlendorf, 21, 25, 47, 144, 149
Zero Hour: origins of the term, 4–6; skepticism of the term, 45, 60, 132
Zimmermann, Bernd Alois, 159
Zoological Garden bunker, 78, 79

ABBY ANDERTON is Assistant Professor of Music at Baruch College, City University of New York.

www.ingramcontent.com/pod-product-compliance
Lightning Source LLC
Chambersburg PA
CBHW061940220426
43662CB00012B/1979